WE LIVE IN ALASKA

⚡Epicenter Press

Epicenter Press is a regional press publishing nonfiction books about the arts, history, environment, and diverse cultures and lifestyles of Alaska and the Pacific Northwest.
For more information, visit www.EpicenterPress.com

Originally published by Little, Brown and Company in [YEAR].

ISBN: (Trade Paperback)

ISBN: (Ebook)

Library of Congress Control Number: tbd

10 9 8 7 6 5 4 3 2 1

To Bud, of course

Books by Constance Helmericks

We Live in Alaska, 1944, Epicenter Press 2018

We Live in the Arctic, 1947, Epicenter Press 2018

Our Summer with the Eskimos, 1949, Epicenter Press 2018

Our Alaskan Winter, 1950, Epicenter Press 2019

Flight of the Arctic Tern, 1952, Epicenter Press 2018

Down the Wild River North, 1968, 1989, Epicenter Press 2017

Hunting in North America, 1956

Australian Adventure, 1972

Books by Jean Aspen

Arctic Daughter: a Wilderness Journey, 1988, 2015

A Child of Air (a novel), 2008

Arctic Son: Fulfilling the Dream, 1995, 2014

Trusting the River, Epicenter Press 2017

Companion documentaries by Jean Aspen and Tom Irons

Arctic Son: Fulfilling the Dream, 2012

Arctic Daughter: A Lifetime of Wilderness, 2018

Rewilding Kernwood, 2019

WE LIVE IN ALASKA

Constance Helmericks

Epicenter Press

Contents

Preface

Preface

1

Here Is the Trail

The motor of the blue and white, six-passenger Lockheed turned over slowly as we taxied down the rough field. The pilot turned us around. At last the moment had come. Now we were rushing forward, nose down, tail up, gathering more speed at each moment. The passengers sat very straight in their seats. None would settle back and relax until we were in the air. But now the ground magically sank below us, and the snow-capped mountains of Resurrection Bay, the flaming Oriental poppies and the falling strawberry blossoms and the wee delicate forget-me-nots of full summer in Seward, Alaska, faded into a dream.

IT ALL STARTED FOR US when we were twenty-one. It might have happened while we were lingering over a coke in the college drugstore, or meeting between classes or walking side by side along the pleasant, palm-bordered walks of the campus. Bud was wearing the loose shirt and penciled "cords" that the Engineers wore and I was in some sort of peasant swing dress, you may be sure. And we both dreamed of going to a lot of far places.

Dreams are thin things spun of air. We told everybody that we were going to go to Alaska (since that was far away!) as soon as we were married. My sorority sister and her fiancé were going to South America at that time. Everybody was going to do something unusual.

There were a few slight deviations from the trail for us, but actually at twenty-three we were married, and we left an hour after the ceremony for Seattle, the Inside Passage, and points north. It was 1941.

We had no job waiting for us in Alaska, and just what we were going there for is hard to tell. Perhaps, because we had talked about it so much, we just had to get out of town.

The early May winds, as we stood on deck watching the gulls, were cold. Even Seattle in summer had been the coldest place I had ever known, after the burning desert of the Southwest. The wheeling gulls looked cold, we thought, and we wondered why, fanning themselves through the air as they did and exposing their naked underwings and their poor bare feet, they did not turn into icicles then and there. At ten o'clock at night the cold sun sank far in the north; then we watched the endless darkened islands slide by on either hand, and jingled the sparse change in our pockets, wondering where we would go and what we would do when we reached Alaska. The lights of the warm interior of our steamboat twinkled on the water, and the sounds of music for dancing drifted out and were swallowed suddenly in darkened fjords. Some of the near-by mountain cliffs rose 15,000 feet straight up from the sea. I said to myself: "This is what you have been waiting for all your life. This is adventure. This is it." But we were on our own now and couldn't turn back if we wanted to. We didn't have the passage back. We knew now, after two years of being bitten by the "Alaska Bug," that Alaska would exact her toll for what she gave. She would retain us for a little while on this detour—yes, longer than we had expected. To see the sights we wanted to see in the way we wanted to see them meant still further waiting and working and becoming Alaskans.

Our fellow passengers on the steamboat Yukon were men on contract for labor for the new government defense projects. We had sensed vaguely that there was something stirring in Alaska, but just what we did not then know. But Alaska is changing and will never be isolated again: the "Outside" will be close to modern-minded pioneers. All but the most blind are forced to see that something altogether new and momentous is at hand. For the first time in seventy-three years, once again Alaska is at the end of an old era and the beginning of a new, like it or not.

There were a few married women, probably no single woman, on the boat, and I realized suddenly one day that there were no tourists among them. We were soon to become used to the inequalities in the population, and would almost regard it as in the normal sphere of things that the proportion of white males over twenty-one to white females of the same age group should be so different from the proportion in any other place we had seen.

Sailing the sheltered inland seas, we were wide-eyed as the vessel threaded the islands of the Alexander Archipelago. Somewhere, at the docks of some cannery long forgotten, I caught the biggest codfish of anybody on the trip.

The capital of Alaska, Juneau, was perched precariously at the foot of the mountains which threatened to push it into the sea. In this it was like several towns along this glacier-fronted coast, although it had a rainbow over it shining through a snowstorm on the peaks. But we knew at a glance that we would not want to live at the little governmental town. And it lay much, much too far south.

Cutting across the Gulf of Alaska we now left land behind us with one last glimpse of the great snowy Mt. Fairweather, over 15,000 feet tall, seventy miles away across the blue, rolling sea. Porpoises followed us.

We had a sort of great-uncle who was somewhere in Alaska. Uncle Fred was a legend. He was an Alaskan sourdough, who had run away from his home in the East to follow the sea. He had had his own fleet of fishing boats, and lost them, some said, when Ketchikan was the wickedest port on the Pacific, and he was a rough companion. It was even rumored that he had been a rum runner at one time. For the past twenty-five years, at least, he had resided in Alaska, and nobody had heard much of him.

When we docked at the end of our week's run at the long- shoring town of Seward, on Resurrection Bay, we fished out a crumpled piece of paper and went to look for Fred. Inquiry revealed that our Uncle Fred was a much-liked person by the many who knew him; that he was nearing the retirement age in the Army Signal Corps, the Territory's telegraph system; that he was now located at Anchorage, 115 miles away. Consequently, we now expended a few of our remaining dollars on tickets and embarked on the Alaska Railroad.

The train climbed slowly through forests of dwarfed arctic spruce, up over a 2000-foot divide, and over receding Spencer Glacier. It tunneled through snowsheds over which spring freshets poured. It wound around and underneath itself in a loop which is perhaps the most scenic in the world, but we learned that not only was it in a bad state of decay which would entail several million dollars for repairs, but that it would be an inviting target to enemy saboteurs as well. Therefore, another line was being built to a new port of entry, Whittier on Portage Bay, which cut off fifty miles of needless tracks. Civilians thought that the town of Seward was dying; doomed for the future.

Everybody should have an Alaskan sourdough uncle. We recall that our Uncle Fred nearly fainted when he saw us—for if anything could surprise him at his stage of life it was the sight of his great-nephew Bud arrived in this outpost of Alaska with a new bride. It seemed Fred knew he possessed many nephews, relations, and the like, but true to the type of the old-time Alaskan, the passing years had found him with less and less to say to any of them. It was all so different here from what they were used to outside. He had sent a brown bear hide and gifts of moccasins, but on returning once had found them relegated to the barn, unwanted. He had sent somebody a case of Cordova salmon and fancy minced razor clams, but his only reply had been a rebuke about forgotten postage—an oversight on the part of a messenger. Fred sent the postage. He had sent a nephew a hundred-dollar bill on his graduation from high school, but had received no reply.

Always game, however, to blow a few dollars on a man just for the satisfaction of observing humanity, Fred had replied with encouragement to Bud's general letter of inquiry two years ago. Yes, by all means come to Alaska. It was the only place to be. "But advise you not to get married, for it is better to get a stake ahead."

As what's done can't be undone, however, and we were married, Fred gave us his bed gladly and slept on a mattress on the floor of the kitchen. After a week, because Fred knew the pioneers of Anchorage, we were able to rent a cabin of our own.

Anchorage, lying on Knick Arm off of Cook Inlet, and incidentally due north of the Hawaiian Islands, was at this time the largest city in Alaska. There is no port in Anchorage because of forty-foot tides and the fact that shallow Cook Inlet is choked with ice for many months of the year. Anchorage had been a railroad town, born around 1915.

By 1941 it boasted the most northern golf course in the world (very rough), a country-club swimming resort (very brief season), and the longest stretch of straight highway in Alaska, which led fifty miles inland to the town of Palmer, Matanuska Valley, and to the outlying mines in the Talkeetna Range. People had their automobiles brought up by rail from Seward just to drive them around town, gaily smashing them and beating them into wrecks within six months' time, as a rule. The road to Matanuska was like a washboard. But there were more cars at Seattle and plenty of money with which to buy them.

Because of the thousands pouring into the section around Fort Richardson and Elmendorf Field, people were living in tents and garages, and buying one-room, cardboard shacks without plumbing for $1500 in order to have a roof overhead. To a depression- bred generation, the newcomers, it looked at first as though one could not afford to eat. Anchorage was a real frontier boom- town, twentieth-century style, leading the procession of the many boom towns which were presently to pop up at quite remote points all over the earth.

Most of the newcomers, or cheechakos, came to Anchorage to make money and get out as soon as possible. Some were tough customers, the fly-by-night realtors not the least among them. Twice a month, when pay day rolled around at the Fort, certain well-dressed, prosperous-looking strangers suddenly appeared in the streets. These were the professional gamblers from Seattle, or Kodiak. Certain women who stepped from planes always had accommodations waiting for them although the wives of the town could find no suitable place to stay. This created quite a disturbance among the wives, who are sometimes forced to put up signs by their front doors: "Private Home." Vice was well organized from Seattle, two thousand miles away.

Grade school and high school were overcrowded and there was a rise in delinquency. The muddy streets thronged with strangers, few of whom ever got much acquainted with each other. Many were burdened with little children and were lonely and homesick. Some were Army wives in slacks and colored sandals, wishing, no doubt, that Anchorage was Atlantic City.

Soldier boys from home commenced to appear in great numbers. They resided at first in a tent city, which was soon to outnumber Anchorage itself in population. Everywhere one looked, Alaska was in uniform now. Congress had appropriated $200,000,000 for its defense against invasion.

Some very fine United Service Organization clubhouses, built by the boys themselves, sprang up in several Alaskan towns, and the USO Building became a much-needed focal point for community activities as a whole. Alaska wives, long dominated by an overpowering numerical masculinity and long suffering from the lack of amusement places for themselves (although there were twenty-eight rough board bars in every downtown block, so to speak), now surged forth in search of war work. The husbands as a whole were antagonistic to the policies of the USO, usually believing in the old-fashioned policy of "Let the soldiers keep to themselves/' It was the women who put the USO on its feet in Alaska, as perhaps everywhere. Alaska women were great readers of the magazines and, while frequently married to slightly antisocial Alaskan men, they watched avidly the doings of their contemporaries in the States.

Among the population should also be mentioned an essential element which the newcomers saw little of in the boom towns, although they were there and had made their homes there for thirty years. These were the old-timers or pioneers. They consisted of the Scandinavian stock of Swedes, Norwegians, and Finns; the aristocracy of the railroad staff, who at one time set the social pace in these parts; and the old people. The Outsiders didn't even know of their existence, but people past forty made up a considerable part of the Territory's population. Fred said in the old days one could see little clusters of pioneers standing and talking on the street corners in Anchorage. They had names like Moose John, Two-Story John, Benzine Bill, Horizontal Bill, Montana Bess, Alaska Nellie, Stucco Johnson, Herring Pete—names that caressed the ear and gave even to the heart of the uninitiated a strange nostalgia. But southeastern Alaska and the coast towns had changed remarkably in the last twenty years. The pioneers either died or moved away. Some of them crawled into their shells and didn't think much of the changes that were coming. Such is always the case when a change comes. The old gives way to the new only with great resistance, and sometimes personalities are broken in the process.

For that whole first year, a period of devoted and awful labors, we newlyweds lived in Anchorage in a log cabin. Water was pumped and carried from a complaining community pump (eighty-seven strokes for two buckets) over paths muddy in summer, icy in winter. It was carried out the same way and dumped from an unlovely slop bucket behind the house after it had been used. Although the city authorities harassed the landlords, neither materials nor labor was available to put in sanitary facilities—well, not until perhaps next year. Meanwhile people had to live some place. They crowded together, not in nice clean log cabins like Abe Lincoln lived in, but in sagging, hastily built log cabins with cardboard bedrooms attached, or in downtown apartments over the groceries which were veritable firetraps. There was no one available to build houses, as all were employed at the "base." The few men who cut and hauled wood to burn in the wood stoves charged eighteen dollars the cord, pile and split it yourself. It was a hard life—the crowding together as in tenements, and yet the loneliness and lack of friends; the complete lack of any place to go or anything to do for recreation; the utter sameness and drabness of life for all when the husband was working the fifty-six-hour week or the seventy- two-hour week without a single day off in the year. Yes, that is the way defense bases were built in Alaska in the emergency. Man after man who couldn't "take it" quit and returned to the States, while the next boat brought a new crowd, willing to have their chance. Even today there is no room for weaklings in Alaska. Alaska has also long been known as a great enemy of marriage, which accounts in part for the large groups of drifting, unattached men.

A neighbor in the next cabin came over and offered to lend us a couple of hundred from his pocket to get started, which was our first initiation into the Alaskan tradition, but we declined his offer. Instead, we lived on oatmeal and turnips until the first pay check came.

Bud first hefted hundred-pound cement sacks as a day laborer on an airfield construction job; but soon he had become a semiskilled sheet-metal worker and had a lot of fun handling iron, copper and the tin for which Outside people were saving their toothpaste tubes.

Every generation must meet its destiny—the destiny of war. We were just being born during the last war, along with millions of Greek and Russian and German and Japanese and Hindu babies. Now all the babies were grown up, carefully trained in the social systems of their forebears, most of whom were dead and forgotten by this time, but their vicious systems lived on, or perhaps were even invented over again by the new generation.

It was hard for me to understand many things at the time I was married. I only knew that, having got to Alaska, I didn't like it. This, incidentally, is usually the case with women. I enjoy pleasure and luxury and have never been a particularly brave person or a particularly realistic one. It didn't affect me to know that women before me had pioneered to an extent that was inconceivable in its endurance. I was a modern woman. I could dismiss all those others with the wave of a hand. The way I thought about Alaska, why—I thought it would be nice to take the roses without the thorns.

But Alaska wasn't like that, isn't like that yet. There were none of our crowd from school to applaud the adventuring heroes now. We doubted if any of the crowd would like Alaska very well actually, except through our enthusiastic letters.

Bud is a farmer's son. He was better constituted to slide easily into the Alaskan scene. He had battled his own way since he was fourteen. In addition to working his way through school he had managed to see all of the States and parts of Mexico and Cuba, and incidentally meet a great many different people under vastly different circumstances. He was used to being alone. As he pounded copper nails bare-handed up on the roofs of the barracks that winter, his mind was with the snowclouds being whirled two thousand feet into the air from the peaks of the untrodden Chugach Mountains. Or, almost unmindful of the cold, he would wonder how the mystic green of summer would look upon those same slopes. Like many boys and young men, Bud had always cherished a desire to wander freely and unhampered through at least some of the great wilderness of the Americas as well as of other countries and continents. We agreed in this—so had I. Bud at least was well qualified to do it.

My contemplations of life in Alaska as the months passed disclosed to me presently that it wasn't only the last generation who had been uprooted and who had suffered and endured. We had thought our generation exempt. It wasn't. I began to see that I was not the only one who was undergoing or who would soon undergo a great change in methods of living.

The world was moving on, and at an accelerated pace. Following the Pearl Harbor incident, the United States declared war on Japan on December 8, 1941. Germany declared war on the United States in alliance with Japan and Italy. England had been fighting for months now turning into years. The magnitude and speed of the process of adjustment to this Second World War on the part of all peoples and nations were inescapable. The activities all over the country were revolutionary in scope. They pointed two ways: to northern Europe and North Africa; and northwest through Alaska to the Orient and Japan. The legendary apathy of some of the Alaskan old-timers was being shaken. The infiltration of global war through and across Alaska, and the subjugation of Japan by the United Nations from eastern Russia, would possibly necessitate a fusion of Occident and Orient which would require all of their united power and strength.

And we, insignificant, young, and very interested, were now sitting on the direct route of the main west-to-east pathway to Asia whether via the Alaska Peninsula and the Aleutians direct from the little town of Seward, or by the natural passes of the mouths of the Yukon! Alaska was the spot of the day.

Citizens of Alaska had followed Governor Ernest Gruening's advice to a large extent. The outbreak of the war found every cabin with about a year's food staples on hand, stocked as only people like Alaskans know how to do. Radios which previously had tuned chiefly to Tokyo and Mexico City, easier of contact than most stations in the States, now enjoyed in Anchorage the improved sending and receiving facilities which hooked them onto the big networks with the favorite programs that the rest of the Americans habitually enjoy—this being one of the growths, no doubt, of the war, and a real blessing. It serves to remind one of how isolated, psychologically and physically, Alaska was before the war.

Evacuation of Army wives and children and all dependents who were not residents began. There was wailing and gnashing of teeth at Anchorage by those who did not want to go. Yet for others it was a free ride, and some promptly came back after they were sent out. Many women suddenly got jobs, so they would be classified as self-supporting persons vital to the lifeline of the Territory.

An interesting local phase of the war situation was the liquor traffic, which continued at increased tempo for some time. Ships docking at Seward carried hundreds of tons of beer and whisky, showing that the powerful liquor syndicates, too, were taking the governor's advice and stocking up for the future. Sometimes there was not a fresh vegetable or any other food in from Seattle because the liquor took so much room. The minority group of the housewives raged futilely to the grocers, who could do nothing about it as their orders had not been filled. Alaskans have always been good customers for liquor—a gallon of whisky per capita per month, somebody said, which is a guess. It's probably more. The Alaska Steamship Company's rates for passengers and supplies became necessarily very high as a result of the dangers of navigating the now unmarked passages of the islands wherein enemy submarines might lurk. The Company demanded a convoy, but was presently relieved of the situation when the Navy took over for the duration.

Bud and I, having survived the rigors of the long winter, were transferred, via slow freight, to Seward, there to work on Fort Raymond. That is, Bud was working on the Fort. I still had the dishes. Uncle Fred, now at Seward, finding that there were no houses to rent, bought a house and installed us in it with him temporarily. We had now resided in the Territory a year, and we were Alaskans. Digging our family bomb shelter, according to Army regulations, we kept this fact in mind and were thankful indeed.

We had been in Alaska a year when we felt we could make the break to see some of the sights which we felt we had truly earned. For instance, we had slept in sleeping bags all of the first year, just waiting to go camping, and had camped in our own home, such as it was. Now it was time for the real thing.

It was full summer in Seward when Bud approached Mr. Cox, his boss: "I've been thinking of going up to the Yukon for a while."

"The Yukon?"

"Yes, you know my wife and I haven't seen it."

"Neither have I," said Mr. Cox.

"We have read that it may be an important place now."

"Is that so?"

"And so—well, we'd just like to take a vacation and see it."

"Hold up your hands for me to see."

Bud did so, palms up and even, before Mr. Cox's kindly eye. The hands quivered uncontrollably, ever so slightly.

"Not bad, for a year," said Mr. Cox, who was nearing seventy himself and who knew the sheet-metal business thoroughly. "Well, of course you've got a month coming anyway. A vacation will do you good. See how you like it up there, if they let you go. By the way, how are you going? Going to take one of them tourist river cruises?"

"Nope. There aren't any river cruises running these days. We wouldn't want to go on one anyway. It's to be a canoe trip."

"Canoe trip! I wish I was going myself. Well, good luck to you!"

"Good luck to you, sir!"

Bud appeared at home and went immediately to the back yard. There by the bomb shelter, he was joined by myself and Uncle Fred in front of a long wooden frame erected just over the carrots and beets. Upon the frame these two weeks past had arisen magically under our hands the form of a canoe, which was to be our only home for the months to come.

2

Initiation

Canoes and canoeing, white-man style, are unknown in Alaska. Everybody simply uses a clumsy, heavy, flat-bottomed river boat with oars, poles, a motor or all three. Most unromantic! Uncle Fred had never seen a canoe, and strangely enough neither had Bud, really. I tried to explain to the two of them what one was like, as I remembered it from my early childhood in the Eastern United States. From the store we borrowed a boat and canoe catalogue which was to be given back when we were finished with it. Then we found that we were unable to buy a canoe any place in the Territory, nor could we get one shipped to Alaska at this time except by waiting perhaps for most of the summer. We would have to build it ourselves!

Down at the lumberyard on a rainy day we selected our wood for the frame. Uncle Fred wanted ironwood at first, until Bud explained that ironwood is definitely out for canoes. The canoe, unlike the ocean-going boat, is not built to withstand the battering-ram of the waves, but to ride over them lightly, like a cork. About the only other wood which Seward's lumberyard boasted at this time was Sitka spruce, fortunately a light and excellent wood for our purpose.

This was war, and nobody was building anything. That is, nobody but us. The man at the lumberyard sleepily looked at us (it was not his lumberyard) and said flatly, "You can't do it." Our order was not an imposingly large one, and he told us that, the manager being absent, he couldn't risk using the power saw to cut our piece. Therefore, our next few days were spent in sawing the gunwales and the sixty-four ribs out by hand, and painstakingly planing them to polished smoothness. Bud, who had by now drawn up the plans and measurements, assured me that care was vital, because the least roughness would tend to make the delicate pieces crack as soon as they were put to the strain of being bent into shape.

The bending of the bow and stern from the keel was perhaps the toughest problem among many problems in building. Bud bent three different bows, but they all broke. Obviously, no one but a professional should attempt to make a canoe; one really needs steamer and clamper facilities to mold the craft into shape, for the great danger is that it will get lopsided and off balance.

Three more of our precious days passed. It was now late June. We were frantic, but we never gave up hope for more than a few minutes at a time. Then it would somehow revive again. At last Bud appeared on the run with two chunks of five-eighth- inch waterproof plywood. After some calculations and drawing out of curves with a stubby pencil, he simply sawed these into the graceful curves desired for the bow and the stern. They were put onto the keel with screws and glue. With our worst problem solved, we knew somehow that we could conquer all the others. We had got our second wind, and Alaska was ours.

The nineteen-foot-by-forty-inch frame was sanded, and a few days of successively sunny weather permitted us to give it two coats of orange shellac in rapid succession. Next came canvas. "You can't get canvas," said the man at the store eagerly. "Haven't you heard of priorities?" We ran quickly to the other store. What could we do with a frame and no canvas? The other store had a thin, eleven-ounce canvas which it was still selling to civilians but which was so light that using it was out of the question. Well, it was better than no canvas at all! We bought a double amount of it from the last roll and put on two layers and went canoeing just the same. The method ultimately proved entirely satisfactory.

We used glue and innumerable tacks along the seams to put the canvas on properly. This step was taken inside the house, with the canoe reaching diagonally across the kitchen from the top of the ceiling in one corner to the bottom of the floor in the opposite corner. It was difficult to open Fred's beautiful, late- model refrigerator door, and we had to crawl on hands and knees to cross the room for a couple of days, but we didn't mind that.

A coating of linseed oil, two coats of tan paint, and the manufacture of reinforced paddles followed. The blades of the paddles were not wide enough because narrow boards were all we could get. But we were jubilant. We installed the seats. Bud's seat was in mannish laced-leather motif, made from an old pair of boot tops. He was to sit in front and I was to have the honor of sitting in back and steering all the way. My seat, slightly elevated, was a frame of laced twine, my handiwork during the past week. In either end were fitted two triangular tin containers for spare clothing and perishables. These were also to act as air tanks to keep the canoe floating if we should capsize. The canoe was wrapped and shipped on the Alaska Railroad to Fairbanks, terminus city located at the beginning of the waterways into the remote Interior.

"I don't believe the Army will allow you to start from Fairbanks after you get there," Uncle Fred remarked dubiously for the fourth time. He didn't want us to work up too much hope for nothing.

Because everybody should properly have an animal totem to represent him while he is in Alaska, we chose the Beaver, for Engineering. Because she was a lady, we titled our canoe *Queen of All the Beavers*. She weighed 130 pounds empty, which was a little more than we had expected.

While the *Queen Beaver* got a head start on us on our journey, we spent three days with Mayor and Mrs. Benson of Seward at their cabin at near-by great Lake Kenai. Not only had we never seen the lake before, except from the train window briefly, but for a whole year, living right among and close to people in Alaska's cities, we had really known absolutely no one. This experience now put us into a festive mood that was like coming out of the long darkness of a bad dream into the sunlight again. We were ready indeed now, with the staunch support of these older friends behind us, to carry on from here. Talking our plans over with someone wiser, even if inexperienced in these ways, had left us with a feeling of glowing gratefulness that was hard to express.

Lake Kenai is twenty miles long, its waters of the peculiar milky green common to glacier country. The milky color is caused by the grinding and powdering of the rock beneath a glacier slowly traveling down an inclining plane for many centuries. The mills grind slowly but exceeding fine. The invisible powder permeating the waters of the lake below is never known to settle.

Now as we winged our way in a small airplane at five thousand feet over the winding emerald lake below, we saw that it was set truly like a jewel amid the all-encompassing spruce forests. Close beside our plane, as though we could reach out and touch them, were the snow-capped peaks and ridges where the bands of sheep and white goats stay; we had seen them from the window at the Bensons' breakfast table. Down below dropped the verdant valleys and the passes between the ranges through which the moose and bears wandered, changing their pasture. Down still farther in the waters flowing at the bottom of the valleys lay the brook trout, the Dolly Vardens, the rainbows, the cutthroats, and, in Kenai, the great sleeping lake trout which have scarcely known an angler's lure. The world's largest record trout and the world's largest moose horns were taken from this great forest reserve area. Believers in the Kenai country prophesy that someday cottages will bedeck the sides of the now lonely lake with its attendant smaller lakes much as they now crowd upon the shores of California's Lake Tahoe. We felt privileged to have the opportunity to see it in a day when few roads penetrated and most people must commute by motorboat to their few cottages, which were Alaska log cabins.

Presently below us appeared Turnagain Arm, and we knew that we were close in minutes to our old friend, unlovely Anchorage. Far out to the left stretched the blue salt waters of Cook Inlet, into which oozed a muddy gray. This little arm, with the second highest tides in the world—thirty-two feet eight inches by Uncle Fred's tide book— had once been the disappointment of the explorer Vancouver when he was searching for a northwest passage. When we set down on the runways at Anchorage from our first brief Alaska plane ride we told ourselves that it was perhaps a good thing that up to now we had had no conception of what we were really missing. Here was the real Alaska, in the wilderness we had flown over, and not in its cities. We were tired of all cities.

At Anchorage the next day we boarded the train for Fairbanks.

By nightfall the endless forests broke to give up to us the elaborate railroad hotel at Curry, only halfway there. Alaska passenger trains run only during the daylight hours, stopping at log roadhouses for lunch. The stationmaster is quite nonchalant as to whether anyone rides or not and nobody cares if the train starts out at precisely ten or is four hours late. Train schedules depend on the arrival of boats at Seward, and during war this is unannounced. Passengers check their own baggage (ours consisted of two sleeping bags, one seaman's duffel bag, and two rifles) and pay six cents a mile for transportation. This, along with the necessary hotel fee at Curry, which cost us eighteen dollars for two for dinner, bedroom and breakfast, makes railroad travel almost as expensive as the exorbitant cost of flying. The railroad was built at government expense to aid in opening up the country, and in this it has done a great service. However, in recent years the government decided that it was time for the railroad to pay back the original outlay. Hence the Alaskans, who are indeed long-suffering in some respects, must buy goods which reach utterly enormous prices before they are received in the Interior. This is particularly retarding in the development of the Alaska natives, who today are almost as dependent on the white man's food as is the white man himself, and who have but small buying power when pitted against the grandiose price scale set up by railroad, Yukon River steamer, and the trader.

The *Queen Beaver* was waiting for us at Fairbanks on the station platform. Since nobody was around, we walked over to her, lifted her wrapping and petted her. She seemed all right. Not knowing what to do with them, we slipped our rifles inside, covered her up in her wrapper again, and went out to a movie.

The movies in Fairbanks were like nothing we had yet seen in Alaska, and how hungry we were for good movies I Fairbanks had showings of the same pictures that the people Outside see, shown in establishments that were like palaces in our eyes. Built by an Alaska millionaire these two movie houses cost thousands, and they certainly looked good to us.

Fairbanks, we thought, was truly everything that anybody had ever told us in praise of it, the resplendent city of the North, the best town in Alaska. Walking down the streets we saw modern, well-built, steam-heated houses and real sidewalks, and everybody looked tanned. The town lies, of course, in the land of the midnight sun. It has a warmer summer climate than points south along the rainy coasts. Many think its experimental farms are much more successful in terms of a growing season than those of highly publicized Matanuska Valley. The Fairbanks Exploration Company, a subsidy of the United Smelting and Refining Company, has been dredging for gold with large-scale operations for many years out of Fairbanks, and it appears probable that the operations can continue indefinitely as far as the supply of gold is concerned.

In Fairbanks the telephone operator chats with you in a friendly way and loves nothing more than to help the stranger out of a dilemma. The stationmaster, the telephone operator told me, obstinately refuses to answer the telephone or talk to anybody who rings him after four o'clock in the afternoon. We couldn't help admiring him sight unseen. Where but in Alaska can one still find workingmen who call no man master but themselves? And such men, when they do work, are both industrious and honest, and their labor comes from the heart, in personal interest.

Discarding the Great Circle Route to Asia for the new Hemisphere conception of geography, airmen now contemplate routes over the North Pole to Asia, or airways to Dublin in three days from Fairbanks. Thus, Fairbanks is thought of as the hub of a great wheel from which the spokes go out to all other parts of the world. It is for this reason above all that friendly Fairbanks may yet become the greatest city of our North.

Four miles outside Fairbanks is the University of Alaska, most northern university in the world. If it weren't for the war, we would have been going to this school. We had tried for two years to get there. Although its student body is small, it has a faculty obtained from Harvard, Yale, Columbia, Copenhagen. Some of the professors are engaged in peculiar and enchanting hobbies. Perhaps one of the best known of them is Dr. Froelich G. Rainey, archaeologist, who has recently attained world-wide renown for his discovery of "Alaska's Oldest Arctic Town" on the far northern coast. Dr. Charles E. Bunnel is the president of the college, the one and only president it has had. He is the man who held it together through the several long years of its wobbly infancy.

It was six o'clock in the afternoon, July 16, when we shoved off from Fairbanks under the bridge which crosses the Chena Slough. We had half looked for some authority to stop us from going on down onto the Yukon from here, but no one had. We hurried rather quietly now to get away before anybody should.

Rain was falling lightly, and we had packed the *Queen Beaver* with ninety-three dollars' worth of food and camping supplies from the Northern Commercial Company. The N. C. Company is a pioneer of Alaska, and we would find several branches of it along our way where we would have credit, except that we did not want to run up many bills. It had cost us in the end forty dollars to get our canoe from the railroad, with little chance of any eventual refund. We were embarking on what was going to be a 2500-mile canoe trip, and although we did not know it at the time, it would be five months, not one, before we got out from the Interior and we would be lucky to get out at all before the following summer. Neither would we receive any mail for five months, for mail sent into the Interior following us could never have found us and we could never have found it. The only headquarters for us was still Seward, despite the fact that we ranged a couple of thousand miles afield.

We had thought we had plenty of money for our undertaking, but when we left Fairbanks it was with a little less than ten dollars on hand, and this is scarcely enough for a night's lodging in Alaska.

I remember an old fellow who came down under the bridge as we were packing. "Cheechakers, eh?" he greeted us, smiling. "Going down the river?"

"Yes," we told him, "but we're afraid we didn't get started early enough."

"Oh, this is a right fine time," he encouraged us in a high tenor. "Most people starts too early in the year."

"We'll probably have to get a plane out wherever September catches us," we explained confidently. "But we kind of had an idea we would try to make it down to Russian Mission on the lower Yukon and cross the portage over into the Kuskokwim

River. Then we could end up at Bethel just the other side of the Alaska Peninsula and the Aleutians, right near home, really. We're from Seward. We could sell our canoe and catch a plane back to Seward, making a circular tour, you see. What do you think of that idea?"

"She's a great old river," the old-timer commented.

"Why, have you been down the Yukon, too?" I looked up, knowing intuitively what the reply would be.

"Yep. I seen Russian Mission once. Open boat, just like you kids. Let's see, that was about 1905, I guess, before you were born."

We agreed. "But I suppose people will still be doing it after we're all gone and forgotten."

"Yep, they keep floating down the river. In anything they can git. I've even seen them on rafts."

"Is that so? Women too?" I asked with great interest.

"No. No ladies," the old-timer admitted with the respect of his kind for the feminine sex. "Aren't many white ladies in this country, ma'am, once you git away from the town. I'm married to a native woman over here for thirty years myself," he explained.

Uncle Fred would call him a squaw man, I thought. Fred had said we would probably see a lot of dirty old squaw men along the Yukon. But this one seemed kindly and not at all dirty. The Alaskans I had known had taught me two derogatory terms which I had never quite accepted in my mind as being an entirely correct interpretation— "squaw man" and "siwash," the insulting name for the Alaskan native or "breed." Literally in the native languages siwash had meant "fish eater," or "one who lives off the country." But with the Alaskan city people it had come to mean any Alaskan not of the white blood, or one of mixed white blood. I decided to reserve opinion. We would probably be guests in the home of many a squaw man this summer and would no doubt be fish eaters ourselves.

It occurred to us that probably few people really know the Yukon River today, the forgotten highway of the great Interior where the small independent prospector and miner once swung his pick. After all, this country formed the greater part of

Alaska geographically, if not in population. A good many Alaskans themselves held their superstitions about their own country, which, being far removed from them, was never seen. The coast people feared the arctic climate almost as would a person from Tennessee. The climate was not so bad, judging from today at least. It was like any summer day in Rockford, Illinois, except that the sun went around in a circle thirty-five or forty degrees above the horizon, rising and setting at an almost perceptibly different angle for every day of the year, never shining overhead, but giving always and forever a romantic dreamy quality to the landscape which, once experienced, can never be forgotten. Colored pictures of the arctic or near-arctic summer as well as of the strange predominant blues and yellows of winter scenes would always have an unreal quality about them.

"Well, I guess we better shove off," Bud said at last, when the old-timer had gone. "Have we got everything?" Apparently, we had, even to "store" paddles.

We shoved off timidly a few feet from shore, where the sluggish current tugged at us and carried us slowly broadside downstream. "Hey, that isn't the right way," I cried, and we plied our paddles industriously. It wasn't a very auspicious start, but nobody was looking or seemed to know that we had left the town, and to our infinite delight we at least floated. The *Queen Beaver* had been well built. We were carrying now about three hundred pounds in addition to ourselves at the start, and would be glad in a certain respect when we had eaten some of it up and so lightened our outfit. Each of us wore a lightweight waterproof ski jacket with hood, and a pair of polarized sun glasses. Each had his big-game rifle slung by ski straps at the side of his seat, and each wore an identical Colt Woodsman automatic .22 pistol on his belt, which felt rather heavy now on stomachs gorged with banana splits and other miscellaneous delights.

As we drifted slowly down the Chena Slough the sun circled and sank lower. We were tired, and made camp at eleven o'clock amid a tempting stand of green spruce, interspersed with occasional white birches. Trees in this country are stunted by the long winters and possibly by lack of drainage, but the timber is straight and sound, averaging around twenty feet tall and six inches in diameter per tree, although it may attain the normal size in favorable localities almost to the Arctic Ocean. There was six hundred miles of untraveled country running due north of us like this and eight hundred or so running over into unknown western Canada to give a feeling of elbowroom. Tall, high-bush cranberries drenched us as we clambered stiffly ashore after our first day at the paddle. Wild geranium blooms and primrose fruit dangled in the grasses, with columbine, foxglove, and occasional dandelions. Small flowers seem to develop more frequently in Alaska, conceivably because it does not take the sun so long to ripen a small bloom as a large one. Except for the tropics, small blooms and small fruits are the rule of the wild everywhere.

The sky was overcast and it began to rain again. Chickadees hopped from branch to branch beside us. We bolted down some canned ham and hastened to spread out the bedroll under the dense trees. Our only tent was a five-by-seven-foot piece of canvas; we had found at Fairbanks that tents were too expensive for our remaining budget, and most commercial tents hadn't suited our taste anyway. We were somehow under the impression that, our sleeping bags being waterproof on the outside, they would stand all things.

"Say, these mosquitoes are something, aren't they?" Bud remarked. They were. They thudded against our jackets audibly, pierced through woolen shirts and pants alike with their long, probing beaks, crawled up underneath mosquito head nets and down necks and up under the hair line into the scalp. The mosquito head net is made of bobbinet or a similar material, with an elastic band at the top to grip the crown of the hat. The material should pass over the brim of the hat and be tucked inside the coat collar. However, from the necessity of raising and lowering our head nets frequently along the river, we got into the habit of not tucking them in at the bottom but trusted the elastic band there to grip our necks tightly enough. They usually didn't, but let a few mosquitoes in.

We used bottles of repellent to some extent, but in living out of doors twenty-four hours of the day a person cannot use it all the time or his skin would be burned from it. As the effect of repellent lasts only a few minutes at a time, the only thing to use day by day in a country of this sort is the mosquito head net. We lived in our head nets constantly, and never went ashore from the middle of the river without pulling them down from the brims of our hats.

The mosquitoes just went wild in clouds about us when they saw us step innocently into that spruce grove. Not finishing our food, we dived in agony for the covers, and went to bed with our hats on and the nets pulled down. Not that that did much good; wherever the net touched neck or cheek there was no protection whatsoever. Evidently, these head nets were not meant for lying down in. The bottles of repellent which composed an impressive part of our luggage at the start of the trip were in the bottom of the duffel somewhere and could not be found; it was too dangerous even to look for them. As the rain pattered softly down we hid our heads under the covers, but since the sleeping bags were of the best, and guaranteed for eighty degrees below zero, we were presently obliged to come up for air. The wonderful property of down to adjust to any body temperature and keep out the climate enabled us in all succeeding nights to be perfectly comfortable in our sleeping bags.

We slept little this first night with the shrieks and howls of our tormentors droning in our ears; and our lips and eyelids becoming puffed up like rubber tires wherever we were bitten. "Well," I said to Bud about midnight, "the states of New York and Pennsylvania and Illinois, not to mention all of the American South, were all just about like this at one time. Fairbanks is right in the middle of this, and it doesn't have mosquitoes, just to show you what a little cultivation of the land can do. I wonder how long it will take man to subdue the North."

But—six hundred miles to the Arctic Ocean, six hundred down to the coast at Seward, several hundred west to the Bering Sea from here, and just nothing but mosquitoes. That must be a lot of mosquitoes. The mosquitoes had already been termed by some travelers before our time as the most serious single obstacle standing in the way of man's subjugation of the North.

The statement is hard to believe until one experiences the mosquito himself. The fact is that a United States Army pamphlet dealing with arctic conditions states that there are probably ten times as many mosquitoes per square mile in the arctic as there are over any equivalent area in the tropics or any other place on earth.

3

Tanana River

The mighty Yukon River owes much of its size to three tributaries: the Porcupine, coming in from the north on the Upper Yukon near the Canadian border; the Tanana River, which comes in from the southeast; and the Koyukuk, coming in from the north again, farther down near the Bering Sea. Most important of these tributaries from the standpoint of a good watershed and of its interest to man is the Tanana. The Tanana is a shifting and treacherous river with many bars. Down it the shallow-drafted stern-wheelers make their way into the Interior from the end of the railroad at Fairbanks with drums of gasoline, rafts of pipe and sheet iron, and all of the traders' goods, which are delivered at approximately sixty dollars the ton.

Our very first morning revealed to us in no uncertain terms that we had left civilization beyond recall when we rounded a slight bend and found ourselves suddenly thrust into the heavily forested and churning Tanana. Fairbanks of course is located on the Tanana River on any general map, but in actuality it lies on one of the many sloughs of the Tanana, and we had come out into it from this.

The first thing that caught our eye was that the color of the water was extremely muddy and that it sprawled out over many acres of brush land in varied and devious channels. Our advice had been: "Stay in the main channel." But which one would that be? We would have to decide instantly and irrevocably the correct channel to take, while being hurled along past "sweepers" that reached out like witches' arms to catch us. These sweepers were often whole trees that had fallen into the water when the banks were undermined but which were still attached by their roots to the land. At every turn of a channel were jammed packs of floating brush, any stick of which, the size of a pencil, might rupture our dear *Queen Beaver*. Bud termed these Mother Nature's Boat Traps. "I think we're now going through Bates' Rapids," he shouted.

I was alarmed at moments, but was thoroughly enjoying it as a whole, paddling furiously, learning by doing, feeling the breeze rush by, free of the mosquitoes at last! It was a wonderful feeling to dodge the boat traps. Imperceptible side drift kept bringing us up alongside the traps almost before we knew it, but we managed to apprehend the danger a hundred or two hundred feet above it, and escape. We kept hearing noises that sounded like people shooting in the distance, and for three days were under the illusion that we would presently find somebody, until we realized that these noises, like the sound of rifle shots, were the sounds of crashing timber as the frozen banks thawed and fell into the water, exposing in their place layers of raw ice. This noise would not cease until the freeze-up, only to begin next year again and continue into the countless centuries.

Now the Tanana settled into a slower pace in more established channels, the sand in the heavily loaded water hissing softly against the canvas sides of the *Queen Beaver*. Presently, there appeared a fish camp and a fish wheel. We brought up against the bank to see it, amid the uproarious and doleful howling of chained dogs.

There is no memory like that of the natives gathering salmon from one's first fish wheel in Alaska. Yet the fish wheel came, interestingly enough, from old-time days on the Mississippi. It was invented by a white man. Before the white man came to Alaska the natives used to drag woven baskets in the water behind their canoes during the salmon run. Today, they have adopted the fish wheel. Anyone may set up a fish wheel, however—not only a native. The mayor of Nenana has one. These twenty-foot wheels, carrying usually two wire baskets, turn lazily with the current, and scoop up the fish. On reaching the top arc of the wheel, the fish shuttle down a trough into the box from which they are gathered by the fisherman. The lazy and creaking rhythm of the countless fish wheels set the tempo of life in Interior Alaska in the summer and sing a funny little song in one's heart.

We tied our boat, stepped ashore, and saw many king salmon, dog salmon, and whitefish, lush in boxes and buckets, and a great many flies hovering over them. It is an interesting thing about the flies—they are bitten and killed by the marauding yellow jackets. On racks in the shed hang the split fish, the backbone and major ribs having been removed and the flesh wedged apart by sticks. The people like to see the yellow jackets come and crawl over the drying fish, for they will kill every fly and lick up every maggot. The fish business, for dog feed in the winter, is still a thriving one throughout that great part of the North where the white man has scarcely penetrated. Some white men also are in the fish business and come along the rivers gathering the fish from the people by the hundreds of tons in large scows. This was a summer fish camp, and the smells, the sights, and the sounds of the fish camps are never to be forgotten.

The man and woman, both Indians, were a self-respecting family, and this was a particularly good specimen of a well-to-do and prosperous fish camp. Their little boy, age eleven, had never been to school, as there are many native children in Alaska today whom the schools have not yet contacted. However, all spoke fair English in addition to their native dialect, for there is scarcely a corner where English has not penetrated as the universal trading and bartering language.

"Come in. Come in," said the small, erect, cordial man, in the clipped accent which we were to learn to know so well. We entered their tent that stood white among the trees. The woman said nothing but only smiled shyly, while the talking was done by the men. I looked about me from the packing box on which I sat and saw that the earth floor was neatly strewn with fragrant spruce boughs. A small stove with a tiny oven was erected in the middle of the floor, although during sunny weather much of the cooking was done outside on a similar makeshift stove. A rope, stretched across the ceiling, held miscellaneous clothing, drying socks, camping gear; one suitcase was in a corner. The bed in which all slept was a pile of rags on the floor. In all our travels we never saw Alaska natives in possession of mosquito head nets. How could they live without them? Could it be that they were not bitten as we were? The answer is that they are bitten all right but are apparently not as sensitive to the poisonous effects as is a person with a white skin, and further, they let their hair grow long in summer, and simply endure the pests.

"Let's go outside," I said to the woman and boy, and I asked them if I could look at their fish wheel and their dogs. They must have been surprised at this question, for to ask permission to see things so ordinary, things that anyone could see with his own eyes any day for the looking, was unusual. But they politely showed me what I wished to see. This family was not far out of Fairbanks, and although not used to visitors was vaguely used to the ways of white people. My approach was but the general way of all white people in making conversation, to ask rudely about their business and to wish to see everything they possessed. It would be a long time before I would learn to take my seat saying nothing, and to enjoy my coffee or my tea in companionable silence. It would be a long time before I would realize that while a creaking fish wheel, a tent, and a half-dozen howling dogs might mean little to me, to these people they meant possessions of pride and dignity.

Endeavoring to meet in some way the mind of this small woman by my side, I floundered desperately to make conversation about the things which I felt she could understand. We came to the fish wheel churning idly in the muddy current, and I said, "That's a swell fish wheel you've got here," and that's all I could think of to say about it. How often were we to say these meaningless words during the coming weeks!

I saw that a heavy, flat-bottomed river scow was tied to the shore, and in it was an outboard motor. These boats are always square on both ends and are long and narrow. The Indians and whites on the river build the boats themselves, and this is the simplest method of construction, in a country where streamlining and the facilities for streamlining have not come in. At the same time the Indian seems today to have no eye for improving any design which has happened to fall to him. The outboard motors, small, cranky, and undependable, are wasteful to the extreme in pushing their heavy loads, and gasoline costs fifty cents a gallon. Into the boat go man, wife, children, tent, dogs, winter parkas and mukluks, and the bundles of unsalted, smoked fish, cottonwood-cured, when the summer is over.

"Where do you spend the winter?" I asked.

"Go to winter camp, then," said the woman.

"Who do you sell the fish to?"

"N. C. Company boat," came the reply.

"Where is winter camp?"

"It is back in woods. We have trap line," she said proudly.

"I see. Do you live in a warm house then, or still in the tent?" I later learned that questions involving choice are apt to be confusing to those who do not understand too well the language in which they are discoursing.

"Oh, in cabin," she said quickly, and with understanding. "We have good home. We have three houses. This is not our home." She turned to me amused. "We are just camping here. Fish camp."

"Don't you ever worry you might get sick or have accident far from doctor on trap line?" I went on interestedly, now talking like a native myself.

"Never see doctor," she said, although she knew what one was. And in that sentence was contained a vast fund of information, could I have perceived its implications at the time.

We now went to pet the dogs, which must have been to the Indians another asinine request. The five huskies, one of them blue-eyed as evidence of a Siberian strain, were chained to separate trees, each with his own pan. They happened to be well-fed, friendly dogs whom it was safe to pet, which is a rarity. Delighted beyond words to have this unprecedented attention, the unmannerly dogs dashed to the ends of their chains and leaped upon me in a frenzy, almost knocking me down. Slightly embarrassed, I petted them briefly and retired to a safer distance.

Bud, who with the Indian husband was discussing the river, called me over to the tent. We were offered coffee, and a fresh fish to take with us, but declined. It was made clear to us that we would see a great many fish wheels farther down, and that free food was to be had at any of them for the taking, for it is river etiquette for the traveler to help himself at any fish wheel for his needs, day or night. How handy this convenient custom would become for us we could not know, of course, at this time. We would learn to live off the fish wheels, and on dried, smoked, raw fish, too, for days at a time on the Yukon.

Accepting a drink of clear water and filling our two-quart canteen, we shoved off and left our kind friends behind us waving on the shore. And how many were we similarly to leave, before the summer's end, waving on the shores of Alaska's great Interior rivers.

All river water must be boiled and then allowed to settle overnight before it could be drunk, according to the Indians, and they were not wrong in this. Although we had not had the least idea of this before we started, we had fortunately brought a pail, along with a shovel and gold pan, and every evening would be spent boiling a pail of water before we could sleep. Springs and side streams were rare to the point of oddity in this section. This, with so much water all around us that an aerial view would have disclosed a thousand unnamed water pockets, the shallow lakes of the arctic, left over from the glacial age and dotted in on every side as far as the eye could see—a veritable world of water. We later ascertained from whites that water samples upon analysis show bacteria from the colon carried several hundred miles down from Fairbanks and into the Yukon. Only the incoming Army with its septic tanks was defying this time-honored Alaska custom of dumping all city sewage raw into the rivers.

Sunbathing in our canoe in midstream where the mosquitoes could not get us was an obsession we satisfied completely along the first reaches of the Tanana River. Another obsession was exploring old houses. Day after day the binoculars would bring to focus before our eyes a romantic house of laced pieces of birchbark stripped from the surrounding trees, standing all by itself, far across the river in the forest. Sometimes it would be standing in what looked like a beautiful meadow. Sometimes it would be back-lighted by the long arctic sunset or the twilight of the night, for already the days were rapidly becoming shorter. Over we would paddle and having successfully gauged the downward sweep of the current would arrive just at the spot. Especially in rainy weather were we on the lookout for these houses and habitations, for we always hoped to find one in which to sleep. We never did. These houses along the rivers, forgotten relics of another day, were abandoned and decayed. Built of ax-hewn logs, with never a nail, the little cabins were sunk into the ground until one on the outside could put out a hand and touch the roof, and they were hidden, except perhaps for a crazy chimney, by grasses which grew six feet tall. They were our introduction to the typical Yukon cabin long before we reached the river itself. The sagging door, provided you could force your way to it, revealed the interior of a hovel which even an animal would not want to live in—a bed of ragged skins, the hair chewed by large black ants and shrews; the floor possibly of mud, for the boards, if any, had been confiscated by the roving Indians; the Yukon stove, meaning a stove made out of anything one can get, such as a five-gallon oil can, lying in moldy ruins; tall, magenta fireweeds, a willow herb, Epilobium an gusti folium, covering all, in an atmosphere of death and decay. The fireweed blooms close to the warm earth during the first part of the season, the blooms climbing slowly up the stalk as the season progresses. Although it actually spreads by means of underground runners, it is named fireweed because it tends to spring up so rapidly on burned-over land.

To take one's chances in the woods or on the river, no matter how wild the elements, was preferable to camping there. Around such places the woods were wild, and the old cache on its four poles behind the cabin loomed ominously against the forest. However, the crazy old houses had a strong lure for us. It was as though we were always looking for something, although just what we could expect to find, only heaven knew—certainly not treasure. We weren't used to a country completely minus human habitation, and we couldn't believe it at first. The one practical lure to which we could claim excuse was the hope of finding some ancient vegetable garden growing wild, or picking the raspberry patch, for indeed the moldering, dank raspberry bushes grew exceptionally well around the spookiest of the old houses.

One day we spotted a place that looked good from the canoe, and after some difficulty in landing climbed up the bank, mosquito head nets down. What we had seen this time was a cache, set up on poles, as we had learned was usual, about ten feet above the ground, to keep the wild animals out. We got the ladder, climbed up, and had a look inside. Remnants of ancient moose meat and hooves covered the filthy floor. In a trunk that looked like a pirate's chest were cached some filthy work clothing and some fine winter parkas. We noticed then a peculiar carved and painted stick on one corner and a bell which Bud said reminded him of a cowbell. There was nothing to solve the mystery of just what the articles might be, but we concluded that they were part of the ceremonial possessions of a priest of the Russian Greek Orthodox Church, who long ago had come here into the Interior. In back of the cache we then found a gaily painted picket fence inclosing a crude graveyard wherein were eight lonely mounds, each with its little cross. A mound and one cross were just outside the fence, which made us wonder for a moment as to just why this one particular chap didn't get in. Then we noticed suddenly that the paint on the fences was new, bright white and blue paint, on graves probably fifty years old. Why were these graves kept up in this way, and who kept them up? What were the Russian influences in Alaska since the United States bought the Territory in 1867? What are the influences still existing in this new world after the fall of Imperial Russia and the rise of the Soviet Republic? If these ceremonial possessions belonged to a Russian missionary or his descendants today, what kind of a man was here?

The Russian Greek Orthodox Church, with a headquarters in New York City, is still active, we were later to ascertain, especially in western Alaska today, where its evidences are not so much links with headquarters as survivals of something else. Bishop Alexei of the Aleutians directs some of this work and a Russian Greek Orthodox bishop still presides at Sitka. The priests may be native and are supported entirely, however, by the people whom they serve in the wilderness.

Exciting thoughts were in our minds as we left the mystery of the wilderness graveyard and the ceremonial possessions behind us, and pushed downstream, on our way towards western Alaska.

The first thing I had done, from my snug compartment in the stern, was to cast out a trolling line upon leaving Fairbanks. None of the spawning salmon would supposedly bite as they came in from the sea, but I knew it was regarded as a great thrill to hook one of the great, purple, sixty-pound "kings" in the bay, and wouldn't it be wonderful if I just should snag one on my spinner here in the muddy water? It would do no harm to troll for a couple of hundred miles as we went along. Seeing tons of fish in the fish wheels during the summer never spoiled my enthusiasm for catching one on a line. But in this immediate section there were no fish wheels, and we were beginning to feel the need of food. Already we had eaten most of our canned goods and our ready-prepared food which was supposed to have been doled out in emergencies. From this point on we had only, in the main, a ten-pound sack of yellow corn meal, a ten-pound sack of cracked wheat, some canned milk, sugar, and bacon. Between towns we would be living largely off the country, which was why I was so anxious to hook one of those salmon.

"Just what is known about the habits of the king salmon, Bud?" I asked, as we zipped ourselves up tight in our waterproof ski jackets and headed into the rain.

"As I understand it," Bud said, "the king salmon is the largest of all the salmon; the king is different from the dogs, the humpies, the cohoes, the reds, the silvers, and all the rest of 'em, because they fall to pieces with rot when they hit fresh water, get stranded on a sand bar, and the sea gulls and ravens pick their eyes out. Kings travel thousands of miles and may live for years. The other day I heard about another salmon, called the jack salmon, which some people think is the young king before he reaches maturity, for a young king has never been found. They don't know whether this jack salmon is a young king or another species. You know that salmon aren't supposed to eat anything while coming upstream to spawn, but the other day I read a new opinion, that they do eat some microscopic algae and water life—well, little insects and things, I guess. So, who knows, you might get a strike yet. I doubt if anyone has ever sport-fished the Tanana and Yukon consistently."

The rod I was using was a new short steel one given me the past Christmas by Bud, and I had not yet fished with it. Bud had a beautiful new telescope job, a real fly rod for trout and grayling, of which neither of us had ever caught or even seen one. This had been a present to Bud from Fred at our parting. Fred gave me a hand mirror which I kept in my end of the boat; I guess he thought I might need it.

Presently we thought we saw a real grayling stream coming in at the side, across the river. Bud spotted it with those ever- ready glasses which he kept up in front, the best field glasses that money could buy, for amateurs. Bud looked for a difference in the color of the water, and sure enough, when we got over there, it was a dear-water stream, with a deserted house standing among the flaming fireweeds. I saw a fish jump in the quiet water in the mouth of the stream, and we trolled over the place. Some fisherman's instinct told me I would get that fish. *Zing!* The line spun, and I had him, fighting on the shallows of the river bar. On bringing the fellow into the boat we guessed that he weighed about eight pounds and ascertained that he was twenty-seven inches long by the measuring stick which we had painted on the side of the *Queen Beaver* for this very purpose. But what kind of a fish was he? The color was gray and white, the head was large, and the large tail fin and powerful flukes had something about them which indicated one thing: salt water.

This surmise was correct. It was a small chee fish or she fish, which reaches the size of sixty or even eighty pounds, and he had doubtless been waiting on the bar of the incoming side stream to spot smaller fish. I was most pleased, because this fish was very rare in these waters.

We had taken to camping for the night, not in spruce groves, or along sloughs and swamps, but on the heads of windy islands in midstream. Now as night descended with the black clouds of storm, we found one of these, with a natural harbor where large logs of bleached driftwood offered a solid anchor. Here we cooked our fish. Bud said, "Let's cook it in mud tonight just for fun, and we can have the practice so that we'll know how in the future, and we won't have to wash the Dutch oven." We built a fire with the haste of campers now fairly experienced, on top of the buried fish. Bud magically pulled out a brand-new bed net for our bed, which had been in the bottom of the duffel bag. "An N. C. Company clerk persuaded me to include this at the last minute," he smiled. He propped this up on sticks at the four corners of the bed. Except for the fifty or so mosquitoes included in that area of space when the drapes of the bed net were tucked beneath the bedding each night, none should be able to get in at us, and we could soon kill the imprisoned fifty- odd by clapping our hands when we, too, crawled inside.

We had also taken to camping, when possible, on islands where the bank swallows nested. We beat on the perforated and honeycombed mud banks, and a million swallows poured out as we set up our camp. The darting birds, catching them on the wing, were eating up all our mosquitoes for us faster than the eye could see!

Presently we thought our fish should be done, so we uncovered him, skinned him, and laid him on the ground on wax paper. We had no knives, forks, or spoons, nothing in fact but our hunting knives, carved spoons of driftwood, and large tin bowls for stews of sorts. And we had no spatula, a real privation in turning things. We sat down upon the beach to eat our fish with pointed sticks from the platter of the wax paper. We found that the paper had melted through, and our fish was now lying upon the ground.

In the near distance a soft chug-chug came to our ears, and we ran to the edge of the island to see our first stern-wheeler, the *Nenana*, coming slowly up the channel on the opposite side. She had been taking on wood just below, and we had thought her a fish camp in the distance until she moved and came toward us. "Steam boat a-comin'!" we cried, and danced up and down with excitement.

She was a magnificent sight, belching sparks to the sky as she labored, pushing a 150-foot barge before her, and her great red paddles thrashing up fifteen-foot waves behind. "Quite a packet, isn't she?" said Bud. "Wouldn't you rather be on that boat now if you could, than here?"

I answered truthfully when I said, "No, I wouldn't. Would you?"

"I should say not. I wouldn't take it if they'd give it to me. Not for this."

We walked back to our supper in the purple evening glow of storm clouds and gold. The fish was well cooked. I took two or three little bites of it as it lay there, and it was delicious. But the waves washing in on the beach brought a bit of oil, a small amount of sand gritted between my teeth, and the very driftwood lying by smelled of fish and foam. I had perhaps become too empty, for my appetite was light. Apparently, Bud felt the same way, for without a word we simply kicked the fish into the river. It had been a fine day, and we just went to bed.

4

Indian Service

Hunting licenses in Alaska are issued from July 1 of one year to July 1 of the following year. January would be an awkward time to issue the new licenses because it comes in the middle of the trapping season when many hunters are scattered far and wide at winter camp and cannot be found. An estimated 8000 whites out of Alaska's total population of 80,000, excluding the armed forces, make their living by trapping.

This year Bud and I were the first in all the Territory to apply for the new hunting licenses, which were our first 1 The forms were late in arriving from Washington, as most things are, so we paid our dollar license fee at Fairbanks and simply started. We would pick up the licenses after the trip was over, at Bethel, if we got there. In leaving Fairbanks we also left all game officials behind for good, but we were our own game officials in a big country. Jack O'Connor of the Alaska Game Commission, a personal friend, simply wished us "the time of our lives," and he was sure we would be only too glad to keep an eye on game conditions in the Interior as we found them traveling along.

The perhaps too generous hunting licenses allowed us for the year included: bull moose, one each; caribou, three each; mountain sheep, two each; mountain goats, two each; large brown or grizzly bears, in most of the Territory, no limit; black bear, including its brown, blue, or glacier bear, color variations, three each yearly, no closed season; ptarmigan and grouse, ten daily in season from August 20 to January

31; geese, two in possession daily as stipulated by the Federal migratory bird laws; deer (most of southeastern Alaska's deer had formerly been exterminated by secret floating canneries sent out from Seattle), a fifteen-day season in limited localities at present. Buffalo are imported, and some day there will be a hunting season on them

as they are increasing rapidly. This was not an area for all kinds of big game, and we were not primarily hunting, anyway.

Hunting and trapping licenses for the "native," meaning all persons of at least half Eskimo, Aleut, or Indian blood, are acquired at birth as an inheritance and are a lifetime affair. Incidentally, just to show the confusion existing between the half a hundred different government bureaus and departments operating in Alaska, while the Game Commission defines a "native" as of half native blood, to be a "native" to the Public Health Department one may have but one-fourth native blood. Many whites in Alaska's cities are not exactly sure what a native is, when wondering if they should invite their next-door neighbor in to dinner. The answer is that some are invited and some aren't.

All persons native and white are required to make a yearly report on a form to the Alaska Game Commission of the numbers of the game and furs taken. Most of Alaska's natives are still in the hunting and fishing stages of cultural development, and they depend on hunting and fishing for their livelihood.

One gets a lot of misinformation on game conditions, as well as other conditions in Alaska. There are people who will try to tell you, for instance, that there are only three walruses left in existence—two in zoos, and one stuffed. The walrus are decreasing, yet the Eskimos still kill them by the dozens if not by the hundreds yearly in Bering Sea and along the Aleutians. It was only a couple of years ago that an attempt was first made to restrict even the Eskimos to a season on this game. Up to this time they were permitted practically unlimited scope in hunting most animals at all times. That the game in Alaska will soon need greater protection and that the day is coming when a different sort of economy should be set up for the native is a thought which strikes the traveling stranger, if not the native Alaskan.

A BRIGHT SUNDAY MORNING PRESENTLY found us sunning and dreaming along beneath blue skies and brought two black bears waltzing slowly on a tangent down an open patch on the hill beside us. I hastily put down my mirror and toothbrush and awoke to reality with a snap, just in time to maneuver us into some snags where we each caught hold of a branch and waited. This was the moment we had been waiting for. We wanted to get one of those bears. Bud had shot two or three bears in his life, one of them with a .45 pistol, and was somewhat seasoned in big-game thrills. He knew his ballistics almost to the last detail, reloaded his own ammunition (had done so since the age of seven), and knew the anatomy of his animals. Best of all, Bud never overestimated himself or his gun, and he had never let a cripple get away.

Now in the generosity of his affection he longed for his wife to be a killer of bears. He had foresightedly bought me one of the largest rifles ever made in America, the Winchester .405, usually used for elephant or rhinoceros. In my own hunting career, I had shot a deer and four wild boars among the larger game, and what I had done of it I had liked so much that I was prompted partially by such desires to come to Alaska in the first place.

As foul luck would have it, however, at this time of all times, one of the few passing motorboats of the entire strip now put in its appearance. We were near the town of Nenana, where the railroad would join us for the last time before the river turned due northwest for the Yukon. As the boat would alarm the bears, there was nothing to do but take to the brush after them before it arrived. We hurried up the mountain, crawling through thickets of tangled slide alder.

Perspiration poured down into my eyes, my breath came laboriously so that I doubted if I had the strength to raise my trembling rifle to my shoulder, let alone hit any kind of a target. Suddenly, looking out from my torn mosquito net, I found myself now quite alone, for Bud, feeling my elephant gun would be ample protection, had left me to my own devices and removed himself rapidly to only heaven knew where in search of the bears. It seems that in his nobility of character he had had the idea that if I couldn't make it up to the bears he would obligingly drive them down to me, much as he had once driven a herd of thirty wild pigs to me in Arizona.

But the more I had seen of wild animals the more amazing and inexplicable their lives and actions had become to me. A bear in a zoo is one thing; a wild bear in a forest becomes an entity whose comings and whose goings are veiled in mystery. The bears had simply vanished. Not a trace of them was to be found.

My visions of fine bear steaks and a fine bear robe exploded. Bud only said, "I kind of wish now I had taken a crack at him through my new telescope sight. I couldn't have missed, could I?"

"I suppose you couldn't have," was all I could say. These were the first bears I had ever seen in the wild, and the only bears, as it happened, that we were to see all summer. Bears are where you find them.

At Nenana kids were swimming in the warm sunshine in a quiet spot at the edge of the river. This was the town famed for the yearly Nenana Ice Pool, which here clocks the instant the ice starts to move out each spring, and on which everybody in Alaska places his bet in a kind of national derby.

Bud sent our mail while I stayed in the canoe to keep an eye on things, after which we took a prompt departure. "We've got to get going towards the Yukon," remarked Bud, as he handed me a candy bar from the general store. "Do you realize it's almost August? We have a long ways to go, and we had better get to paddling. If we make a run all night tonight we should be able to clip off thirty-eight or forty miles. And maybe we could see some bears when it's still."

"Did you ask after the war news?" I questioned.

"Yes, it doesn't look so good for the Allies. It's going to be a long war this time."

We paddled all night, a twenty-hour stretch in all, leaving Nenana and the railroad far behind us. Rustlings and snorts in the brush attended the darkest hours of the night, which were from 11:00 to 2:00, war time, when the sun dipped briefly below the rim of the world, its progress presaged by a weird red glow behind the scraggly, skinny spruce trees. Dodging the boat traps was by now second nature to me, and, gaining confidence, I took all kinds of fancy channels and cuts between the islands, some that were only a few feet wide, where the red and golden waters assumed a glassy appearance that was unreal and deceptive. I was playing quite a game, and I knew it; Bud had gone sound asleep sitting up, and our safety was in my own vigilance. Bud was as yet no canoeist and being in the bow he had no power whatsoever to direct us, but only to follow my command instantly.

Mists rose from the water, the river seemed to take on a stillness, and the mosquitoes descended, following me in clouds as I guided us out into the center again, and, in the clear once more, confidently pulled down my mosquito net—a rather successful blackout for me, for I could now see practically nothing. In the distance the boom of a caving bank came familiarly to my ears.

Then suddenly something loomed up dead ahead. "Bud, paddle on the left," I screeched. Bud awoke with a jerk and dug in, just in time. A twist of the rudder scooted us past a six-inch log which rose two feet up from the waters before us like the nose of some battleship cannon and plunged again to the hidden depths. "Boy, that was a close one!" Bud said.

"I guess we'd better quit and go to bed after that," I suggested, but it was already getting daylight again before we found a good island on which to land.

Across the water from this island was the cluster of log cabins which was marked on our map as Minto Village. Dawn streaked the sky with gorgeous purples and reds intertwined with silver just over this sleeping village of native muskrat hunters as we staggered wearily onto firm land again. Somewhere in the past hours Bud had gathered three fish from a fish wheel. Now he filleted them on a log—king salmon, dog salmon, and white- fish—and flung the carcasses into the river. We had wanted to try them all. The fish meat was left in the bucket in a salt solution and then we wearily turned in. Sleep came as the noises of the day commenced.

The day after this stretch was spent barefooted in the sands of what was a real South Sea island paradise, eating, sunning, and stitching a new canvas cover with a sailor's needle. The cover was made to protect all our outfit, with a rope at the edges which slipped snugly under the gunwales. It was detachable, to be used only at night and in case of rain during the day. It stopped necessarily at the junction of our seats, but a loose projecting flap at my end would cover my lap, and Bud could wrap up in the other small piece of canvas so that we could now travel in all-weather quite comfortably. We had learned within a few days that to travel in this country in an open boat was out of the question.

It was late in the afternoon, and we were glad to be traveling, eager for what the next turn of the river might bring in the way of a new scene before we would rest again; traveling had gotten into our blood as it never had before. We camped again, and I slept under the white mosquito head net while Bud took the camera and glasses and went inland. He didn't go far, for he was soon stopped by one of the innumerable puddles of the Minto Lakes district, but he came back and got the canoe, and paddled slowly and with some trepidation to a lake, in which he saw two moose. At this season of the year all the moose lay quietly submerged in the inland lakes, communing with nature and dripping with water lilies. To escape from the insects, they closed the flaps on their flaring, velvety nostrils, and headed for deep water, while the great northern pike looked at them askance with fishy eyes. The thick skins of the moose, with their under layer of fat, insulated them completely against the icy water. On the way back, Bud mistakenly tried to tie the canoe to a wasps' nest on the bank and was obliged to retreat behind his head net in a hurry, although he got a picture before he left.

I had fallen asleep to the cries of a strange bird which haunted me in my dreams. Coming from the inland lakes, it filled the atmosphere with a medley of sounds, as of someone idly strumming his fingers over the strings of a giant harp in the dreamy distance.

It was on the following day that a motorboat with a white man and woman in it came into our lives quite suddenly. It was rather late in the morning, and we weren't making much progress although we labored at the paddle mightily. There seemed to be no current here to speak of and since yesterday we hadn't seen the rest of the river, which was strange. "Do you suppose we'll come back to the main river all right?" I fumed.

"Sure, we're bound to," Bud reassured me. "There's only one place in the world that I've heard of where you can go down a river and not come back to the main river again. That's some place on the upper Yukon, in the Flats."

It was then that we saw the boat, coming easily up behind us.

"Hello!" the occupants cried excitedly.

"Hello there!" we returned warmly as they stopped their motor alongside and grabbed hold. We saw a white man and woman, and between them a silver-tipped, wolf like dog.

"Where did you ever come from?" asked the small, bright-eyed woman with the quaint hair-do.

"Where are you going off the main river?" interposed the man with interest.

"I guess we got off the river by accident," said Bud. "My wife and I are taking a canoe trip."

"I should say you are! But you're a ways out of your course. This slough here is fifty miles long and there's nothing along here. It empties into the Tolovana River after about thirty miles."

"There's nothing like that on our map." I cried out against the unfairness of it all.

"I know, but lots of Alaska isn't on any map, you know," the man said, "or it's usually wrong. Just ask the pilots. But you'll get back to the Tanana all right. Just keep going like you are."

"We're the Hollands of Minto Village, and we're so pleased and surprised to see somebody down our way," spoke up the woman then. And to me: "I only get to see another white woman about once a year when we go into Fairbanks to order our year's supplies."

We introduced ourselves then and climbed into their boat at their invitation. "Now you women can really talk," said Mr. Holland, as I made myself comfortable. He didn't look as though he was going to do so badly himself at that. The Hollands were, as we might have guessed, Indian Service people.

"If you had only stopped over to see us," Mrs. Holland told me. "You know our natives told us there were a couple of white men camping over on the island, but a white woman—I never dreamed!"

"If we had had any idea there were white people at Minto Village, we certainly would have stopped," I said. "You must have a very wonderful and unusual life there. How long have you been in the Indian Service?"

"Five years. Yes, we think we have a rather nice life. When we first took Minto Village it had the reputation of being one of the very worst posts in Alaska. Nobody wanted it, I guess. The Indians were terrible. Oh, we haven't done all there is to do, as it's something you can only live day by day, and it takes infinite patience, of course, but we think we have helped them some. Other things going on in the world don't seem to mean a great deal, after getting into this work.

"When we go Outside on furlough, people try so hard to show me a good time for what I've missed, staying here, and they feel so sorry for me. We show them pictures of our lives here, but they still can't understand why we should want to live here. They think it's just ice and snow and loneliness. But as for me, I couldn't live away from Alaska again. When I go Outside, *that's* when I'm lonely, among people I don't have anything in common with any more. I'm lonely then to get back to this big, beautiful, free country. You're your own boss here. You don't have to mark time for anybody. It seems strange that some people do, doesn't it? Just look at it—" and she indicated with a sweep of the hand—"where any place in this world today could you find a day more perfect than this?"

It was indeed glorious. We were pioneers. There was still pioneering to be done in the world, and we were glad. No other human being within miles, and the free earth singing.

Her opinions were but typical. I had long since drawn the conclusion generally that Alaskans like to live in Alaska.

I next asked her about the Indians in the Interior. That was something I had been wanting to know, for I knew that they must have a name.

"They are Athapascans or Athabascans," she informed me. "Either is correct. They are very degenerate in many respects, however, as they have forgotten their origins and most of their tribal customs and their pride since the coming of the white man. That is what usually happens. Their culture never was as highly evolved as that of the Eskimos."

"Are they very diseased?"

"Yes, pitifully so. The draft board took one look at our village and just crossed us off the map as far as they were concerned. There is some venereal disease, but mostly it's the tuberculosis I

Active tuberculosis in adults was estimated at the Sixth Pacific Science Congress in 1939 to be around 85 per cent. Since then, I don't know if there has been any change. Someone has said that the average life expectation for the women is thirty-five years, for the men forty years of age, although they move around so much from village to village that it is hard even for missions to keep really accurate records that can be trusted. You see your Alaska natives are citizens as well as wards of the government. The problem in both medicine and education is to get to these people, because they are always roaming. Private medicine cannot reach them, and a public medical campaign proves very expensive. They remain at Minto Village, for instance, only because they like the teacher. We can't make them do anything. They are free to come or go as they wish. Nothing is accomplished except by persuasion and by gaining their friendship and confidence. The government offers them certain advantages, but it's up to them if they want to accept them. The bright children get free transportation to a free high school education at Eklutna near Anchorage, and they all get free medical care at the Indian hospitals located about here and there. But they are just like children in many of their attitudes. They never look into the future but are extremely improvident. We also find them very jealous and a very unappreciative people in some respects. Their hunters will bring back bear and moose and divide it in the middle of the village right in front of our door, but as long as we have been with them, they have never offered us anything. We always pay them for anything we get from them and for all services done, of course."

"Do you folks ever have to play the part of a doctor yourselves?" I asked.

"Oh, yes, we get the medical book down from the shelf every now and then, and we bandage lots of cuts and sprains. Usually their own midwives deliver the babies. We are everything to the natives—doctor, lawyer, game warden, postmaster, and my husband is commissioner for the district. He marries them and buries them and has a seat in the tribal council.

"One of the big problems with these people I feel is nutrition.

I have often wondered if the terrible craving of the Indian for alcohol might not be partially nutritional as well as psychological. Incidentally there is no alcohol in our village, but they go to Nenana in their boats and get drunk, and we can't stop them. Natives can buy liquor in Alaska. We try to discourage the extensive use of "white man's grub," especially sugar and flour, of which they eat four times as much as a white man and which seems to hasten the decay of their teeth. I've got all the women raising gardens of potatoes, cabbages and rutabagas—if you had come over you could have seen our gardens! Sometimes the hunters of our village rather turn up their noses at vegetables, though. They really like meat best."

Mr. Holland, who had been talking to Bud, now turned to me.

"Well," he said, "we might as well be getting on. Won't you folks come along with us and pick blueberries for the day? We can't let you go now. We won't take you much out of your way."

As we sped along, the *Queen Beaver* towed alongside, the cool air on our cheeks was as heady as wine. Mrs. Holland told me about how her husband and she cut each other's hair, and how he was going to give her a homemade permanent wave soon. She told me how classrooms for the natives were located in the same building and under the same roof with the Indian Service residence quarters so that the teacher stepped across the hall to go to school. She told me about her electric washing machine and about her "icebox" at the village. The icebox, holding barrels of blueberries for the winter, her butter and her canned whipping cream from Fairbanks, and in inner compartments whole moose and caribou on occasion, was simply a cavern dug into the frozen earth, and it worked the year round. Two thirds of Alaska has perpetually frozen subsoil, on the arctic coast extending down as deep as some three hundred feet. In summer the frozen area lies from ten to eighteen inches beneath the heated surface of the ground, and gardens are planted upon this. The areas of perpetually frozen subsoil are highly irregular and undependable, as they have exactly avoided the irregular paths of the glaciers of 20,000 years ago. Where the glaciers once lay, the earth has kept warm.

Picking blueberries far up the Tolovana River, we dabbed on mosquito repellent by the bottle, and kept a sharp lookout for bears. The country was wild and rolling, the sky of an unclouded blue. Our picnic lunch consisted of fish and beans, donated by ourselves, and dried fish and hardtack donated by the Hollands.

Afterward we sat and talked until suddenly it was sundown and we realized that the day had come to an end. It was eleven o'clock at night, and the Hollands could not remain to camp with us in the blueberry patch but must be getting home. "Our people would be worried to death if we didn't get back," they explained. "The chief would have everybody out looking for miles around."

We thanked the Hollands for the perfect memory of one golden day spent in the Interior picking blueberries.

5

Wilderness Family

The Hollands had mentioned that they had one neighbor, forty miles away, on the Tolovana. "You'll be going right by his place," said Holland. "He's a very peculiar and interesting man, a white man. Said on his draft questionnaire that he was educated at Princeton. You can't miss him. He'll probably want you to stop and stay with him a few days. Don't mention that I told you, though, because we don't get on."

The current of the Tolovana River was sluggish, and we were sunbathing along when the sound of chopping was brought to our ears. Time had stopped. There was simply the river, without beginning and without end, and we were drifting on it. We were bringing with us a couple of small teal ducks as our offering, as we would always try to bring some sort of gift or service to those whom we visited. Again, came the sound of chopping and the flash of a double-bitted ax in the sun. The chopping stopped amid a weird chorus of howls as vicious chained dogs lifted their muzzles to the sky, and now came the useless shouts of a man, trying to stop them. It was a scene which was to grow familiar, one which would become less shocking to the senses at a later time. As the cabin came into sight we saw the familiar fireweeds growing on its roof—an old trick, sodding a roof to keep the heat in—and smoke was issuing from the chimney, rising up in the little clearing. A fine plank houseboat and two Indian canoes were nearby, and our eye fell upon plots of thriving early cabbages and potatoes. The dogs huddled by their kennels, panting miserably in the heat, their fur crawling with mosquitoes and the hard-packed ground about them giving up a vile odor where they were obliged to lie in their offal. The eyes of the dogs followed us always, noting every least movement.

A great tall man, in rags and moccasins, on his head a skullcap made of an old sock, and with a long flowing beard, turned vacant blue eyes upon us from the bank, staring as though unable to comprehend what he saw. This, as we were presently to learn, was Dick. The slant-eyed boy of twelve who came to his side was Tommy. Tommy was not Dick's son, but he was Mary's son, and he had half white blood. Mary was standing in the doorway, Dick's wife of ten years. Only four feet tall, for she was a hunchback, she was half Chinese and half Eskimo. She was blind in one eye from what appeared to be a cataract and had black and broken teeth.

As he helped us ashore the white man now appeared highly excitable. Ordering his woman to prepare food, he ushered us into his house.

"Nobody comes down this way," he told us in rapid-fire speech. "This is a big day for me. I got nobody but the woman here and the boy to talk to. You don't know how lonesome a man gets to talk to his own kind—but I wouldn't want to live with 'em! It's fine to hear somebody's voice and thoughts besides your own just talking back to you. Do you understand? I guess you must think, 'He's a funny old bird,' huh?" The man laughed now at himself, rocking in almost voiceless mirth.

Did we understand? We did. At least we hoped so. This was our first experience in talking with a person "bushed," but by putting ourselves mentally in his position we knew that any of us could soon get the same way.

I noticed that the table on which food was set before us was of inlaid, polished wood, a table made by a craftsman. The food itself was strange to me: canned moose nose, considered an Alaskan delicacy, black coffee, and slices of sourdough bread spread with moose "butter."

"You ain't eatin' much," the trapper observed. "You don't like it, eh?"

"Oh, yes, only I'm not very hungry."

"If they don't like it, throw it out, Mary, and give them something else. These are our guests."

I hastened to assure him that I did like the food, which was the truth.

"Our life here is simple," he told us. "It's just as you see it.

Only things mostly we buy from them damned bean peddlers is gasoline for the boat, a little sugar and flour, and the coffee and tobacco a man needs. You people looked all gone when I saw you come in. Are you trying to siwash it?"

"I beg your pardon?"

"I mean, are you living off the country as you go?"

"Well, a little," Bud said. "I always wanted to see if a man could do it. You never really know until you try. Besides, it doesn't do to carry large amounts of cash on you on the river, and N. C. stores are far between."

"I seen you kids is inexperienced and don't know how to get by. But this country has nothing. You get down on your blessed Yukon now and it's all been hunted over by the Indians before you were born."

He got up and went to the door. "Why not bring your boat up on the bank? You're here to stay awhile now, you know. We couldn't just let them run off, could we, Mary? I see"—he cleared his throat—"that you are taking a look at my books. So, what do you think of them?"

On the built-in shelf I had spied some volumes of the philosophers. In one hand I held Friedrich Nietzsche, in the other Voltaire. "I used to take some courses in this sort of thing," I said, looking him in the eye. I wanted to know about this man. Strangely enough, it was Mary, the little brown woman with the warped, crippled body, who answered me, speaking for the first time.

"We read together largely from Nietzsche, my friend," she said softly, coming up under my arm. "Dick has taught Tommy to read, too," she explained. "You read, don't you, Tommy?"

"Sometimes," replied the boy.

I liked the way in which Mary had said, "my friend." Later she and I and Tommy went to the blueberry patch growing wild as jungles by the side of the house, where with a native blueberry comb we soon gathered enough berries for a pie for supper.

Then we went into the woods at the opposite side of the house and immediately returned with two buckets filled with the Alaskan "beefsteak" mushrooms. These we sorted, the smaller, hard ones to be carefully cleaned and fried for our evening meal and to be combined in bear soup; and the larger fly-blown ones filled with maggots to be boiled in junction with a large pike and thrown as slop into the dog pans. The pike were caught in fishnets Mary wove rapidly with a shuttle. She could make the loops almost faster than the eye could see; the vicious pike threshed a new net to pieces each three weeks.

"It's a funny thing, we tried for hours to hook one of those pike on a line along the Tolovana," Bud told Dick. "Do you ever do any sport fishing here?"

"No," he admitted. "I don't think they'll take anything. Those fellows live on game—young ducks, birds and things. They'll drive the muskrats out of a country, too, when they get started."

"Some fish," we breathed, and looked at each other, realizing that this was but the beginning, that there were literally hundreds of rivers like the Tolovana in Alaska that had never known an adventuring fisherman. Even Uncle Fred had tried to convince us that it was too far north for such fish to live through the winter conditions of an almost uninhabitable country. Yet there they were. Tommy, the wilderness boy, was interested in our fishing poles because he had never seen one or conceived of catching a fish in this way, other than that some people did it in the magazines.

His house, his garden, his toolshed and cache, Dick showed us with pardonable pride, talking a steady stream of conversation which lasted ten hours the first day. "You have to give him credit for the ways he has contrived to make a living in this wilderness," Bud whispered to me privately. "Do you think most of the people you know could do it? Whether you agree with the man or not—do you know he cuts all his boards and planks just with an ax? Have you noticed his device for filtering his drinking water through gravel? He has figured out everything. It's just about an ideal primitive life as one man sees it. He catches bears in snares. He's learned a lot of things from the Indians and then he can beat them at their own game."

The sleds and snowshoes that the wilderness family made even I could see were works of art, each created with a lasting care. Far out into the trackless forest the husband and father of the family would go in his eternal quest for food. Lean and hard, his endurance was limitless, although he was a man crowding fifty. Sometimes he would come upon a birch tree of just the right age and size for snowshoes, and these he laboriously carved. His courageous Mary, with her varying weights of sinews tanned from caribou hide, or sometimes, in fine work, from the tail of the muskrat, would patiently follow Dick's design and weave in the rest. They were beautiful and unusual designs.

Bud was enthusiastic over the ingenious household chairs and over the Daniel Boone fringed moose jacket Mary had made for Dick, and over the caribou socks (the heel corresponding with the hock of the animal) which the family wore in winter. "Mary can teach your wife to make them," Dick said easily. "Why don't you stay awhile?"

Slowly I myself began to reverse, just slightly at first, some of my opinions, as there began to form in my mind the picture of their daily labors for life and of their conceptions of the universe. And as for these conceptions, who could say that they were entirely wrong? Life was different out here from the easy life lived by townspeople who bought their ease with the slavery of their life's time devoted to the comforts of the body. These people disdained many of those comforts but particularly that slavery.

Breakfast the next morning was waiting for us after a refreshing sleep within the houseboat, where we had put up our usual mosquito bed net and made camp. Sourdough hot cakes with blueberry syrup and bear bacon comprised the meal, which with a reviving appetite I heartily enjoyed. "You've got to eat if you're going to work," Dick said to me, which made me, I must confess, slightly apprehensive as to what was coming next. I knew that Bud was wild to go out on a hike with Dick for the day to see some of his trap-line country. "He can teach me how to call moose right up to me and that's something few white men really know," Bud argued.

"But what will I do all day? What can I find to talk about with that woman? What is my place here? How am I to act?"

"Just act like yourself. Mary makes very good bread. You don't know how to make bread," Bud suggested reasonably.

It was after the men were gone that I began to see that a really fine mind, for her limited education and opportunities, burned within my friend Mary.

She showed me her sourdough bucket. "My husband is of course a sourdough addict," she informed me, smiling. "We use no baking powder here. I used to cook in white ladies' houses in Nenana, and I can make lemon pie, strawberry shortcake, roast lamb and mint jelly—anything you please. But Dick wants to get away from all that. He believes baking powder is very harmful to the system, for instance."

"So that's what a sourdough is?" I asked.

"Yes, they only use soda. But Dick doesn't believe in letting the batter get as sour as many of them do."

"I suppose they find it hard to agree even with each other on certain points," I murmured.

"How true," she laughed. "All men think they know best. But you should have a sourdough bucket. It makes everything." It certainly did make everything at that—bread, biscuits, pancakes, cakes, and even liquor. The sourdough "starter" consists of one original cake of yeast, which is allowed to ferment with a little sugar, water, and flour. One starter can be used for a thousand years without replenishing it if a person so desires. All you ever add is flour and water to increase the quantity of your batter. Just before using, you sweeten your batter with a pinch of baking soda, but always leaving a small amount of the original sour batter in the bottom of the bucket for the starter of the next batch. Thus, at last I learned literally the meaning of being an Alaskan sourdough—a word grown famous about the world.

When we washed the dishes Mary used no soap, but again, following the typical sourdough policy, used baking soda in the water. Many sourdoughs believe that the use of soap on dishes causes many maladies in human life, including cancer of the stomach, although I have been unable yet to find a housewife who will agree.

Mary explained to me briefly (the explanation was brief, but the process was long) the two methods of tanning skins. There is the "alder" method and then there is the "native" method.

The first consists of softening the green skins in a solution made from boiling the bark of the alder; the second of softening them by the brains of the animals killed and by soap, if available. Mary sometimes also made her own soap from tallow. Human urine is saved by the natives, both Indians and Eskimos, for its tannic acid, which is excellent in tanning the skins. Thus "native-tanned" or "squaw-tanned" implies to white people a garment which is much too odoriferous to be worn around civilization. Both methods entail long hours, days, and weeks of laborious handling, smoothing and rubbing, for only patience can turn out a creditable skin; the reason, no doubt, why our own early endeavors along these lines had never made the kind of skins that Mary made.

"Did you like your life in Nenana, Mary?"

"Oh, sometimes I get lonesome for the city life—you know how it is—but this is the best. It is so peaceful. No troubles. This is much better than working for white ladies—to work for yourself, to be free. I used to have to work harder to support my little baby scrubbing and cooking for the white ladies than I do here."

An outcast from her people at Bering Sea, this hunchbacked child had been raised by the mission at Holy Cross, whose teachers are monks and nuns. When Dick found her doing housework in Nenana some time later, she had a baby, half white, and no father for it, which is a common predicament among native girls. Dick took her away and taught her his version of the lost arts of her people once again. In doing so, he sincerely believed he was doing the right thing, and he stuck by her.

She told me the cause of her deformity: when she was about five years old her cousin was pushing her in a swing. Swinging was a pastime acquired from her Chinese father, who had once been a laundry boy for the forces of the United States Army in Alaska. He had been a devoted father. Later the Eskimos collected enough money to send him back to China in his old age—his great desire—and he was not heard from again. But neither he nor anyone else thought of a possible accident, apparently, in the fact that there was a sharp, freshly cut stump beneath the children's swing, for when the swing broke one day, it was upon this terrible instrument that the child fell, never to rise erect again. There was no doctor. She never saw a doctor until much later in her life when her people came up the mouth of the Yukon.

When Bud and Dick came in sometime later they had walked at least twenty miles. "There's a seven-thousand-foot mountain range just back of the house, dear," Bud informed me. "You can't see it from here, but to Dick's knowledge it has no name, and nobody has ever been on it, not even Dick. We lay in the sun on the lower slopes and ate raspberries from bushes ten inches high, for a long time. Wolf tracks as big as my hand all over the place. Dick says they'll go 140 pounds. And I saw some of Dick's other cabins. They live here only in the summer, you know. His other cabins are all outfitted just like this one. He has about fifty miles of trails cut in, all carefully hidden from the Indians, who resent him. It's just one man's private park."

"You like it then?" I asked.

"He says we could have one of the cabins to live in if we'd like to stay this winter and be trapping partners. Marten season—sable to you, darling—has just been declared open this year for the first time in ten years."

I romanced greedily on sable for a moment, then put it out of my mind.

"What I'd like to know is who this Dick is, if he really is a college man, and where he comes from and why he's living like this."

Dick answered the question of where he came from that evening, when he told us he was born at Nome and had lived all his life in the woods. He said it so convincingly that I was forced at the time to believe him. "Not to be curious," I asked a little later, just bursting with curiosity, "but do your people know about you now?"

He took this overstepping of the bounds of familiarity in good grace, fortunately. "No. You have to give up all that when you choose your own way. I have a daughter older than you, in Seattle," he said quietly.

After that we changed the subject.

"The mystery deepens," I said to Bud beneath our mosquito net the second night. "Do you really think he might have gone to Princeton?"

"It's hard to tell," was Bud's candid opinion. "He claims to have seen India, and I don't doubt that. He's a pretty well- rounded man, aside from his peculiarities. He gets jittery out here sometimes, do you know it?"

"No! Really? How do you know?"

"Oh, I know. He told me something about his feud with the Indians, and of course they'd kill him in a moment if they dared, and the world would scarcely know the difference. We're not exactly in town, dear. Another private feud he's wrapped up in now is with one of those big brown bears. You know that's one of the few animals that will hunt man. They'll lie in wait behind trees sometimes. One of those big boys has come into this territory during the past few weeks and Dick knows the bear is around and the bear knows Dick is around, and they're kind of playing hide and seek with each other. What he worries about is not himself, but his family. He gets to thinking what might happen to them if he should go out on one of those trips sometime and not come back. There's a lot of things can happen to a man alone. He's afraid Tommy might drown in the river. He has never been able to teach the boy to swim because of course the mosquitoes would eat him alive. Last year he came back from a trip and found Tommy had cut himself with the ax and almost bled to death while he was gone."

"Yes, Mary told me. When Tommy bled till he was unconscious, do you know what she did? She just left him lying on the bank and ran into the house to bed, because she was afraid to look. I tried to teach her a little first aid."

Bud was no longer listening. He was sound asleep.

When we awoke the morning was late. We went into the cabin, and the radio, which was Dick's one concession to civilization for Mary, was saying: "Every college and university should be turned into an Army and Navy training center. The bullets that a high-school boy or girl makes can kill a Jap. No person shall be allowed more than five automobile tires—"

"Turn that damned thing off, Mary," Dick was saying disgustedly as we entered.

"I guess we've got to get on for the Yukon," said Bud, his shoulders back in a way that meant business.

"You're not wrong there if you intend to go," replied our host. "There's an old saying, you know, that there's but two seasons in Alaska: winter, and the Fourth of July. But have a bite to eat first and think it over. What's there for you out there? No rush, no rush. You people seem to be in such a hurry, just like they are out there, hey?"

Before we left, Dick got his old moose antlers down from the cache and we took pictures of them. They were so large they would scarcely go through the door except by the utmost efforts of two men. "It was not an exceptionally large animal these came off of," Dick explained, putting them back in the cache, "but I've just been keeping them, I don't know why. You can have 'em if you want 'em."

Bud longed to take the antlers with us more than I knew at the time, but that was next to impossible. As it turned out, they were the world's largest and most perfect spread of moose antlers ever killed by man, numbering 76 inches from tip to tip as against the 75 15/16-inch spread of the world's record. One larger set was found on a dead moose on the Kenai Peninsula, and now exists in a museum.

To Mary I gave our next to last can of tomatoes, a favorite food of hers of which she had dreamed nights but seldom tasted because Dick's theory of dietetics did not include it. To Tommy I gave our last can of orange juice because he had never tasted it.

"You know one of my cabins stands right by the wildest grayling stream you ever saw," Dick said persuasively. (He had been told of our weakness for the elusive arctic grayling.) "And the geese come over here by the thousands in the fall. And the caribou have their calves right over here in these hills. We eat T-bone steaks and wild goose with cranberry sauce around here all winter, you know. You would like the snow in the winter, and to break trail for the dogs, eh?"

But we didn't weaken in our determination to go on. "It's been nice knowing you, since I can't make you stay," he finally said, smiling, like a man who is taking his medicine. The preparations for our departure were made complete.

"It's been wonderful knowing you, Dick, and you, Mary and Tommy," we said, holding out our hands to them.

"It's not my name," said Dick at last. "But names don't make any difference. I never rightly knew yours. But we know each other, don't we?"

Yes, we knew each other. We wished Dick and his wilderness family happy hunting until we should meet again—and all of that strange race of men, like Dick, who even today live quietly and alone along the trickling tributaries of the Yukon.

6
Living Off the Country

In Alaska many young men were rejected by the draft boards because of bad eyes or bad teeth. People who have never had tooth decay have sometimes been known to have their teeth practically fall to pieces after a year or two of residence in the Territory. The reasons for this are rather interesting. The waters of Alaska, unlike those of most places, carry no lime. The only natural food giving calcium in any quantity, outside of the bones of animals and fish, is milk. Fresh milk in Alaska is used by people like our Uncle Fred, for instance, only as a medicine in case of illness. It costs thirty cents a quart or forty-five cents a quart with the bottle and is obtainable in limited quantities from small dairy herds on the outskirts of the cities of Seward, Anchorage, Palmer, and Fairbanks, along the railroad. Ice cream costs a dollar a quart. The cows, incidentally, do not thrive easily, but tend towards early tuberculosis from lack of enough sunlight, and part of their winter hay, at least, must be shipped in from Outside at the cost of from $65 to $150 a ton, depending on the locality. It is not, however, that Alaskans cannot afford to buy milk in these vicinities. I have seen Uncle Fred flavor his fresh milk with canned milk until it suited his taste. The fact is that some old-timers have completely lost their taste for milk and dairy products, and actually prefer the familiar canned milk which sits, like an old friend, in its little brace on every Alaskan lunch counter.

The lack of any quantity of the calcium- and phosphorus giving milk is coexistent with another interesting scarcity: lack of calcium in the water throughout the Territory, and lack of Vitamin D in sunshine, which physicians tell us is curiously necessary in the body for the assimilation of what calcium we do get.

Although there are more daylight hours in the Arctic and Antarctic Zones than in the other zones on earth (as refraction of light in the atmosphere increases with a decrease in temperature), these hours are largely twilight, while the sun circles near or below the rim of the world. When one of the rare sunny days comes in summer, the Alaskan perishes with the heat. He is as afraid of the sun as he is of death itself. But all winter long he may sit by his stove in the subtropical climate of 90 degrees Fahrenheit. As someone said, "The only thing that keeps some of those old fellows alive is that they have to get out and chop a few sticks of wood once in a while." The Alaskan cannot stand the sun, but he cannot stand cold either. His complexion may be pale and pasty. He lacks Vitamin D, but you must never mention it to him.

Along with the lack of calcium and Vitamin D comes a third lack, which in combination with the other two makes a bad situation for ideal health: the lack of fresh vegetables during most of the year. Vegetables and fruits from Seattle also are obtainable at times along the railroad, but by the time they arrive they have lost so much of their value that a public lecturer employed by the Department of Agriculture through an extension of the University of Alaska councils that vegetables in cans, scientifically packed, are superior, and much more economical. The Alaskan even in the larger cities lives from cans; in fact hundreds of pounds of cans are necessary to sustain his life each year. As the contents of the cans grow tiresome, one finds his appetite for the protective vegetables frequently diminishing as the years pass, and although every person is different, and it is dangerous to make generalizations, there seems to be a tendency in the North for people to feel that they can get along without vitamins altogether.

With the coming of some new families of women and children to Alaska, however, civilization is asserting itself in several small respects. There are people in Alaska who take many bottles of all kinds of fine vitamins, beginning in the fall and lasting until the spring, for nine months out of the year.

We took some vitamins on our canoe trip.

There has already been much speculation as to just how the original, primitive Eskimo, as first found by the white man, had such magnificent health and such magnificent teeth—teeth that were even used as tools in his daily life and as weapons for fighting! He didn't brush his teeth and he thought nothing of it, and he lived in a land where calcium was not supplied by milk or water, nor Vitamin C by oranges and grapefruit nor Vitamin D by sunshine. He has been termed the most marvelous example of the adaptation of human life to a hostile environment that has ever been known in the world. The Creator supplied him with sunshine in the rich fats and blubber so thoughtfully furnished to the animals and fish inhabiting all such climates. In my sightseeing in Alaska I always failed to see anything funny in the sight of a native eating these natural things.

Yet science still fails to admit an understanding of how the Eskimo or any "primitive" can get at least two necessary and vital qualities to life out of a straight fish and meat diet: calcium and Vitamin C. The books say that meat and fish don't have enough of these, no matter how much you eat. Perhaps this is because the books have only paid attention to the cuts of meat that a white man would eat. A nutritional expert has recently discovered that the livers of seal, walrus, and sea birds, especially eaten raw, are satisfactorily rich in Vitamin C.

Vilhjalmur Stefansson, the great arctic explorer, who explored 100,000 square miles of the "Lifeless Polar Sea" north of Alaska, and whose word is explicitly accepted by the Army today on all matters pertaining to the arctic, lived on meat alone for five years, without even salt. Although he is still at odds with some stubborn nutritionists, he and Ole Anderson furthermore lived on meat and water exclusively for a year in New York City in an experiment carried out with the Russell Sage Institute of Pathology to prove that meat is an adequate diet, not only for the polar explorer or the "native" but even for the average city dweller. Stefansson's meat eating had two secrets or conditions to which its success was due: first, the meat was eaten undercooked, or in most cases practically raw, as many would conceive it, and thus preserved a greater amount of Vitamin C than we usually get in our meats; and secondly, for every two pounds of lean meat, Stefansson ate around one third of a pound of fat meat—he claims this comes natural and according to taste when one is living altogether on meat. We found it so. Not to eat fat under these conditions is to court nephritis or "rabbit starvation" which can cause death within about three weeks.

Bud and I had been Stefansson fans long before we came to Alaska. But the nutritionists still replied that just eating straight animal proteins is a burden on the kidneys which would be bound to show up in later years. The amino acids and the fatty acids of meat cannot be broken down and burned chemically by the body, they said, without a certain percentage of carbohydrates in the diet.

My aging father, a physician, surgeon, and member of the American Association of Scientists, wrote, humoring me: "I should certainly eat all the meat I wanted if I were hungry on a canoe trip, and I should not be afraid to live on meat. Its very composition is largely carbohydrates anyway. A person living a vigorous outdoors life would probably have no trouble in burning the carbohydrates."

Uncle Fred said: "I saw Chief Kot-le-an of the Tlingits at Sitka, and everybody at Sitka will tell you so, no matter what the historians say. Nobody knew how old he was, but he was a young man when the Russian explorer Baranov met him first in the spring of the year 1800. Later he organized the Sitka massacre. He lived on meat."

I had become really interested in diet in planning adventures in the wilds, for I knew that ignorance in the matter of food requirements is not bliss by any means, and neither are the nutritional theories of sourdoughs or ordinary hunters and fishermen altogether to be trusted. I wanted to know the real truth, as it would apply to me traveling in Alaska.

But actually, when it came to our own food, in spite of my fine theories and technical knowledge the matter was rather haphazard. Our diet was the most abominable one in the world for choice, and also for regularity, the way matters turned out. Still, we survived remarkably well, the fact being just another proof of how good nature is to us. The food was chiefly my problem at first, matters pertaining to the canoe, aside from my own personal housekeeping and homemaking, being in Bud's realm. Later on, we shared both problems together. In fact, I might say that Bud had more to do with the food than I, for if it weren't for his ability in shooting things, sometimes there would have been no food. We wouldn't kill such large beautiful animals as moose, when we couldn't have used but a fraction of the animal, but we were going to try to supplement our diet with the commoner kinds of small game.

For one thing, we wanted to taste them all. There is scarcely a bird or a fish or an animal that is not perfectly good to eat, and we used to delight in giving our friends ground-hog and marmot sandwiches. We were good siwashes because we had few food prejudices to begin with, and less when we were through.

From Dick and Mary's cabin it took us two days to get out of the Tolovana and onto the main river again, fighting an upstream wind. Bud had traded our new .22 rifle for a combination .22 rifle and .410 shotgun which Dick had. First, he shot little red tree squirrels, about the size of a chipmunk, treeing them one by one and returning from the forest drenched. The labor was exhausting. I waited in the canoe, or sometimes took the canoe and joined him below. Then we found a raft of arctic snipes standing on a spit of sand. Beneath the cruel, withering crash of the shotgun, four snipes fell dead, turning up their little pink heels to the sky. But they wouldn't have comprised more than a half pound of meat in all. Two more stood tottering as another withering crash cut them down from a distance of thirty feet. "Good night! What a gun!" wailed Bud. Miraculously the pattern of shot had somehow passed through and around most of the tiny creatures without even touching them. It was the fault of the cheap shells, and we learned then the inadvisability and cruelty of using such shells, which should never have been sold in the first place, because they wound and maim and do not kill.

We crunched on some raw rhubarb stalks disconsolately. We had not wanted to accept food from Dick's winter larder, although he had offered it. On his third attempt in stalking ducks, Bud retrieved three beautiful mallards shot from close by in the grass, and oh, that was such a joyful moment that we forgot our tiredness. However, we weren't so very hungry at the last, so we ate nothing until the evening of the second day when we arrived at the one-man town of Tolovana. Conserving our few dollars for the many hundreds of miles to come, we bought one can of creamed corn there, price fifty cents. The price on all cans, indiscriminate of contents, the trader had marked as fifty cents, for it is weight in shipping that counts in Alaska. It was fortunate that we reached Tolovana just as a heavy rainstorm burst from the skies, and here, kindly provided with a vacant cabin, we spread out our outfit for the first good slumber we had had in three days. The next morning, I summoned energy to cook all of our food, including game and corn-meal mush, and we had a gorging, with blueberries for dessert. We were to have many such feasts, after three-day fastings during which it was too miserable to cook. Our systems got adjusted to eating only once every day or so, or when it was convenient. We grew peaked during the first part of the summer, when there was little in the way of wild life to find along the river, but one good meal of anything could revive us completely and could last us for days.

I discovered with the thrill of the explorer the bird that had made the exotic, "churring" call which I had often heard since starting our trip. "Those strange calls always turn out to be a little gray bird," said Bud, but how wrong he was this time. The bird was gray, but hardly little. It was a crane standing tall as a man, and when it flew over the United States from its nesting grounds in the arctic to the countries of South America, it never stopped, and it flew so high that it was not seen. "I have never seen a sandhill crane before, but I've heard my grandfather tell about them," said Bud. "They are supposed to be a species that are practically extinct. But I believe that's it." Stratosphere bird! He with the enchanting voice, speaking of reedy and marshy places!

We dined well on a sandy island in mid-river on duck chile con carne and a rhubarb shortcake. This, after the stern-wheeler *Kusko*, passing in the night, had almost drowned us in two feet of water as we slept packed in beneath the canvas of the *Queen Beaver*.

It was not two days after this that, with a bed sheet improvised as a sail and with the American flag flying, we wobbled slowly up a seven-mile, fresh-water slough beneath Bean Ridge and found the sheltered little town of Hot Springs.

The food at Manley Hot Springs is something wonderful to talk about. Here, on about fifty acres of land, the snows of winter never gather, be it fifty below zero, but melt away by magic as they fall. In summertime now we saw tomatoes, cucumbers, squash, celery, cauliflower, and watermelons thriving on the vine—warmed by the sun above and the earth below. And tall stalks of an old-time familiar friend of other climes, golden corn, was lacking just two weeks of being ripe upon the cob! The tropics in Alaska! It was a wonderful sight. Scattered about Alaska are many similar hot springs in far-removed parts of the Territory, most of them, up to this time, completely undeveloped. Alaskans rarely get any of the vegetables in from Seattle, even in the summer. Fresh corn, string beans, melons, are unknown. Why could not these hot springs eventually be the answer, with hothouses and a developed air service, to Alaska's problem of fresh vegetables? Perhaps hothouses and local canneries will be built at these spots. But the great objection to all enterprises for the past seventy-three years has been that they always prove somehow to be more expensive than getting the same products from Outside, and these same objectors also state that the population of Alaska is not large enough yet to support such home-grown industries. Perhaps when a large enough population does come to live permanently in Alaska, it will create such demands of itself.

Fresh peas and carrots and small early potatoes the telegraph operator gave us from his garden, and we hastened to prepare them, camping by an icy-cold spring. "You know," the operator said (it was a private line, and he owned as well as operated the telegraph himself), "in Canada the government Mounties keep an eye on everybody who goes into the woods, and you check out of one fort only to check in at the next. But here—nobody knows or cares much, it seems. So, we try to be neighborly. Holland told me about you by radio telephone." We thanked him for his concern, but were glad we did not live in Canada. We were checking in at Bethel anyway, after a few months.

The springs themselves, we found, are owned by one family, who raise a few vegetables, mostly for their own and local use. There is a Civil Aeronautics Authority station and airfield with its attendant families, who live in standardized, modern, up- to-date houses with all the conveniences. And we had an idea that there were more of these C. A. A. Airways Communicator Stations mushrooming up overnight all over Alaska than the maps indicated.

A piece of automobile road at Hot Springs connects the town with the main river landing for purposes of freighting, and with adjacent mines which handle a few trucks and machinery. A man also had a fox ranch nearby, and it was he whom we happened to ask if there were any fish to be caught in the many channels of the beautiful slough. "Sorry," he answered. "You know you're the first folks what's asked that. This slough used to be just packed with pike. But for seventeen years I've fed 'em to my foxes by the ton." The man, too lazy to set up a fish wheel in the river below for salmon until forced to, still had his nets stretched across the slough at this time. I caught one small pike and let him go.

We headed for the Yukon.

7

On the Yukon

The Yukon is a big river for canoeists. It can rise seventy-five feet in two days at break-up time in the spring. Starting in latitudes far south of Sitka, and taking a great curve into the north, it flows west and then south again, and then north once more in a final swing before it empties, by several different mouths, into the Bering Sea. A native Eskimo guide with his age-old knowledge of tides and winds and channels directs all seagoing vessels that would enter the mouth of the great Yukon whose shallow passes are but four feet deep at low tide.

Twenty-three hundred miles long, filthy yet paradoxically clean by its immensity, carrying the silt of half a continent, rotting with "stink banks" where the bones of prehistoric animals become exposed each summer anew, life artery to a handful of forgotten people whose lives follow the Arctic Circle, the mighty Yukon flows on. The day is blisteringly hot. In fact, it is the last hot day of summer in a land where summer is short.

From the trees on the cliffs nearby come the cries of young American ospreys or fish hawks; their parents are teaching them to fly. "Let's go climb up and have a look," you think. But there's little use in that. You could find nothing when you got there. The birds are just as big as their mother. You may see a few bald eagles. It is estimated that there are upwards of a hundred thousand eagles in Alaska, mostly in the southeastern part, and they are quite destructive. Most of them evidently live to a ripe old age, as no creature bothers them. The Audubon Society took the one-dollar bounty off a pair of eagles' feet since the war, for patriotic reasons.

From the distance comes the lonely *squeek-squawk* of a slowly revolving fish wheel. Above your head the sky is of a deep cloudless blue. Along four thousand miles of inland rivers on a day like this, salmon, hung on racks, are drying in the sun, and are attended by brown people in bright calico dresses or, ridiculously, in dresses of green silks or satins.

Only a slight breeze stirs the birches. A pair of glaucous or burgomaster sea gulls in slow, lazy flight are seen wheeling over the water, followed by their single rapacious offspring. Yes, some numbers of gulls come up these larger rivers a long way from the sea to nest. These parent gulls are anxious, and they give encouraging calls, sometimes fluttering down upon the now placid bosom of the river to rest. That large, timid gray bird with the absurdly high-pitched voice is their infant born this spring.

The entire scene is timeless. Old-timers have a saying that the Yukon is going backward rather than forward. By that they mean that thirty years ago there was more human activity along the Yukon than there is today. Today the trails are overgrown, the roadhouses are closed, and the telephone wires, if any, down. The airplane carries much of the mail that was formerly carried by the dog sled. Except for the few traders perhaps, the men along the Yukon completely lack worldly ambition. For this reason, it is a restful, out-of-the-world place to be. Yet there is no one Yukon personality. Far from that, it is a land where everybody is an individual and a law unto himself. That is why, if for no other reason, you will like the Yukon.

On the mud banks before every river town you will see things that you will not like, however. You dog lovers, for instance, will see sights that are enough to break a dog lover's heart, for here on the waterfront are chained the dogs of the Indians. And they are not the kind, lovable dogs that you know. These are cruel, inhuman dogs with dull eyes, whose only occupation is to dream of revenge upon man, their perpetuator and their tormentor. They are insane dogs. They should not be held accountable for their actions. Some of them will die on these chains. Just ask the traders who deal in dog chains. These dogs are within sight of water and of food, but their pans are empty and dry. They are prisoners undergoing torture and slow death as a reward for their long winter services. The owner is sometimes present; sometimes he has wandered off drunkenly or sociably and forgotten them, for "dogs breed easily" and their worth is not much in summer. The Indians do not understand that dogs have feelings, too. Besides, there is a superstition: one should never kill a dog in cases of their overabundance. If he dies because he does not eat, then it is his own fault.

The few white men who hear the howling of the dogs as they pass pay little attention, for they are used to it. The dogs howl all the time anyway. You are far from the Humane Society now. The trader, around whose frame house the wretched little hovels of the Indians cluster, does not interfere.

You are in a possession of the United States, but you are visiting a land which, for all the thousands of words that have been written upon it and entombed in Washington files, is but little known to the general public. The people you will talk to day by day speak and understand English to an extent, yet seem largely ignorant of where they are on the map of the world or even on the map of Alaska. They do not know where Fairbanks or Seward is and perhaps have never heard of them. They have never seen the railroad, but know only the Yukon River, and at that, a very limited part of it for a hundred miles or so. These people will not tell you their name when you ask them at their fish camps, for to tell one's name is bold and immodest. You find out their names by asking somebody else. You will not like the odor of these people at first, but you will grow accustomed to it in time; when you close your eyes at night you will associate the people with the sharp smell of fish camps and the sound of howling dogs. When you have once seen Interior Alaska leisurely from a small boat and have stopped at every fish camp and every town, each with its different trader and teacher and missionary organization, the memory of this way of life will remain with you forever, and you will have seen and heard, tasted and smelled, Alaska.

The few hours before we reached the Yukon itself were not uneventful for us. We knew we were very close now; the Tanana River was five miles in width as we drifted down upon island after island through Squaw Flats where the stern-wheelers must ply their sounding poles and cry, "Mark four Mark six! Mark twain!"

The current caught us in its immense sweep and did with us about as it wished. "We've got to keep to the right," Bud kept reminding me, "or we're liable to miss the whole town." He was referring to the town of Tanana which would be on the opposite bank across the Yukon and which we would make for before the current carried us below it. Dick had advised us to enter the Yukon by Squaw Point. There are three mouths of the Tanana entering the Yukon, and we wanted to take the one which was farthest upriver of the three. The extreme lower entrance comes in three miles below the town.

It was around ten o'clock in the evening when we finally decided that we could not make the Yukon that day. To stretch our legs, we tied the boat securely, clambered up a crumbling mud bank, and trekked off towards some low hills in the distance to look for mushrooms, berries, and bears. It was a last look at the Tanana country. One needs to get away from the broad highway of the river just a short distance to get a fair idea of what this country is really like. When the surface of the ground thaws out in the north it is pitted with pockets of water which have never drained in a million years. It is all one great big soured swamp—mosquito country. The circling midnight sun incubates the mosquitoes relentlessly twenty-four hours out of the day, as it increases and forces all life at this season. The water pockets, lying beneath a covering of spongy moss sometimes two feet thick, are every place you step. They are even on the sides of the hills, where hummocks of earth have frequently been distorted and thrown up by the frost of winter and carved into queer shapes. There is not a human being, not even a native, to be found inland during the summer for trackless hundreds of miles of mountain and swamp. Only on the arteries of the big rivers can you find a human being.

It does not take a wise person to keep out of these trackless muskeg swamps. Cross-country hiking over this terrain is just unknown; nobody does it. As we stumbled along through the "niggerheads" this realization struck me as it never had before. Across niggerhead country you cannot go. Niggerheads are puffed-up, deceptive clumps of moss, through which even the sharp-pronged bushes can scarce force their way to daylight, and as you step from one clump to another over more or less open water, they roll beneath your feet, pitching you sooner or later head first into the slime. This gray glacial mud or slime is almost as dangerous as quicksand in some areas. Its sucking and adhesive powers are immense. Engineers building the Alcan Highway through western Canada to Alaska have had whole tractors and trucks sink from sight in it. Niggerheads may grow as high as ten or fifteen feet. Even sledding in winter is impossible, because then the rough hummocks become frozen into solid iron.

The country we were in was not as bad as that, but it was the most exhausting over which I had ever floundered and thrashed. After about an hour and a half of constant effort we had progressed perhaps a mile, and our low mountains were no closer. Bud tore his mosquito head net ever so slightly as he wandered among the scattered spruce trees of the darkening swamp. This set us to wondering just what would happen to an unclothed man turned loose to the mosquitoes here.

It was our belief that such a man would become blind within three hours from their bites and would be a dead man possibly within the next thirty-six hours. "In fact," said Bud, "that's just what the Indians did at one time. They took the clothes off their prisoners, tied them to trees, and turned them loose to the mosquitoes." Since the mosquitoes of the North carry no fevers or diseases and there is but relatively little poison in each insect, others of greater experience have told us that the cause of death, aside from exposure, would be from loss of blood.

It was midnight when we arrived back at our boat, dripping with perspiration, and followed by such swarms of insects that they looked like clouds about our heads. Clapping Bud on the back of his once-white ski jacket, between the shoulder blades, my gloved hand covered as many as a hundred or more mosquitoes in that small area, black, crawling, bobbing, probing with their beaks. We were alive with them.

We fled, paddling four miles furiously down the middle of the river to shake ourselves of them, when suddenly we were on a bar! There had been no warning whatsoever; no island was near. The fast current washed us inch by inch farther onto the bar before we knew it. Bud, fortunately living in long hip boots these days, climbed out instantly, as he had done a few times before, to help us off. It was dangerous work because it was the darkest part of the night now, and the bar might pitch off suddenly at any step into deep water. Bud got us off and we drifted downstream along the side of it. We were very tired and were looking only for a place to sleep. The opposite shore towards which we were heading looked dubious, but we couldn't be choosers. We had no desire to enter the Yukon by night.

I tried to cut across, and we were stuck on the bar again. Apparently, it ran down the center of the river for some miles. To camp in the muskeg was impossible. We simply must cross, and we must get into the right-hand channel. It was one o'clock in the morning and pitch dark. Suddenly a wind began blowing, an upstream wind, turning up little whitecaps which rapidly became larger, followed by lightning and the roll of approaching thunder in the distance. It was the first and only thunderstorm we had ever seen in Alaska, which has few indeed of them, and it chose a fine time to burst upon us.

It seemed as though all nature were conspiring against us, but we were still determined to get across. Bud, cautiously leading the canoe, walked along the bar trying to find a break in it, and he eventually found one. Although stopped by a couple of successive bars again when we got on the other side, we at last achieved our goal. Gathering all the wood which we could find in the dark, we started a large fire. Bud was able to secure our pot of uncooked duck and upland plover and the makings for tea, along with the five-by-seven-foot canvas; then the storm, long brewing, burst upon us.

The night was spent in drinking bucket after bucket of hot tea and gazing into the cherry-red heart of the fire, watching the castles of the coals build and crumble and fall. No rain, however persistent, could reach the heart of our fire, even though it might run down our faces. The mosquitoes flung themselves against us as the night wore on until we would put our faces practically into the fire. Even this extremity bothered them not at all, for they could apparently bear more heat than we could. Bud fell asleep with his head in my lap as I sat on the ground draped with the small piece of canvas. I persistently swatted each mosquito that settled on him, but they kept coming, almost faster than I could swat. My grasp on the physical world about me tightened for a moment—the rain, the mosquitoes, the night, the fire, the Yukon wilds about us—then relaxed. I too was asleep, crowded close to the fire, with my head lying in the mud.

AT FIVE IN THE MORNING Bud awakened me from the blissful state of exhausted sleep. We ate duck and plover. I was unable to get a comb through my hair, but I put on my hat. The river was silver and serene; the skies were clear. A three-toed arctic woodpecker hammered nearby, awakening the early echoes of the neighborhood. We started traveling again immediately and within a few hours found ourselves entering the Yukon upon a day as bright and placid as paradise itself.

At first, we thought the Yukon was running the wrong way, and we tried to stop ourselves, churning with our paddles against the hard gravel of the shallows over which we were being hurled. We couldn't stop, but the Yukon managed to straighten itself out before our eyes anyway. We finally stopped on the lee side of an island, to observe a settlement of wooden houses across the way, shimmering in the sun. "Whew, it's hot!" Bud said, mopping his brow. We didn't know it, but we were as sunburned as two beets. He peered across the river.

"Well, if we can just make it across there, we can go above town a little, make camp, and dry our things on the rocks in the sun. We couldn't have picked a smoother day to get across the river."

We were just a little wary of what the Yukon might do to us, as we shoved out into it. But we found that in contrast to the shifting Tanana it at least traveled in a more established bed, and was, on the whole, less whimsical and not so dangerous.

Thirty minutes later found us with all our outfit spread out in the sun to dry, and ourselves lolling on the hot rocks like beachcombers. Even so, our dampened sleeping bags would not dry quickly. The Alaskan sun seems to have little power to evaporate moisture at any time. The village we had seen appeared to be completely native. We were just discussing whether we should go swimming with our soap along the edge when we were faced by a handsome young white man in a long black robe and clerical collar.

When we saw this ordained Episcopal minister step onto the beach, we could hardly believe our eyes, for we had thought ourselves quite alone. We didn't know that our approach had been eagerly observed by white people on the Yukon bank.

"Welcome to the Mission of Our Saviour," said the minister, holding out his hand. "You're the first visitors, that is, the first white people, we've had in these parts for some time. I'm Mr. Files. Where are you from?"

"From the Tanana River," we told him, introducing ourselves. He whistled aloud, and we smiled at his amazement. Bud pointed toward the distant settlement. "You're just about the first white person we've seen in three hundred miles. Is that the town of Tanana?"

"No, this is our Mission," said Mr. Files. "It's an all-Indian village. The town itself is three miles below. I have just been conducting a funeral, and I have church services coming up now at Tanana, but if you'll just step up to the house and introduce yourselves I know Mrs. Files will be very interested in meeting you."

"Thank you. We'll certainly do that. You said you just conducted a funeral? Do you have many of them, then?"

"Well, yes. We've had nine the last week. The natives, you know, are very susceptible to white man's diseases, and they seem to have little resistance. It's the measles, this time. Have you had them?"

"Yes, we have."

He seemed relieved for our sake.

"Well, I'll be seeing you then." And he departed, as suddenly as he had appeared. Bud and I looked at each other, still in a state of surprise.

But that was nothing to our greater surprise when, five minutes later, another canoe drew up on this very same beach right beside ours, and from it there stepped a laughing young white man and girl just our age. The girl wore bright lipstick, and both were sunburned and healthy-looking. It was almost like seeing ourselves.

We immediately asked them to sit down. Things had certainly started happening fast as soon as we hit the Yukonl

They were Indian Service people from a village seventy-five miles above on the upper Yukon and had arrived by a route at right angles to the one by which we had arrived, but within twenty minutes of us. They were off for a vacation of three weeks. At Tanana they would leave their canoe and take the steamboat up the Tanana River to Hot Springs, where, taking the trail starting over Bean Ridge, they would hike fifty miles or so home again. It was high country, exceptionally scenic, and there were cabins along the way. Both wore light packs, but they hoped to live more or less "off the country," they said. It had taken them, three days to make their canoe voyage, and they too had been drenched and mosquito-bitten all the past night, just as had we. They knew Mr. and Mrs. Files, and had come to visit them on their way.

Mrs. Files that night had unexpected company. As she had already invited the pair of Indian Service teachers from Tanana to dinner, the six guests made, all in all, with herself and Mr. Files and baby Willie, the largest number of white people to be under her roof at the same time for more than a year. It must have presented a food problem. Planning meals is difficult on the Yukon because you cannot buy fresh meats or just run to the market. Only occasionally does the local trader have on hand a haunch of beef or some reindeer meat. When the caribou migrate, crossing the Yukon at several different points each fall, everybody lays in his stock of meat, which is kept frozen fresh all winter. But in summer there is no meat except that which is canned. Not having tasted fresh meat herself since March, and this being early August, Mrs. Files cheerfully opened some canned pressed meats, and filled in with iced tea, potatoes and green salad from the garden. If the menu was worn and familiar to her, it tasted wonderful to her starved guests.

Of course, in this momentous get-together everybody fell to talking about his village, and comparing the problems arising therefrom. Aside from Bud and myself, every person in the room was wrapped up in his life's work with the Indians, almost to the exclusion of everything else. They lived with them and worked with them and saw few other white people or spoke words much longer than two syllables during the year. The Fileses for example, had more Indians to tea in the rectory day by day than they had white people. They practiced in actuality what they preached in theory: race equality and the brotherhood of man. The people from upriver, the Youngs, had resided in Alaska only a few months, but during that time they seemed to have assimilated a good deal of general information and to have formed their own concepts about their environment. It promised from the first to be a highly entertaining evening.

"I believe our village is quite a bit different from yours, from what I've seen," said Mr. Young at the first, addressing the Fileses. "You see, we have quite a predominance of white blood at our village—from the old Russian stock, some of it. Some of our people look just about as white as you or I. It's kind of hard to think of them as Indians."

"It's too bad these half-breeds have to be treated as outcasts by everybody when they grow up," said Mrs. Files. "Some of them are attractive children, too. But they lead lonely lives. They don't fit in with the white way of life and they don't fit in with the Indian way of life. They fit in nowhere."

At this Mrs. Young sat up straight. "I don't see a reason in the world why they shouldn't fit in. It's not the child's fault that he was born that way, and it isn't as if it was the first time it had happened. Migrations, with cross-breeding of whole populations, have been going on since the world began. The world ought to be used to seeing the half-breed by now."

"Yes, I think you're right," Mr. Files agreed. "In the case of Alaska, at least, cross-breeding is exactly what is happening, and it is happening all over the world as the world grows smaller, whether we approve of it or not. The social barriers set up against it don't seem to make much difference in preventing it. Some students of the subject prophesy that the future population of Alaska will be composed of the original Alaskan natives completely absorbed by the white. Of course, we try by every means we know, by church and school, to prevent it, but that is what is happening."

"I won't come back to that old worn saying, 'How would you like to see your own daughter marry an Indian?' but it is frightening, isn't it?" said someone.

"Why? We've got to believe in the future of our education if we educate," Mrs. Young pointed out. "We can't in fairness just put up a sign, 'Blind alley here,' and expect a normal adjustment. No, we've got to come down off our high horse and accept the responsibilities of admitting the native to our fellowship as an intellectual and social equal. Otherwise why go to all the work and useless expense of an educational program? It's either one way or the other, for me. What would happen then to our half-breed or full-breed Indian or Eskimo girl from Alaska is that she might marry."

"You mean a white, American boy in the States? You would encourage it?"

"Yes, indeed. And why not? An educated, lovely person—and pretty good-looking in her own right, with a charm altogether her own—I have an idea that the boys would find her quite attractive."

"But then, the children!" we cried. "What would become of the children of such a match? How they would suffer! All of them would be outcasts!"

"You're thinking of the situation fifty years behind the times, perhaps," Mrs. Young suggested dryly. "You paint too gloomy a picture. She should go east of the Mississippi, of course. There she'll find lots of company. New York University would be delighted to offer her a professorship in art, perhaps in the specialty of Alaskan art, I might say. You see our Alaskan girl is not in her home environment now. She is a traveled person, from a remote, strange land that is of interest to everybody. In her veins run generations of slow, unhurried living; she is stoical, courageous, resourceful. It is good blood—nothing to be ashamed of. She really has something to offer, in her own right, don't you think? She is our newest American."

"You are very visionary, Mrs. Young. Do you really think that the crossing of the races is desirable?"

"Well, of course these individuals I speak of are exceptions," Mrs. Young admitted. "Not even all of us can become professors yet by a long sight. The point is that I believe in the future of Alaska as the Forty-ninth State of the United States. And when Alaska or any other place produces individuals who can rise above their environments, the rest of us should give them a hand and not try to hold them down. The usual low type of squaw-man situation I'm afraid has given us the wrong impression of the whole problem, and naturally the drunken, irresponsible white man who marries in with primitives and accepts them on their level, at the same time adding to their degradation and to his own, is not desirable. But you ask about the harm resulting from the crossing of the races. A friend of mine who is a professor of sociology said this to the class, on this subject—these are his words exactly: 'There is no known degeneration of the mind or of the body that results from the crossing of the races.' However, I shall say this myself: 'If our Alaskan girl could marry an Alaskan boy of her own race whose intellect and whose ambitions were congenial to hers, and they could be offered a guiding and helping hand by someone who would take the interest in helping them in their careers, perhaps that would be the best.' I think all educated people experience a keen pleasure in seeing fine specimens of distinct racial types."

"That is the way God made us," somebody said. "If God made the different races perhaps He wanted them to remain distinct."

"I don't think history goes that far back," offered Bud apologetically.

However, this observation was quite in keeping, for the Fileses, like many intelligent ministers and priests today, accepted the indisputable evidence of the prehistoric life of the earth before mankind commenced to keep its records, and the fact that the earth has been and is in a constant state of evolutionary change. To Mr. Files, biology, astronomy, and geology combined to bring him but a greater knowledge of the workings of God than ever before.

"Well, it is quite a problem what to do with the native after we get him educated," said Mrs. Files, who admitted she was just now beginning to realize the ignorance she had had concerning the native and the native problem during her first years of mission work. "I guess all we can do is go along day by day and do the best we can. Since you can't take all the Indians and Eskimos out of Alaska, most of them will still be living here."

"Certainly, the Indian Service is doing a practical job," one of the older people said. "I guess it's just on the ground floor now. Although the Department of Education had the natives for some years, the Indian Service itself has been established in Alaska only since 1931, and has made remarkable strides. First things have to come first."

In this, we all found a compromise. It was time to go to bed.

8

Old Jim's

Some hours after we had been asleep in the "house tent" shown us by Mrs. Files, I awoke with a vague feeling of uneasiness. The wind had risen. "Much as I hate to do it," I said to Bud, "I think we'd better go down to the beach and look at the *Queen Beaver.*" We ran down the slippery path amid the clamor of dogs and lifted her farther up on the bank where the dash of the waves could not reach her and rock her against the stones. But it was too late. The rising winds had already pounded two holes in her sides. However, these were patched by Bud and Mr. Files the next day. They were our only leaks of the entire trip.

After three days of cold wind and rain, we left the really Christian hospitality of the Fileses, who, as Bud put it, had considerably "fattened us up." Although advised by Mr. Files and by two other white men not to risk the choppy waves, we felt confident that we could make it. There are days on the Yukon when even the big steamers tie up. We must learn what kind of seas we could take were we to make progress at all from now on.

At the practically all-native village of Tanana we stayed just long enough to mail some letters and push on again. Much sightseeing was out of the question because one of us would have to stay to guard the boat. Although the natives surrounding the Mission village would not steal we were warned to watch out for those who lived at the ordinary river village but three miles away, for tough and irresponsible characters hang around these villages. At Tanana the government has in recent years set up both school and hospital over and above the former institutions handled in this locality for years by the Episcopal Church. Churches and missions in Alaska still flourish but seem to be going out as the governmental agencies come in with their more standardized services.

We camped on an island, cooked beans, and made a real houseboat out of our canoe, revamping with the canvas we had. Bud did this. He cut willows and bent them into a covered-wagon like frame, and over this stretched the canvas, which he waterproofed with boiled linseed oil. The old canvas had leaked whenever it had touched anything. Although stitched together in pieces like a patchwork quilt, the "covered wagon" extended to our seats, where a projecting flap could make all tight for the night. From now on we would keep dry nights by sleeping inside the boat, and we could even sit up inside! We had to take out one thwart to do this, but the "house canoe" still managed to hold together.

"Do you remember," reminded Bud, "how we slept the other night during our big rain? Do you remember the night before that, and the night before *that*?" I certainly did. It started to rain lightly in the middle of the night, and we didn't get up. What was there to get up for? There was no place to go if we did. So, we stayed in bed, taking cat naps, and trusting to keep dry. As the hours continued, we realized that slowly we were becoming flooded. It is a peculiar sensation to sleep in water. It drained in downhill from our heads, in little trickles at first, and slowly engulfed us, until at last we were lying in a lake, wet all over. It was a warm lake, though, as the water was warmed by our bodies, leaving us quite cold. But no more of that! We also rigged our first small sail, although we did little sailing until we approached the lower reaches of the Yukon.

It was lucky for us that we lived in a house canoe and had a cozy place to crawl into when need arose. We were in for a summer so rainy from now on that scarcely would we see the sun in days except briefly, as a novelty. Every mile that we approached closer to the Bering Sea coast meant consistently heavier precipitation, but we got so used to it that we scarcely noticed it. We hiked in the rain on "exploration" trips inland, we ate with the rain pouring down our faces and into our little bowls, we ate standing up because logs and rocks were too wet to sit on, and we went to sleep at night with the eternal rain pattering softly on the roof. The heavily forested Yukon country became so soaked that it was difficult to find wood, even the usual bleached driftwood, that had not turned into rot. Hours were spent cooking food.

But much praise should be sung of the long, ankle and wrist length, 100 per cent woolen underwear which we now donned and never took off for the rest of the trip. This seemed largely to adjust our body temperatures for us under all conditions of the North and insulated us against the prevailing dampness. Bud lived continuously in his long hip boots, and I should have had some too, for, miserable as they are, with them I should have done much more of the actual hunting of birds, which was one of the great enjoyments of the late summer and fall. Except for occasional hikes and stays in people's houses where I wanted to "dress up," I discarded my smart laced boots for clumsy rubber-soled shoepacks originally bought to accommodate four pairs of woolen socks in wintertime. At intervals during the summer, and altogether during the autumnal and wintry part of our voyage, we donned our fur trappers' caps. They were of Hudson Bay seal, which is a special processing of the skins of muskrats and came off the collar of mother's old opera cloak, 1920.

When we left Tanana, we were leaving behind us the last, the only doctor, in an estimated twenty-five hundred miles of wandering canoe travel in the Interior. This doctor of the Indian Service Hospital at Tanana was shortly after drafted into the Army, and there was then left nobody to help the dwindling natives, when, the measles epidemic of summer past, mumps came to annihilate them by winter.

On our right hand arose a mountain range whose patterned slopes we watched through sunshine and through rain. A break in the clouds showed that far above the timber line stretched a land of sunshine and prairie, the eternal highlands. "It's about time we climbed a mountain, isn't it?" remarked Bud. "You know I've been looking for a good one for a long time. Do you think we have time to take off a week or so?"

That suggestion didn't sound so bad. It had adventure in it. The longing came to me to be lying on a mossy mountain slope in the sunshine once again and looking out over an expanse of seventy-five miles of country, high up in some warm sheltered nook between the snows that only the wild goats know! We realized sadly that it would take a person all summer to explore the big mountain range, even if he started right now. We hadn't the time.

"Well, we can stop and ask the name of our mountains anyway," I said, as I steered us past a fish wheel choked with driftwood and brought us alongside the first inhabited Yukon cabin we had seen in a couple of days.

It was occupied by an elderly white man, and a gentleman if one ever lived. His hair was snow white and his eyes were kindly and wise. Two slant-eyed, furry huskies of magnificent build galloped beside him as he stepped down to the beach to greet us. We had stopped at the Yukon home of one Old Man Jim, who had resided at this spot for the last twenty-five years, or somewhat longer than we had been alive!

"You'll have to stop over a bit and go up to the Dome, come a sunny day," he told us when informed of our interest in the mountains. "There's a mining outfit just back in. They have a horse, and a small caterpillar tractor, too. Then there's a good trail from then on. But come into the house."

We placed our boat safely upon the beach, and entered the dark interior of the simple, low-roofed, one-room cabin, its chinks stuffed with arctic moss. Behind us filed several natives silently and took their seats.

Old Man Jim lived alone, but these were his friends and daily associates in a land where all human beings are scattered and far. We all sat around in the evening listening to the Tokyo broadcast which was filled full of war propaganda for the Americans. It was doubtful if the Indians got much out of it, but it amused Old Jim.

The native woman Maggie who lived next door to Jim was an outstanding personality to me in a way that made me realize definitely, if I had never done so before, that even simple, primitive people have deep-seated, elemental differences in their make-up. Maggie wasn't shy—far from it! She was a natural-born extrovert, with kindly, shrewd eyes and a slightly crafty expression, much as one's next-door neighbor frequently appears to one. Maggie burned with curiosity to know everything that was going on. She was vigorous, prided herself on the domestic arts as she knew them, and was fond of snaring rabbits and hunting grouse and spruce hens, called "chickens," with the .22 rifle. About thirty years of age, full-breasted, and dressed at this season in a light calico dress and cotton stockings worn in moccasins or shoepacks, she had very possibly survived as many as four or five, or even seven or nine brothers and sisters, who would now all be laid to sleep in the graveyards along the river.

As even missionaries, teachers, and the occasional traveling public-health nurses who have spent years in Alaska do not become so interested as to remain in a native camp overnight if it can possibly be avoided, I was certainly the first white woman Maggie had ever had a good chance to talk to. Possibly we were too enthusiastic, but we enjoyed these experiences as much as we enjoyed, at times, the buffeting of the elements. And these within a short time buffeted into us a realization of certain facts about human existence which a person living in a house or even traveling in his large power boat between villages can't easily assimilate into his system.

Jim gave us two freshly baked potatoes, one each, which, with salmon that I cooked on the beach, went down so quickly that they scarcely touched top, sides, or bottom. Three Geodetic Survey men now arrived from the inland trail and departed by boat for Tanana. They were accompanied by a bearded prospector, Martin, and the pack horse. The men had been investigating a tin deposit in connection with the war needs. Old Jim, who had seen the last war come and go in this very spot, had known them all for several years. We planned to hike up the same trail the next day.

The next day broke with sodden rain and leaden skies. As we lifted the flap and stuck our heads out of the *Queen Beaver*, rain in fine particles caught us right in the eye. But we went on our hike anyway, taking the camera in hopes.

At twelve noon we arrived at the Grant Creek Mining Company and gained our first impression of what gold mining in Alaska is like.

As we hiked up men were clustered about the washbasins outside the crude dining shed, puffing and blowing in their ablutions much like rhinoceros. It was the largest congregation of white men we would see for a long time—four of them. The fifth man, when he finally arrived, was the owner of the diggings, Fisher by name.

Accepting Mr. Fisher's hearty invitation to stay for lunch at the mining camp, we took our cue from the miners and plunged into the washbasins, and then stepped inside the shack and seated ourselves on the board benches by the table, where first to grab was first served. The fare was simple and exceedingly generous, being the most food we had seen at the same time for quite a while. The cook was a middle-aged woman from Fairbanks who received eight dollars a day. Miners had certain food habits, she told me privately. No left-overs could appear on the table more than twice or the cook became exceedingly unpopular. The cook could traditionally expect to be "kidded" when she took the job anyway, and certainly had to watch her step not to break the mining camp traditions. The men didn't want any new foods tried out on them. They liked to eat just what they had eaten at other camps all their lives. No local game, berries, or fish in the country was considered by them as fit for human consumption, but everything must come, and daily, from the cans in which they put their trust. Price didn't matter. Bottles of catsup and every imaginable sauce and condiment must appear on the table, and fried potatoes and some sort of pie must be served at every meal. An airplane came over on occasion by an arrangement with a Fairbanks meat market, circled, and dropped fresh beef by little parachutes. We would see more of the mining camp when we returned.

The trail after dinner became exceedingly narrow, and pushed through a tropical rain forest which, except for the absence of giant ferns and the dishpan-leaved devil's-clubs, was almost a replica of the coastal jungles around Ketchikan. It was for this reason that we had confined our "explorations" to a trail, for while disliking trails in general, we realized that at least they enabled one to get into the desirable country within the shortest possible time.

The end of the day found us about nine miles back in the hills hunting for a supper of mushrooms and blueberries in a great highland marsh at timber line. For all our efforts we had not shaken the mosquitoes. While Bud in his greater energy set out with rifle to explore a part of immense Grant Dome for possible marmots, I sat myself down gratefully in the blueberries which in amazing size and profusion covered the landscape on their low bushes as far as the eye could see. Failing to grow fruit of any size or on trees in the North, nature does the next possible thing and brings forth from her ever-resourceful soil for the brief season the miracle of the wild berry—strawberries, cranberries, currants, blueberries, raspberries, gooseberries, salmonberries, bearberries, and even mossberries. The berries grow close to the earth where the reflected heat reaches its maximum intensity and warms and ripens the small perfect morsels through and through, although it cannot sweeten them too much but leaves them more sour than the fruits of other climes.

As night came on Bud returned to find mushrooms already prepared and boiling merrily. Being near the trees was a comfort, but Bud quickly used their soft wood for logs, because it took no experienced glance at the sky to tell us that we were in for a night of it again.

Our meal consisted of the mushrooms, which had boiled down to nothing, a couple of left-over burned biscuits, and some chunks of cold fish unwrapped from waxed paper. We ate few blueberries as we both had sampled generously of these before dinner. Extra food consisted of one pound of yellow corn meal.

All night long it rained or dripped while the fire smudged damply with wet fuel, and we sat, or half lay curled around one another for warmth, on the hummocks of the moss, mosquito nets pulled down.

Had we known it, a mile or two beyond, over the hump, Martin, the prospector, had a cabin stocked with grub, which he would have been more than glad to have us use. He had mentioned this, but we had not understood that when a man offers you hospitality in the North, he means it, and he is possibly even offended if you do not accept.

What we should have had for a tour of this sort was a couple of pack dogs, or, if we carried the packs ourselves, we should never have gone without the sleeping bag and an adequate canvas which would do for a tent. In order to avoid the heavy backpacking, we had tried to live like the birds. Unless a person is protected from the elements and has proper rest each night and proper food, he weakens.

The next morning, we felt terrible and we wondered whether to go on or to turn back. We had just begun to get into the interesting country. Enchanting prairies and buttes like those of Wyoming or Montana beckoned us. We finally decided to go on if it would only not rain that night.

However, it did rain, and we were wise in turning back right where we were. In the rain Bud located two spruce hens for me in trees, which I shot with the .22 combination of the .410. These we gave to the cook at the Grant Creek Mining Company, who had never eaten any. Once again, we dined sumptuously with Mr. Fisher and his miners, who enjoyed tremendously our adventure when they heard it. No one had ever dreamed that we were hiking up the mountain with the intention of staying out in the rain all night. They considered us amazing people, and probably a little crazy.

Mr. Fisher needed men badly, for the extent of his profits was largely determined by the number of men he could employ and accommodate in the limited time remaining before freeze-up. The men worked on their respective shifts twenty-four hours out of the day, at this season, never slackening for a moment. Pay of course was sky-high.

"Well, if you would rather work for yourself now," said the soft-spoken and easy-going Fisher, "I wouldn't be blaming you. Now is the time to look ahead. You can use my camp as a base if you want to, to get started. You'll just make enough to stay alive if you work for somebody else all your life. Why think in terms of cents when you can think in terms of dollars? There's plenty of room in this country, and you would be wise to just get you an outfit and prospect. If I was a young man again that's what I'd do. It's a clean game. You're not taking it away from anybody else. You're taking it right out of Mother Earth. If you want to hang around for the rest of the summer you're welcome to pan for yourselves here what the scoop misses."

"Oh, thank you," I said. "But we couldn't be taking your gold away from you. That's your gold."

"Oh, that's all right," he said genially. "If I couldn't afford that I guess I couldn't afford to stay in business, could I?"

"No, I suppose not," I said.

We stood and watched a little bright-crested yellow bird skitter along the ground and in behind the great treads of the dragline, now standing idle in the raw mud as Fisher talked to us. Suddenly it came to me that the little dragline was quite a toy. Every minute that this man in a dirty shirt stood talking to, us in the rain was costing him money of some kind. Yet he was in no hurry but was interested in us and anything we had to say.

I surveyed with interest the plot of mangled ground which was the evidence and results of fourteen summers spent in hydraulic mining here. He had spoiled a good grayling creek, but actually in all this time he had only torn up a few hundred yards of the forest. He was working slowly up a little valley, clearing the timber as he went, so that the great hoses could be turned on the earth and chew it to fine particles, washing down the gold through sluice boxes. Grant Creek furnished the water power; the water was driven through great iron pipes which were as cold as ice.

"Yes, I prospected this spot fourteen years ago," Fisher told Bud. "After I took out a million, one hundred thousand, for the Fairbanks Exploration Company, I decided I would go into business for myself. It's like anything else, it takes time and work. At first, I had only one helper, and it was slow. We dug a ditch seven thousand feet long—you saw it up there—to detour part of the creek. We camped in a tent and the mosquitoes about carried us away."

"You mean you dug that tremendous seven-thousand-foot canal all by pick and shovel?" I asked incredulously.

He nodded. "Then of course we had to make a trail in for the machinery, and assemble the dragline, get a camp together where men would be willing to live. There's still a lot to do to the place." He nodded to us and walked off.

We returned to Old Jim's, heard Tokyo again, and the next morning decided it was time to be on our way.

They stood on the bank waving good-by to us; Old Jim, white-haired and saintly, and the bearded prospector Martin leaning lazily against the neck of his affectionate pack horse, in the Yukon sunshine. The picture doesn't fade. One wonders when we shall meet again.

In his Alaska Diary the late Dr. Ales Hrdlicka, curator of the National Museum in Washington, tells of meeting Old Jim at his home on the Yukon in 1924. Jim had driftwood stuck in his fish wheel, and hurried off to fix it, not taking time for a word with the great anthropologist. There was no other white man within miles. The gentle and lovable Dr. Hrdlicka, who saw his Yukon from underneath an umbrella and whose findings and theories of Alaska have become world-famous, comments on Jim's poverty and isolation, prognosticates that these poor old fellows cannot last long. (But Jim's hair was no whiter when we met him in 1942—it couldn't be.)

I have been meaning for some time to write Old Jim a letter, but it is difficult to know quite where to send it. It will be addressed:

Old Jim
Right-hand side of the Yukon River
About thirty miles below Tanana.

9

Wilderness

U pon inquiry about mastodon bones we had learned that there was a place called the "bone yard" not five miles below, where possibly we could hunt souvenirs. Now as we drifted towards it, on the opposite side of the river, we were all enthusiasm.

Our channel of the river became narrowed in by two-hundred-foot promontories rising in some cases straight up from the river and in some cases on an incline. Far above, the forest was broken off abruptly, disclosing the thawing and caving strata of raw earth, from which little rivulets ran in trickles. We gazed above in interest, but were obliged to keep a sharp lookout ahead, as unfortunately the current seemed to be very swift through these straits of the bone yard, and we didn't want to add our own bones to the collection. No one in fact had remembered to mention that the big steamers kept away from the bone yard, whose small whirlpools had a tendency, unless riding the outer water, to draw any craft toward the danger of the cliffs. Well, we were in it before we knew it, in a season of unusually heavy rains and unusually high water, and there was no turning back. Doubtless our informers hadn't seen it for at least a season or two, and these places change rapidly all the time. Still, I thought I could make a landing in some of the recesses of the banks should I be notified in time. Bud felt that he could instantly recognize any exposed bones, which would be stained gray and would appear much like weathered wood.

At the time we went through this particular bone yard, the water was too high for any exposure of bones. Bud felt it to be a doubtful place to take chances with anyway; we only made one landing, and then had a difficult time getting out into the current again, for we were almost marooned by reversing whirlpools which churned near the cliffs. We had to start out again by turning upstream, in spite of the fact that the sweep of the river was rushing downstream viciously just thirty feet away.

The possible loss of the boat, due to being dumped out, or as a result of tying it carelessly to the branch of a tree, was another consideration more serious than might appear on the surface and was again a thought which was kept constantly in our minds. To float down the Yukon is one thing; it is a broad highway and quite safe in a, small craft if reasonable precautions are taken. But to walk out to the next town or human habitation along the way is another thing. Seen from the air the river is serpentine, making great turns of fifty or a hundred miles to the loop, winding and squirming as it turns, and intercepted at numberless points by whole rivers or wildcat sloughs, and swamps of mosquito-ridden muskeg that are treacherous and interminable to a person on foot. To be cast afoot in this country, especially without a gun, would be as unpleasant as being cast afoot along the Amazon. There would probably be less food to find to eat; you can't catch the fish in the river and the small game is negligible in summer or else is particularly adept at hiding; the rabbits are like ghosts because they only come out at night to dance briefly in the moonlight and then retire again completely. A rescue by either whites or natives could not be counted on, for their powered boats usually follow one of the main channels.

It was principally with these thoughts in mind that we conscientiously started on the trip wearing at all times our ten-shot automatic Woodsman pistols so as never to be caught unarmed. Bud's job, as he sat up in front, was to keep all our guns oiled and in perfect working condition as I steered hour after hour, and this job he attended to regularly and often. This is particularly important with such a fine mechanism as an automatic, which can quickly jam in but one of its many small parts with dampness and gritty sand and become a useless lump of steel in one's hand. When given the right care in the hands of one who knows how to use it, this small-caliber gun becomes a fine weapon capable of killing even a large animal in an emergency. Since the beginning of our trip our vigilance had somewhat relaxed as we gained confidence, and now at most times we kept our pistols simply slung in their holsters by our seats. But at times like this of going through the boneyard we could strap them on again at short notice.

We passed through the six or seven miles of the bone yard, and came out onto a calm, broad, sky-lighted stretch of river, peaceful and serene in the late afternoon light. We were drifting along watching the big islands slide by, when over on the other side again (it's always on the other side, with several channels in between) we heard a sound that made us suddenly lean on the paddles. It was the sound that a wild mountain stream makes tumbling down through green forests.

It was only by some strong stroking and very good luck that we reached this noisy little creek without being carried entirely below it. Bud leaped into shallow water and pulled us ashore where the riffles cleared magically of their smoky color and green- blue, turquoise water met the muddy waters of the Yukon. Together we lifted the canoe up on the sandy beach. This was the spot we had been looking for, for a long time. Uncle Fred's telescope fly rod was taken reverently from its case, and a can of assorted leaders and lures was taken from the recesses of the front bulkhead. Quickly selecting a very small black fly, with hands that fairly shook with impatience, Bud attached it and disappeared with no more ado into the forest. I sat down to wait for him. Solitude is the heritage of every fisherman.

Then I saw a structure upon the hill a few yards away, overlooking the river. It looked like a terrible place, even from afar. I crossed the shallows of the stream, the water just going over the tops of my shoepacks. Once again, an old vacated cabin had risen to haunt me. I took the .405 in the crook of my arm and went towards it.

I went inside. It felt like walking into a trap, as there was only one entrance leading out, and at any moment I expected this entrance to be blocked by a horrible apparition. I stayed only long enough for a quick survey. An old newspaper on the wall, dated 1909, reminisced of Boston. "Boston is a long ways away," I thought. This site was no location for a fish wheel. This spot had been some white man's idea of paradise at some time, some white man from Boston. He had chosen his location from a poetic rather than a practical view, his cabin on the Yukon. What had he looked like and what were his dreams, in those days before my time? I wondered. He had been a young man of a wealthy family, adventurous, intelligent, throwing conventional Boston to the winds for a time, until he went home and married the girl who waited for him, and she was very beautiful and he became a banker and just stayed in banks after that. But to me he was perpetually young and splendid, this adventuring Yukoner of long ago.

But I vowed that I would never explore an old cabin alone again. It was too depressing. As I plunged into the valley our first real partridges roared out of the gloom by my feet, so startling me that I fled to the boat, there to wait until Bud should return.

When he did return he brought with him the first genuine arctic grayling which either of us had ever seen. The grayling has unusually large fins, which, although they appear colorless, reflect the colors of the rainbow when he is held up to the sun. He must be, as Bud mentioned, the result of a perfect job in streamlining such as man has not yet achieved in his inventions, because he can lie for hours head-on in a current so fast as to sweep a wading man off his feet, yet he seemingly makes never a wiggle, but is apparently asleep. His meat is as sweet to eat as the waters in which he lives, and it goes clear up to his eyes!

The next day we waded fourteen hours. After the first hour I ceased to notice the coldness of the water any more, and I never felt better in my life. Wading was the speediest and best way for the most part to navigate the overgrown stream which was, I am sure, as wild as on the first day it was created.

Early in the day we came to a small crystal pool into which the sunlight was sifting mistily in green subterranean patterns. The rim of the pool was banked with white foam, forced against a fallen spruce log on which one could cross. Small twigs dropped into the vortex were instantly sucked from sight by an unseen power and were not seen again. This was also what happened to our tiny flies, which were suspended on slender leaders that were invisible to the fish and of but four-pound test.

Lying close to the bottom and at the lower end of the pool reposed the largest grayling we had yet seen, although it was difficult to judge the exact depth or the fish's exact size.

The trick was to cast the fly into the stream above him and let it drift down in a tempting way, hoping that the small sinker would bring it near the bottom at the time it reached him. But the fish lay in an almost unattainable spot for us, because of the currents, and he seemed quite contented where he was.

When it came my turn to use the long limber fly rod, I frequently hooked the foliage behind me and once the seat of my pants. We were both just learning. Once I cast into a pile of brush just across the creek, and Bud patiently leaned far out on stones to hand me the rod so that I could reach the end of it from the opposite bank. As the water boiled over my wrist I got the tip end of the pole and dragged it through the water to safety, where, holding on with the other hand, I managed to thread the tangled line between the bushes and unhook it without completely crashing into the water. Such feats as this are the proof and the making of the sport fisherman. I have always thought that people who pose smiling with long strings of their legal limit of fish look rather ridiculous.

When Bud got the fly rod again he cast a few times, and suddenly the big fish struck with no warning at all. "I've got him," he cried, as the rod bent double. He held the handle of the rod straight up, pointing at the sky, and kept a tight line, so that as the fish leapt, no slack would gather in the line to afford him a chance to rush and break it. Back and forth dashed the frightened fish as Bud attempted to bring him into the shallows, and then he leapt three feet out of the water in an endeavor to shake the hook from his mouth, and, ping! he was gone. Down below in his favorite spot again was this fish, three feet of line dragging from his mouth. We could have wept with exasperation.

Bud had carved out with his jackknife two wooden pegs which he attached at either end of a stout fourteen-inch cord, and we now had several grayling on our line. Bud also carried in his pocket a specially carved little wooden club with which to hit the aristocrat fish over the head. We fished every pool in the stream for several miles back into the immense mountain range which was known as the Birches. Late at night, while I fixed supper, Bud was still trying for that big fish which was still swimming with our one and only lure, known as the Alaska Ann. We wanted the lure, but besides that, we were thinking that it must be very unpleasant for the fish. We wished for his sake that we could get him.

The next day was largely devoted to waterproofing the bottom of the canoe, where the paint was scarred, and while it was drying in the sun Bud was back at the pool, looking through the clear waters at his grayling, eye to eye. In desperation, he even shot several times with his pistol in hopes of blasting the fish out of the pool but had no luck. Then he contrived a spear, but the fish dodged. Failing in this, he again tried to win the confidence of the fish.

He had already found that there is such a thing as wearing the nerves of a fish down through sheer persistence. The fish may not be hungry at all, but finally strikes in anger because he can't stand seeing either the lure or the fisherman any more. At least that is what we concluded. After two more hours, during which I begged and cajoled Bud, for heaven's sake, to leave, the fish at last began to show definite signs of agitation. For more than twenty-four hours this fish had been nerve-weary. As I gazed at him myself, he looked, in plain words, tired. Bud worked on him psychologically until he darted round and round the pool at a faster and faster speed, backing off before the lure as though it was detestable in his sight. Apparently, he never thought of leaving the pool altogether, for this was his home. At last report Bud said he knew the fish was going to strike now, at any minute.

As I picked up our camp dishes and wrapped all of the fish Bud had prepared and put them into a box, Bud returned at long last from his solitary occupation. The fish had struck, wearily, and allowed himself to be brought gently into the cup of Bud's hand. "Well, let's have him," I said.

"I haven't got him."

"What?'

"That's right. I let him go, the biggest grayling of them all. He just sort of seemed like an old friend."

Bud reported that the fish seemed to know what was happening when the hook was removed from his lip, and made scarcely a struggle, but submitted to the operation tamely. That the slime might not be removed from him, allowing parasites to enter and cause disease (for many released trout are reported to die), Bud was careful not to take him from the water again. When released he swam slowly down into his usual position. The last seen of him, reposing there in the unnamed grayling creek, he had a grateful look in his fish eye. "He seemed to know me," said Bud. "I think that in a few days I could have had him eating from my hand and coming up to be scratched under the jaw. He was quite a guy."

There being a fair wind, we ran up our small sail, the five- by-seven canvas, and sailed away, with a canoe full of fish to eat for some days.

Now for the first time the subject of wild geese became our main topic of conversation. It had all started fairly early in the summer when Bud unsuccessfully stalked his first flock of around a hundred blue geese on a bar. It was kind of funny, because he found when he got there that they were separated from the main island by a small channel. So, he took off all his clothes, waded the icy channel to his neck, and then all the geese flew away.

The second attempt was made on a small flock of eight white-fronted geese, which was easier, as there were only sixteen rather than two hundred different eyes to watch him. Bud was clothed this time but barefooted so as not to break twigs or jar the ground (so many birds and animals getting their feeling from the ground), and much of the distance was navigated on knees, elbows, and belly. I watched the stalk with the field glasses. I saw all the geese suddenly raise up their long necks and look. As Bud put it, "You could have raked their eyes off with a stick." They flew away again; gone was our goose dinner. Bud had revived his old cowboy knowledge of baking to perfection light, fluffy, golden-topped biscuits in the Dutch oven, we had canned butter, and cranberry sauce was to be had at any picking. All we needed was the goose. My stomach did a flip-flop every time Bud commenced a stalk with his short-ranged little .410 shotgun, so inadequate now. We continued to subsist on the usual cereal and fish.

Later, another grayling stream was discovered coming down from the same range of mountains; in fact, there were two of them right together. Selecting the smaller of them we pulled into it and up and around a tranquil bend, just at sundown.

How can one describe the thrill of discovering each new solitary camping place along the Yukon River? Here was a perfect campers' beach, looking as though it had just been swept for a Sunday picnic. The only creatures who had ever picnicked here, however, were the creatures of the wild, to which a multitude of tracks could attest. Around the bend a flock of ducks came floating serenely towards us, while back in the forest a beaver trail practically three feet wide and cleared of debris led toward some distant lake, following the contours of the land like some surveyor's line.

Here we fished for two days until pitch-black midnight would catch us in the woods, where we would tangle and stumble and fall our way back to camp, breaking leaders and losing flies on every bush. I remember Bud caught one of his fish while perched in the crotch of a tree overhanging the torrent. He successfully got his strike, reeled the fish in, but as the deep pool fell directly below the bank, there was no place to land it. Squatting on the grass, I leaned down and down. Bud brought the fish into my grasp as I attempted to lift the slippery thing up to safety. Whiz! Out went my feet from under me, and the fish, hitting the ground, bounced up and back into the pool, having broken the line with no effort at all, while I barely saved myself by clawing the earth with mosquito-bitten hands.

But the fish looked sick. He floated sideways downstream out of reach, giving faint struggles. Bud drew his pistol and shot him through the middle, and that was worse. He sank. Rushing down to the next bend we gouged him with a long pole and secured him just before the treacherous undercurrents would have taken him into the riffles. The peculiar end of this fish was that he was lost somewhere in the woods at night on the way back to camp.

We took some monstrous grayling from this stream, and although plentifully supplied with enough mosquitoes here to keep them fat, it was chiefly not on mosquitoes that the big ones fed. Autopsies on them showed beetles, cranberries, yellow jackets, small frogs, and shrewmice in their stomachs.

Bud used the undigested shrews on hooks to catch more and bigger grayling. "It's fish eat what he can in this life," he said philosophically. "Do you remember the case of the hungry shrews?"

I did. We had slept once in an Alaska cabin infested with shrews in wintertime. Only at night when the house was still did they come timidly from their hiding places in the chinks and reveal their real character, and to judge by all sounds they must have come by the thousands. I lay paralyzed by the noises that I heard from these silky, less than three-inch animals. The night became horrible with their howls, wails, and shrieks, and the crunching of their teeth. The lives of the shrews, I learned that night, are lived in darkness and horrible bestiality. The man of the house had traps set. Crack, would go a trap, and a moment of silence would ensue as the tribes gathered. The victim was caught by the end of his tail or by a leg. You waited breathlessly, knowing what was about to happen. Now came hair-raising shrieks of anguish as the victim's voracious parents, sisters, brothers, and cousins commenced to eat him. "Crunch, crunch, crunch. That must be the backbone," you think. After a couple of hours of this repeat performance, you think you are going to lose your mind.

In the morning light each trap would hold its pitiful skeleton as the evidence of the ghoulish feast. Unfortunately, people living alone will tell you, this method of trapping seems to diminish the tribes of the shrews but little, for it enables the survivors to keep alive on their victims and reproduce again. At least, that is one theory about it. The man who had this cabin told us of his diabolical scheme to be really rid of their unpleasant company. When he went out for a few days he planned to set out tall tin cans about the floor, accommodated with inclining ladders of little sticks, and in the bottom of the cans he was going to place small pieces of moose meat, which is a better bait by far than cheese. He figured that the first shrew would jump into the can and eat the bait. Not being able to jump out again, and becoming weak with starvation, this shrew would presently be leaped upon by another shrew who would in his turn lure another, and so on, until they had every one been eaten by another, and the last one, alone in the can, would starve to death.

It would be terrible, I thought, to be a person living alone and fall sick with pneumonia or in some other way be abandoned to the charities of numbers of these coal-eyed, shark-faced shrews. No doubt, like their larger relatives, the rats (Alaska has neither snakes nor rats), they would become bolder with each passing day that one was down. Our informer told us of a man who died in this way alone in his cabin and was not discovered for seven months. When the cabin was later opened, and the bearers reached down to move the body of the large man, they found it as light as ashes. The shrews had gone in from the cheeks and down inside, hollowing all out, until there was naught left but a shell.

We had been on the river a month exactly when we left this second grayling stream of our experience. In a wild forest pasture off a slough I saw two of my great cranes grazing. Gobbling down a large jointed grass larger than the goose grass, they strode along with seven-league boots, walking leisurely, conversing amiably, and with their long necks bobbing from one side to the other. Their eyes were telescopic in vision. They kept always in the middle of the field and on the watch for enemies, uttering on occasion their churring, trumpeting cries. These were the sandhill cranes all right, the only existing American crane that does not eat fish or carrion, and a bird once prized, when plentiful, as an epicure's delight.

Around the great bend of the river there now appeared before us slowly a town which we had not known was on our map. And it was a big town. We couldn't believe our eyes because the modern frame houses seemed to be brilliantly painted in colors of red, green, and blue, and their spires and steeples projected into the empty sky.

10

River Towns

Watching a Yukon River town appear as you float with the current is a slow business, but a fascinating one. Uncle Fred used to have a saying concerning the towns of Alaska: "When you've seen one, you've seen them all." This is true to an extent, and yet at the same time towns are different just as people are different. It must have taken us an hour to two to reach this town, during which time we made dozens of surmises and changed our minds about it at least a few dozen times.

It wasn't until the last two miles that the field glasses revealed once and for all what we were beginning to suspect—that our brilliantly colored and bedecked "town," with its many American flags flying overhead, was a graveyard! The houses which we saw were only little houses not more than four feet tall at the most, and they were erected over graves upon and surrounding a lonely Yukon hill.

However, a graveyard quite often means a town, and presently we saw the town itself right by it, brown and drab, and dwarfed into insignificance. We could see that it was a town of perhaps seventy-five people in all, when they were there. Most at this time would be at fish camp.

We pulled up amid the usual uproarious howling of the captive huskies, who lunged at their chains again and again. We couldn't help but hope they didn't break loose as we walked up the vile paths among them to the narrow boardwalk which was the town's single street above the summer mud. Both human and dog excreta covered the banks of the waterfront and surrounded the paths between the houses and the whole town. This was typical, since the Yukon outhouse, that poem of expediency, is unknown to the natives, who will not be bothered to build one. Realizing the dangers which can result from such lack of sanitation and trying to promote a more civilized outlook, the Indian Service has made at least one attempt to remedy the situation. In some localities it has attempted to set up septic toilets in connection with the school for the children. Teachers whom we talked to many hundreds of miles from here in a similar situation in another village told us that along with their many other chores of fire-building and water-carrying and filling in of Indian Service reports on the progress of each child or spending their evenings scaling an exact diagram of the living quarters they inhabited, they carried and emptied the school septic buckets for some weeks amid blizzards and snow. Then they were through. They would resign if they had to carry another bucket, for the buckets in actuality were futile. The children, never trained to use them properly, treated the situation as joke, performed the wants of nature at any and all places, and the village remained, of course, as filthy as before, since their own homes were right next door to the schoolhouse anyway.

When we walked up to the trader's frame house on the boardwalk, we could feel eyes upon us. A stranger of course is an event. An Indian boy with a pair of cheap field glasses had run out and blown a police whistle as though to arouse everybody, and he continued looking at us now through the glasses until we approached to the last dozen feet.

The old man in his seventies who had the trading post, a branch of the N. C. Company, we found in bed with the measles, and we were greeted by a rather beautiful, gypsy-like girl with page-boy hair and long lashes, who was taking care of him. Vivian was just our age and certainly one of the most attractive young women we met on the entire trip. However, she looked pale and had big circles under her eyes right now, for many had died recently and had had to be buried, and most of the village was still down in bed.

"Indian Service?" I asked.

She nodded. "I don't mind telling you," she said, "that at this point I'm about to lose my mind. But won't you come over to the house and meet Joe?"

Joe was slender and dark, and I concluded that he must be of French-Canadian stock. There were three little boys, with round mosquito-bitten cheeks and mosquito-bitten arms and legs.

"You people in the Indian Service certainly have courage," I said, glancing about the expensive-to-build, but rickety, rambling house which was their quarters.

"Do you really think so?" asked the young couple hopefully. They looked so tired and so wistful that we certainly forgot our own selves, if we never had before, at the sight.

"Yes," Bud answered truthfully. "I wouldn't have believed it unless I saw it with my own eyes that such situations as yours really exist today. You people aren't equipped educationally or otherwise to handle medical problems, and yet you are put in a position where the lives of these people are in your hands." Neither one of us could recover quickly from the fact that our friends had seen several human beings die during the past week and even during the past twenty-four hours. It made our little adventure look ridiculous by comparison.

"I guess this is one of the out-of-the-way places," Vivian smiled wanly. "Having a radio, you know is voluntary and you have to buy the set out of your salary. We haven't been able to get an electric plant put in. There doesn't seem to be much anybody can do when the natives get sick anyway. It only takes a strong wind to blow them over," she said, showing perfect white teeth. "This place is hard to heat in winter. It's hard to make it into much of a home, it's such an old barn. But Joe's going to get a better post, I think, as he works up."

"We haven't seen anyone in weeks," broke in Joe, who was older than Vivian, perhaps in his early thirties. "You know the people thought you were a couple of men when you came up. Vivian gets lonely for women to talk to."

Although we had planned to stay only to learn the name of the town and then push on within a few minutes, something in Vivian's wistful glance utterly refused to let me go.

"Do you like to hunt?" Bud asked Joe. "You know, I've been kind of wanting to go hunting."

At this Joe definitely smiled for the first time, and his whole face lit up. We learned that he had not been far out of the house all summer. He perhaps had needed just such an excuse as Bud to entice him to go out. As the crisis had passed and the village was somewhat recovered, a small vacation was now in order.

While the boys went out with their shotguns, Vivian and I, with a helper, Anna, hopefully set about preparing for dinner, and meanwhile we talked. It is never hard to find something for conversation on the Yukon. We found people openly and candidly telling their entire philosophies of life at every stop.

Vivian was from Klawock, a town ninety miles out of Ketchikan, where her father ran a salmon cannery and she was one of a family of twelve children. It was not hard to imagine what popular girls she and her several blond, brunette, and redheaded sisters and cousins must have been with the men of the community if the others were all as attractive as Vivian. She described the dances, parties, and "potlatches," a custom borrowed from the Indians wherein gifts are exchanged, that the sociable fishing communities would have one after another. It must have been a happy existence, as she described it. Vivian and her favorite cousin began working in Seattle winters at an early age, doing housework and going to high school. I caught a glimpse of that small army of people who in summer move up to Ketchikan in their fishing smacks and each fall again, like the migrating birds, return to Seattle. To commute between the two towns is just a couple of days' run. It never gets below zero at the "rumming" town of Ketchikan.

Vivian married Joe at the height of her popularity, at the age of sixteen. He was much quieter in nature than any of her other suitors, and in fact for almost two years she had heartily disliked him, while he doggedly persisted, following her from Ketchikan to Seattle and back again, where he even secured a job in her father's cannery. Joe was a student of philosophy and the arts, who never had any desire in his life to impose himself on anybody and added to a modest and retiring nature was the handicap that he was not too strong and that he had had one lung collapsed after a period in a sanitarium. The breakdown was supposedly caused by overwork although in actuality probably by fears and worry, working his way through a Washington university, from which he eventually emerged with honors. Of her many admirers, none could have been finer than quiet Joe.

Since that time three children had arrived, and now the pair were located at an exceptionally lonely post on the Yukon. Both were a little worn by their cares but perhaps were in some ways better than new.

It was the last place on earth that sociable Vivian had ever wanted to be, but here she was. She told me about delivering babies. This is one of those optional services on the part of Indian Service people, and we met many teachers who flatly refused to do it, no matter what the extremity. The Indian woman, Vivian told me, has delivery from a position on her knees by custom, and the local midwives are of course hopelessly superstitious and abominable according to our standards. Vivian's first delivery was a dry birth.

She told me a weird story about the teacher who had been here before she and Joe had come to this post; the scandal of their predecessor, who had been removed and transferred, was known far and wide, as such things are. This predecessor was in the difficult position of being a stubborn, mentally set, older single woman. These instances of single women do occur at posts in the field of Indian Service, but as a rule are not deemed desirable. Too many things can happen to a person alone. They are usually small things, but they are big things, too—a breakdown in the electric plant, the lack of a proper draft in the kitchen stove pipe, an overly sensitive nature come from too much battling of the world alone. In this case, it was the latter situation. Lying in bed at night in the silence of sixty below or at higher temperatures listening to the flopping and banging of the shutter in the wind, the distraught mind of the lonely, forty-year-old woman brooded on the small happenings of her day, magnifying them. The children in school simply would not behave. For some reason they were mischievous beyond her control. She believed that the scattered sourdoughs and trappers of the outlying vicinity were talking about her, because when they came into town they held long whispered conversations with the trader. She did not get along with the trader, who was married himself to the ugliest native woman in the village. She never felt close to the secretive Indians, possibly because she lacked the prestige of having a husband. She felt that even the children laughed at her about that. When the wind would blow and bang the shutters she began to imagine that it was the children outside her bedroom at night tapping on her window and playing pranks on her.

This teacher presently made that fatal mistake which spells the end to the Indian Service teacher when, along with her growing peculiarities, she commenced to seize the opportunity and temptation to impart some of her own religion to the children at school. As an organized missionary group, in this instance Catholic, naturally had this village covered, within their territory, the interference caused confusion, and it was not many months before the teacher was removed. Before her removal her growing lack of self-control had long placed her in the position for the ignorant to tease. She correctly realized that the whole countryside was making fun of her, something revolving around the subject of her being an "old maid." She became obsessed with the insane idea of proving the fact of her virginity to the sourdoughs and she managed to contrive and secure, apparently from a visiting doctor of some sort at one of the river towns, a "certificate of virginity," which, when authorities came to remove her, was nailed up on the bulletin board in the classroom for adults and children to see, despite the fact that few could have read it or cared a great deal in all probability. No one knew what eventually became of her.

It wasn't until the third day that we got around to asking about the interesting graveyard which had first attracted us.

"Why do the Indians build those houses upon the graves?" Bud asked.

"It's, like most things, an accumulation of several layers of culture," Joe told us with interest. "You see originally the Athabascans didn't bury their dead, but they did pile rocks on top of the corpses so that the dogs couldn't get at them. Then the Russian Church came along and built their domed churches and taught the natives to bury their dead Christian style, as they conceived it. The natives buried them beneath the ground all right, and through the generations they became increasingly ornate with the stuff on top of the graves, which was originally rocks. Like native peoples everywhere they accepted unquestioningly each new missionary cliché which came along, but they only added it onto the old, and still continued using their own magic and their own gods as a double charm. This they still do today in spite of the missionaries, and they are really superstitious about many things which they will not admit to a white man because naturally they don't want to be laughed at. Today the little houses are made for the spirits to live in after death. They are spirit houses. It is every man's ambition to have a better house for his relative than the rest of the village has, so it becomes a sort of social mark or distinction. Some of these houses cost a lot, too."

"I'll say they do," Vivian agreed, with her dark eyes flashing fire.

"Roofed with tin or iron worth maybe a hundred and fifty dollars down this way. You never see anything like that on the village homes. Wouldn't you think they would think a little about the living once in a while instead of just the dead?"

"I gather a native thinks differently than we white people," Bud said to Joe.

We learned further that the graveyards are quite a social center of activity, where the old women especially will gather in the afternoon to chat and make a pot of tea. What they chat about nobody knows. But it is apparent that to the Indians there is not that separation between life and death that the civilized white man feels, but to them death is the natural order of things. Indeed, more of their friends and relatives are lying on the hill in the graveyard than are alive. They might as well laugh as cry. A funeral is the signal for large preparations of a social nature. It is widely attended and is usually followed by a dance that night.

Later that day when Bud and Joe were out of the room, Vivian turned to me. "It amused me," she smiled, "how your husband said to Joe, 'we white people.' Don't you know that Joe and I are both Indian?"

"What?" My eyes popped. "Please don't fool me, Vivian."

"I mean it," she said, and in amazement I realized she was serious. "I'm half white myself, but Joe is a full-breed of pure stock. Maybe I am wrong, but I don't think of us as being on a level with the people we are supposed to teach, though."

Then every person in the town was Indian outside of the old trader with the measles! It took me a moment to recover my breath from the unexpectedness of it all. Vivian and Joe were Tlingits and did not speak the language of these people, and were believed by the village to be whites, because they occupied the position of whites!

Bud and I hated to leave this charming couple, but we said our farewells and found ourselves out on the river again, and the little town, with its colorful graveyard and the American flags flying in the breeze, was only a dream receding into the distance. There was only the river. We were faced immediately with the problem of finding something to eat. Bud stalked a flock of Canada honkers, the largest goose of all, and we ate the last emergency can of meat in a delicious meat pie for supper. Bud refused to eat perfectly good fish out of fish wheels. He said I somehow always kicked sand into the fish.

The town of Ruby eventually made its appearance. Although several white people lived there, including even four or five hard-rock mining women, "out on the cricks," we only stopped to charge a little food at the N. C. Company. The food included canned milk, one dozen cold-storage eggs, canned butter and peanut butter, biscuit mix, and a couple of cans of oysters.

Ruby got the vote for the most tumble-down town of the trip. Of course, there was no paving; few towns in Alaska have any of that, and you don't expect it. But much of formerly prosperous Ruby has been abandoned. The shacks are both log and frame, unpainted, and they lean every which way, huddled together like rats' dens, like a crazy town. A sawmill spews its refuse into the waterfront. We thought of fire, that greatest danger of all in the North. Nome, Seward, all of the main towns in Alaska, not to mention such camps as Ruby, are frequently burning down.

At Ruby, however, we were able to buy the first and only fresh beefsteaks of the five months' trip; most of the food we bought vanished within the first three days, and then we were hungry again. We picked up a telegram from Fred telling us our affairs were in order as we had left them, that he had received our one letter mailed at Nenana on leaving the railroad and wishing us bon voyage.

The prospector Martin had imparted to us an interesting bit of information concerning Ruby, which, although otherwise unverified, I will pass on. He said that $5000 worth of pearls had been taken from fresh-water clams lying in the Yukon by Ruby.

Bud had unsuccessfully tried to make a trade for a twelve- gauge shotgun. His claim was that we should by all rights have eaten goose several times already had we been properly equipped for these noble birds.

A large river, known locally as the Melozie, comes in from the north across from Ruby. I can't remember exactly where it was, because I was almost sound asleep inside the canoe, as we drifted on.

11

The Army on the Yukon

After days of successive rain and dampness, all our outfit was wet again. Bud arose at dawn and deciding that at last it would be a clear day urged me to tumble out that we might have a session of repairs. By nine o'clock, just as he had unsewed the canvas from the top and had washed out the mud from inside, it started pouring down, and it rained all day. I cooked beans and a dried-apple and cranberry shortcake and much hot tea while Bud worked. The bedroll was saturated again, the mosquito netting a clammy cold veil when it touched one's face, and my cotton pajamas were well soaked, from the atmosphere, not to mention the vast accumulation of wet socks and gloves which had previously collected. A seaman's * duffel bag held fresh ones that were dampened. Bud went along the beach and felled a forest giant, a very wet one, and in the rain, we chopped and sorted the spruce twigs and lifted them in bundles inside the boat, where they were bedded down levelly to form a mattress. "I don't see how we'll ever get really dry again sleeping on that wet stuff," I complained.

"Well, if we waited for a sunny day," replied Bud sagely, "we might wait all summer. Spruce needles are waxy and shed water, and I think we'll find ourselves dry." He was right; we did. We continued traveling, I enjoying the luxury of crawling inside now and then when things got too bad. However, it was best to keep busy and exercising.

We arrived at one possibility of why we never saw any bears but only tracks—namely, that the men passing on the river boats shoot at them continuously. The number of bears that crawl off to die, often with a .22-rifle bullet in them, shot in idleness, must be considerable.

Through winds and rains we persisted. One day we got caught in a sudden treacherous gust while crossing a wide reach of the

Yukon, and the old *Queen Beaver* lifted up upon five-foot, white-capped waves, and fell with a bang into the troughs, while we pulled like mad for our lives. After that Bud made a sort of canvas wave-splitter on a curved willow, so that the bow could actually plunge beneath the waves without shipping water. During such travelings Bud rode howling and sometimes angry through a continuous icy bath.

For three days we fought high winds, and ate practically nothing. A night came when we camped on a great flooded-over area of the land, much like a desert with streams flowing through it and enticing inland ponds of fresh, filtered drinking water, which would have made good bathtubs had one found them at a warmer time in the summer. As for bathing, we had little desire to do that! As a matter of fact, we scarcely washed our faces all summer, as we found washing chapped them. I used a little cold cream now and then when the mosquitoes were not too adherent; Bud had his beard, now growing red-gold and curly. At Tolovana Bud had shaved one side of his face and sent me over to the trading post for a new blade, as the one he had was dull, and it was his last blade. Alas for Bud! The storekeeper had only single-edged blades and Bud's razor was a double. That had settled it; Bud simply washed off the lather and called it a day. The only thing was to let his beard grow as it would for the rest of the trip. In good faith I had bought a liberal supply of both laundry soap and face soap in the beginning. We were hardly to wear the surface off one bar during the whole summer!

In contrast to the close, impenetrable brush we had known, this site of open land was a paradise for the walker and hunter. Far off the beaten track of the river boats, it fairly called to us to walk over it. This we did together for some hours, the stormy clouds of an early night furnishing the backdrop for large, three-toed tracks of cranes among the sand dunes. This then was the true habitat of the sandhill crane, for which he had been named.

"I think the time has come when we'll have to eat meat," said Bud, looking at the tracks fondly. "Don't you?"

In discussing the situation, we had agreed that if we really got hungry enough, we would try to stalk and kill a crane. We weren't exactly starving, but our heads were getting light by the morning of the third day.

"Well, if you think we are hungry enough," I said uncertainly. "But where are the cranes anyway?"

"Over there. You stay here, and I think I'll have a try with my .30-06 and 'scope." The fact that Bud's seventy-five-dollar, All- Weather telescope sight, of which he took such loving care, had remained clouded much of the summer did not deter him. It was the only possible chance.

From a half mile away came the melodious voices of the sandhill cranes. They would be standing motionless on some long spit of sand projecting into the river, with a clear view of several hundred yards on every side, their small heads on top of periscope necks continually turning and missing no detail of the landscape. Or they might be inland on these flats, surrounded by two miles of scattered, low new willows struggling to survive the winter frost and the springtime floods. Great precautions must be taken in approach. Bud was fairly good at snaking his way over bare ground on elbows and knees, but I fear I lacked that attribute. I was like the new Army rookie first being trained in field tactics—I got my head down low all right, but the posterior generally remained high in the air, a target for all eyes.

However, I couldn't stay still very long. I wanted to witness the shooting through the field glasses, and with this in mind I kept continually changing my position, slipping along after Bud many yards in the rear. The cranes became disturbed, but not alarmed, flew off clamoring for a distance, and settled down again. When they flew near me, it was never over me, where I hid hopefully in the bushes with the shotgun, but always over bare country and usually following the shore line. One pair departed completely, leaving but two more birds, who were uneasy.

There was a long period of silence, during which Bud was swallowed up into the landscape, and I decided to go back to the canoe before I got shot myself. I stepped across the sand, and there were the two wise cranes, about eight hundred yards away from me, walking actively about. They stopped and so did I.

I was sure they saw me. I should have stayed perfectly still, but I turned rigidly in slow motion and put one foot backwards away from them, towards a bush. That settled it. Up the suspicious cranes rose with a mighty clamor and disappeared with measured flight at the rate of fifty miles an hour into the immensity of distance.

From a quarter of a mile on the other side of them, Bud had just cleared the sand carefully for an elbow rest, had pushed aside the screen of twigs to thrust the muzzle of the gun through gently, and was just holding his breath to put the first pressure on the trigger!

We had practically reached camp when Bud agonized: "Down, down!" and we sank into the mud again. A flock of geese was coming in. They were rolling and squirming in the air and giving high liquid chortles, and they had come so quietly that we had not known they were there until they were upon us. They were waveys or blue geese. They wheeled and settled down a few feet from the canoe. "Now this time you stay still," admonished Bud sternly.

The plan was that he would snake around quartering from me, and try to get a still shot, prone, through the screen of willows. We would hope that when the geese rose they would pass low over me, where I could get the first shot of my life at a goose with the .410. Bud never got his still shot, as the birds suddenly rose, taking off low, near the ground. Wildly I put in my shot as they came over, but nothing happened. Then a rifle crack followed, and the leader of the flock of blues pitched from the sky and fell onto the sands with a thud. I couldn't believe it; the action had been so fast. "Down, down," lamented Bud again as we reached the goose. "I got their leader. They might come back." We hunched down, the geese whirled, took a look at me struggling for my ammunition, and were gone. But we had our goose! Bud had somehow shot it on the wing through the clouded "scope of his .30-06 rifle, and the bullet had gone through the neck, breaking it while the bird was traveling at forty to forty-five miles an hour. We grabbed the bloody goose and each other, and made preparations for a feast.

The following day the sun came out for one hour and then disappeared again, leaving us in a thick fog. We were slowly approaching the Bering Sea. Silently as the driftwood amongst which we moved, we passed by great towering walls where the river lay three hundred and fifty feet beneath its curving right- hand bank. Trees of the forest above lay strewn upon its tilting slope at weird angles. Bank swallows had perforated it with their holes in some places. These little birds went halfway around the world and back each year, yet each knew his summer home upon the Yukon, among the thousands of similar ones of his neighbors. The swallows whose nests were narrow tunnels sometimes four feet deep into the bank seemed to know which banks were crumbling and which were sound.

Presently, as the cliffs fell away, we came upon a fine little cabin in a niche of the river. Alas, it was locked up tight. It was the first locked cabin we had found, and this caused us to believe the man must have something pretty good inside. The real reason, however, was that we were nearing a tough new little town, built and supported by a U. S. Army fort, to which many and devious characters naturally were attracted.

We explored up the man's creek in the fine misty rain, passing his harbored fish wheel safe from river floods. There seemed nothing better than this to do at the time. It was one of those times and circumstances in the open that one feels the mystery of the universe poignantly. We were taking our little home right with us, with each stroke of the paddle, and we had nothing to lose. Our stomachs were filled with hot savory goose meat. If we got too cold and wet, we could always tie up, crawl inside, and go to sleep within the down sleeping bag. Our hope was to make our way inland and sleep this night on some secret lake or chain of lakes far in the forest behind the great cliffs.

Two days below the Army post, we found in the middle of the Yukon what Bud called a "goose island." Feathers and droppings covered the mud flat at the lower end of it in a confusion of such wallowing and muddy footprints as neither of us had ever seen before, and this was what we had been looking for. It looked no different from any other island to us, but for some reason the geese liked it and met here, as if by agreement, in their travels along the airways of the great North—or of the world, for that matter. From now on, as the elders trained the young geese for the long journey south, they would begin to flock up and travel about on test flights all over the country, and the airways would be echoing with their calls.

To camouflage our tan canoe, we found that only a few bent willows were necessary. They concealed nothing yet seemed to conceal everything to the incoming geese. It was left a few yards upriver next to the forest. There was just one thing to be careful of. Bud had shot only one goose in his life as a boy before coming to Alaska, but he had shot ducks, which, at least in the case of the male mallards, are just as smart, and he had found that any papers, cans, or especially shotgun shells dropped on the beach by the hunter are enough to warn the prey. For extra precaution we were careful not to leave our tracks in the mud, although we subsequently found that geese have no conception of human tracks.

When, seated at my station among the willows, I saw my first flock of wild geese come in, drop, and settle all around me like so many airplanes, I just couldn't shoot, but let them all get away in the willows. Bud shot one goose when he heard no report from me, a skinny Hutchins's, or what we called lesser Canadian, which we retrieved with considerable effort, chasing it across mud flats and finally downstream in the canoe and back again.

In order to kill a goose, a large and heavily feathered bird, with a .410 shotgun, one must be almost upon it. Bud dug me a trench behind a log and covered the top of it with brush. Here I huddled hopefully for two days in the mud, shivering, counting the mosquitoes, completely miserable, while it rained and rained. I would come out of my hole only to stretch my legs, grab a quart of hot tea, and go back underground again. Bud was cooking for us back in the brush a few yards, a thin spiral of smoke dissolving into the rainy air. Fortunately, the humidity was keeping the smoke close to the ground. I didn't feel too well. I reflected upon the fact that we were not getting the proper food and that our systems were becoming upset. Why did Bud insist upon waiting senselessly upon this island just in vain hopes? That young man's passion to hunt, to make me into a hunter, sometimes surpassed all bounds.

Suddenly, the sound of shouting voices came to our ears. Rifle shots from high-powered rifles poured into our island from a traveling boat. They approached closer. "Oh, oh!" I thought wildly. "They must be shooting at a bear and they're going to hit us!" Taking the initiative, I ran out to the beach and stood in full sight, where I was joined by Bud. Enter the Army. Instead of the Indians we expected—for contrary to romantic opinion Indians long contaminated by the white man will behave in this way—it was a boat packed to the brim with young soldiers in uniform which approached. They had certainly come a-shooting. It had just been, unknown to us, pay day at the fort for the first time in four months, and I suppose the boys felt like "blowing off." The boys had rented a boat from a native, a very unwise practice, incidentally, and a single bottle of whisky, costing on the Yukon in the vicinity of fifty dollars, was up- tilted and seen to be going the rounds as the boat ran with a fancy showing up onto the beach.

"Hello there," and the half-dozen boys, surprised, stepped up on the beach in the soft mud, adding their tracks to those made by the wild geese. "Say," said one fellow in a loud voice, "do you know where we can find something to drink? They told us there was a saloon down here some place."

"Do you know you might have shot my wife just now?" said Bud, inhospitably. "And also, my canoe?"

"Ah thought it was a log. Sure am sorry, sir," said a Southern voice. "Hope we didn't inconvenience you-all."

We grudgingly had to admit that we didn't mind. Personally, I wasn't sorry to see the Army at all; it had been a long time in our sober lives in Alaska since we had heard any young people laughing and shouting. There weren't many young people in Alaska.

"Someone must have been kidding you about that saloon," Bud informed the loud boy, who came from Chicago. The others crowded up. "There's nothing here but what you see—the Yukon River. The next town, Koyukuk, is thirty miles down from here."

117

"Come on then, fellas, what are we waiting for?" said another one from Florida.

"I wouldn't do that if I were you," Bud advised. "When you go out on the river you should always go upstream. You are in wild country. What would you do if your motor should give out?"

"She's leaking right now. Walk home, Ah guess," the one from Alabama laughed. "Hey, you guys?"

I had never realized we had learned so much about the river until now. Although these other people had been on the Yukon four months, they had been, no doubt, chained up. Now they were lathering at the mouth, and wild to go. One of them, who seemed somewhat more sensible, asked us if we knew where any wild geese were. I wondered what Bud was going to say to this.

"No," he finally said, thoughtfully. "I can't say I do." Of course, it was out of season, although season means little on the Yukon. But even had it been in season and perfectly legal, it would certainly not have been legal in a moral sense to tell them. Giving one personal friend a hint about where there is good hunting is one thing; telling whole groups and armies and egging them on to kill is another. Everyone should find his own game. That's what we were doing.

The boys got back into their places in their heavy wooden boat, while three attempted to shove off. No luck. Already the boat had settled into the mud, and the boys' uniforms were muddy to the knees. "Get in," said Bud, and they did. Wading out into the slime, Bud braced his shoulders against the boat, and to the surprise of all of us, it moved. The boys moved off upstream in the direction of home.

"You are certainly getting to be some man of the North, Bud; but don't get conceited," I tempered my praise.

"You have to be," Bud replied seriously, and I could see that he was not joking.

"I wonder what kind of stories those guys will tell about Alaska when they get home after the war?"

"It does make one wonder, at times, doesn't it? But maybe by the time the war's over, they will really have something to tell about, some of them. Who knows?"

No sooner had we got back to our hunting and the echoes quieted into silence again than we had a second group of visitors to our island, two men and a girl in another boat. These three also were out joy-riding and seeing the river after pay day. The girl had bright red hair and was extremely pale. She didn't look at all well. One man was a civilian and the other man was the highest officer of his outfit, there being two outfits quite distinct from each other at the post. The officer had come to question us as to our business, where we were from, and where we were going; we subjected ourselves to this examination in good spirits and found him a congenial, friendly person who would assist us in any way he could and who sent by us friendly greetings to the commander of the post at Bethel when and if we should arrive.

We went back to waiting for geese again. But we had not seen the last of the Army, by any means. Early the next morning, we were just making the last preparations to shove off when we looked up from our labors to see one of our friends of yesterday approaching on foot, the fellow who had been interested in the geese. By his appearance, we wondered immediately if some tragedy had occurred. Covered with mud, mosquito-bitten, he staggered into camp.

"What's happened?" Bud quickly asked, all business. Once again Bud was a pillar of strength by his very voice and manner.

The boy, who was only twenty-one, and who had a wife at home in Texas, explained what had happened. Bud seemed ageless as he listened. The boys had spent the night on the other end of this very island, three miles or more away. Their motor had failed. They maneuvered ashore. There, before they realized what had happened, the boat had silently settled. It was at the moment filled with water, with only the tip of the bow sticking out. They had nothing to bail it with. They could not budge it. Having no lunch with them, they had not eaten in twenty-four hours. (No news to us—neither had we.) Used to a hearty breakfast each day, our friend's stomach was plainly "caving in," although he was a very good sport. The night had been spent standing miserably around an open fire, while it rained ceaselessly and coldly upon their backs. They were not equipped for walking over this type of terrain, and their brimless caps held no mosquito nets. This morning they had voted, like shipwrecked sailors, on what to do. Some thought they would hold onto logs and swim and paddle across to the main shore, where they thought they might walk back to town. We gasped, for this idea would have proved suicidal. Subsequently this boy had volunteered to come down to our camp and borrow an ax.

"How do you think you could walk back to town on that side?" asked Bud, not unkindly.

"Why, can't you?"

"No, I'm afraid not. That's just another big island."

"Oh."

"Didn't you notice that the river splits into three big channels? The island we are on now is in the middle of the middle channel. The river spreads out over an area of, oh, maybe fourteen miles wide at this place. It would be very dangerous to use a log. Trying to float and swim across, you would never make it. The water's too cold. If you made shore you would find many swamps and wildcat sloughs. You have got to learn that it is not always possible to walk home in this country. Besides, the post is not over that way; it's over there."

"I hope they start looking for us this morning," said the boy, and sat down on a log. "We sure wisht a thousand times last night we never come down here, boy."

"If you'll chop a few sticks for me and lay them over my wife's goose blind, I'll see what I can do about taking you up in the canoe," said Bud.

"So that's what you're doing—hunting geese here," said the boy, displaying more animation than he had yet shown. "Don't it get awful cold sittin' in there, though?"

"Yes, it does," I said. "But that's goose-hunting. How do you ever expect to get all those fellows in our canoe, Bud?"

"I don't know yet."

Unpacking the canoe again took a short time. With our accumulated possessions stored at the edge of the woods beneath the canvas, Bud left me. "Can any of you paddle?" I heard him ask the boy as they shoved off. The answer was no. The boy

picked up his paddle with good intentions but small art. Bud was not used to steering. They wavered uncertainly upstream, just missing the treacherous sweepers which thrust out at them. Could they ever make it, with five boys packed in like sardines lying down inside the house canoe and only two to paddle, after they left the shelter of the island and met the full sweep of the current in mid-river? "And for goodness' sake," I called, "remember I'm stuck on this island alone, and remember the right channel to find me when you come back."

Had we all but known it, there was someone else who had been out in the cold downpour of the rain all of the past night other than the boys. Someone else, right in this vicinity, close by.

I installed myself uncomfortably in my goose blind when they had gone. We needed food. But no geese came. Bud had cautioned me not to build a fire, as he believed the geese were seeing or smelling the smoke. I gave up, suddenly. Taking the ax, I selected some long dead poles lying in the forest, and holding them vertically, propped against the ground, chipped the strips from them until, underneath, I found those that were dry. When I thought I had a liberal supply of them I stacked them carefully, for everything was waterlogged from the continued rain, and I was completely alone and growing more thoroughly chilled and ill every moment. For once in my life I started a fire with only one match, in the rain. Although flint may still be used in the far North to some extent, the old boy- scout method of rubbing sticks does not go. Happily, and independently I boiled a brew of river-water tea, which floated with twigs and goose grease in our long-unwashed bowls, and drank it standing in the drenched woods. With my jackknife I opened and devoured the last canned food, corn, except that one can of milk and one can of oysters remained for Bud to have a hot oyster stew when he got back. And just then there came to my ears the call of the wild geese. "Loot. Loot. Honk." Geese! Down! Down! Out with the fire! But alas, I couldn't put the fire out. It smudged with wet leaves like an Indian signal. Oh, here they came, low over the trees. They were coming in the wrong way, by land instead of by sea. Tensely I held my gun ready to shoot. Wouldn't Bud be happy and proud of me if when he returned

he found his pupil had shot a goose! It was a lovely vision, but that was all. The hundred Canada honkers all suddenly saw the great cloud of smoke which issued forth from this end of the island. At the last moment they flared, and as suddenly were gone beyond all recall. There was no use.

I was back in the goose blind again quite obediently when from afar off across the river came the sound of a shot. I listened. A pause. Another shot. I listened now intuitively. Finally, a third shot came, muffled by distance. That was all. All was still. Three shots evenly spaced is the universal distress signal. Perhaps someone was hurt over there! I gave a single answering shot of encouragement with the shotgun. I watched the opposite shore line with the powerful glasses, but nothing moved there. There was nothing I could do until Bud came back with the canoe. The hours had seemed endless already. Where was Bud?

A low whistle, and, sometime later, Bud stepped out of the brush. I almost cried with relief. Rain, mingled with grime, bedewed his bearded face. He was soaked to the skin, as his waterproof jacket was fast wearing thin. "Food?" I asked first of all. "Did the Army feed you, dear? I've been thinking of it all day. I kind of thought they would. Did you get any for me?"

He shook his head. "I got them all in the canoe all right," he explained. "Four of them had to lie down inside. Must have been half a ton she carried. What do you think of that? Some *Queen Beaver*, eh? But they couldn't paddle. I never saw such guys—not one of them could paddle," he repeated incredulously.

"You couldn't either at one time, dear," I reminded him.

"Well, I'm worn-out, now. Completely worn-out. When we just got within sight of the town, there was the biggest officer in a boat just coming back after looking for them among the islands. It's just like trying to find a needle in a haystack. He took them back in his big power boat. They gave me ten bucks, though. Then you know that .22

revolver I got on a trade with Dick on the Tolovana? Well, I sold that to one of 'em for twenty bucks. So even if we didn't get any geese, we got thirty dollars' profit out of this island. I've been thinking, sweetheart, that I haven't been doing right by you. This life is too tough. It's too much to expect of a girl. You haven't been getting enough to eat lately.

No wonder you aren't a very good hunter yet. I am going to take better care of us, somehow. If you want to, we can stop at the next town or two and go back on the river boat and give it up. We can wire our bank or make arrangements somehow to get out. Any time you say."

"First you must eat your hot oyster soup," I said, disregarding this for the time. "Until you've eaten we can't do anything. But I have something to tell you. A couple of hours ago I heard distress shots from the other side. I think we had better go over there and have a look."

"Oh, I'll tell you what that was," Bud explained. "Do you remember that officer and his party who came here yesterday? Well, I forgot to tell you, he's lost too, and the other officer and his bunch are out looking for him."

"Oh, dear," was my first thought. "That girl. Was she out all night, dressed lightly, as she was, in high heels, in that downpour?"

"She must have been."

"I wonder what could have happened to them?"

"Oh, just a breakdown, I suppose. Certainly nothing they couldn't fix in time. They were headed to go up Bear Creek when last seen."

"Do you think we should try to rescue them?" I offered timidly.

"I wish someone would come and rescue me," sighed Bud. I'm in no shape to rescue anybody after that workout. I mean it."

"But do you suppose we should try?" I persisted.

"We can't do it," Bud replied finally. One good thing to know is what you can do and what you can't do. "It's out of the question. They're all right. The only thing for us to do is head downstream towards Koyukuk as fast as the current will take us and spend some of this thirty dollars getting some food. Do you realize that we've been practically living on air for days? Just try and do some hard labor and you'll see the difference. I found it out. We're both dizzier than sick cats. I don't even want food any more, but I have to force myself to eat it. That part of the Army which is lost has got the rest of the Army out looking for them, and they'll find each other eventually. They're right near home, and we aren't. Say, it's a good thing pay day doesn't come very often, isn't it? But I have a little present for you before we leave."

Bud pulled from a hiding place something which I perceived to be a small totem pole about sixteen inches high. It was carved out of spruce; and consisted of figures which would have dismayed any Indian by their strangeness. The first was the head of a man, smiling; this was followed by a jackass head just beneath, which was followed by the sole of a woman's shoe, projecting viciously; and the final figure at the base showed the same man as at the top, looking very sad, with his mouth drawn down grotesquely. "I carved this for you while we were waiting for geese," he explained. "You know all totem poles tell a story. Let's see how good you are at reading the story."

It was only a guess, but I guessed right. "The man made a jackass of himself," I deciphered. "That's clear, isn't it?" Bud admitted that it was clear. "Then he got the boot from the woman, who was angry with him."

"Correct."

"Finally, the man is very sad, and wishes to apologize. But it isn't necessary, for she holds no grudge against you. We're in this together, however it turns out. And we're going to finish the trip, just as we planned, all the way to Bethel!"

Placing my totem pole in a safe place, I now took up my paddle and we headed for Koyukuk.

12

The Koyukuk

Bud would not eat fish from the fish wheels any more. Mushrooms had made him sick twice. Small ducks we got were slightly "blown" with young maggots before we could find a good place to cook them. We cooked beans and ate but a mouthful because we discovered they were full of gnats. Our diet certainly hadn't turned out to be all that I had planned for it. Bud, being larger and needing more food to keep him going than I, was rapidly starving before my eyes at this point. A swell wilderness dietitian I had turned out to be! All he wanted was tea and more tea, on which he was living. Indeed, it was a temptation to subsist merely on a little tea, as its comforting warmth filled up the emptiness and both of us were too lethargic to make the effort to cook the foods of which we had grown so tired.

We sat in the canoe motionless hour upon hour as if we were drugged, letting the current do with us what it would. What it would do, whether we made an effort or not, was to carry us on the longest route around the bend of the river, and then, when the river immediately turned in the opposite direction again, leave us stranded in the shallows brought up against some bank in water that was not moving at all. This is how we traveled much farther actually, in navigating the Yukon, then does a powered boat. I used to think in the beginning that one could greatly shorten the distance one had to travel by drawing a straight line and cutting off some of the turns, but this is not so in a canoe. The perverse sweep of the current will not allow it.

"I think the time has come," Bud said significantly once again as we prowled a beach in a daze. There were three cranes squatting by the edge of the water or hip deep in water about eight hundred yards below, as revealed by the glasses. We dived into the wet fringe of willows and skirted the shore. What a golden opportunity of a lifetime—there was, for once, perfect coverage for a stalk.

"I'll make a sporting agreement with you," said I. "Let me make the shot this time if it's to be done."

Bud agreeably maneuvered me into a wonderful position. "You mustn't miss this time," he said. I didn't answer him.

Two hundred yards out on the beach the cranes were seemingly asleep for the night, although I wouldn't testify to it for a certainty; to all appearances their long legs were curled up under them, for no legs were to be seen. They looked exactly like stumps, so perfect was their natural camouflage in this position.

I lay on my stomach as wet as a lizard, the rifle cocked and ready to go. Last of all, I raised my mosquito net so as to see less darkly. The moments during which I took perfect aim a thousand mosquitoes descended upon my face and neck, and clung, as we both held our breath. We concentrated on the gray objects; they were revealed but dimly in the partially water-clogged telescope sight and to a person looking without the aid of the sight they were scarcely revealed at all unless one knew in the first place that they were there. Bud greedily eyed all of the huddled objects, realizing we could have but one at the best; his concentration on the business of hunting was this time not beset by other interfering thoughts, I could see. I selected the gray object which appeared to the casual observer to be the most broadside, and fired.

The startled cranes departed clamoring. Did one, just one, remain behind? We ran to the beach. We hunted the water's edge over carefully. There was no crane. But in the middle of where the cranes had been was one solitary gray stump which looked just like them. Bud would never recover from this, that I had selected the stump as my target, and hit it, too!

We had had the satisfaction for a minute of thinking that a sandhill crane might be ours, I reflected as I watched Bud's face. Bud was glad the episode was over and that it had been decided in this way. No one should shoot the sandhill crane at this time. I was sure now that the episode of the cranes would never arise for us again; the crisis was past.

We made a two days' stopover on another goose island, and

Bud brought down one more goose from the air with the .22 rifle. I think our enjoyment was intense and savage and really too terrible to tell as we devoured this plump creature; the stop was one of mistaken strategy, however, because a high wind marooned us at its will on the island, leaving us afraid to cross to the shore and proceed. We were fortunate that it relented after a couple of days.

Although we did not know it, for nobody had warned us, we were now approaching perhaps the most dangerous single spot on the lower Yukon—Bishop Mountain. A traveling bishop of the Catholic Church had once been murdered by his Indian guide here, and he lies buried at this spot.

We perceived a tall, undercut cliff suddenly facing us, at a double bend, where the whole river poured abruptly through one narrow gap. The red walls of the cliff were sheer, about five hundred feet high. We weren't worried. We didn't even cross to the opposite side of the river but allowed the red wall to approach closer and closer in our ignorant curiosity. By that time, it was too late to attempt to get to the other side of the river.

It was around seven in the evening, sunset. In the lingering twilight we found a small river flowing from a valley just at the edge of the cliff, and we even explored carelessly up it for a while, Bud securing the first and only rabbit seen on the entire trip. Later we were to find out that this river was but a channel of a short cut running twenty miles back of what was just another gigantic island in this wilderness of islands. Up this river I crawled close up to a flock of a hundred or more geese in the grass as they were bedding down for the night. I took much too much time in the stalk, and eventually missed my shot, to have not a hundred but actually a thousand geese who had been hidden from sight boil up around me. I certainly seemed to have a genius for missing targets, however one looked at it.

The long twilight had dimmed to a late blue. The cliffs were red no more, but black. We shoved out of the mouth of the quiet little river. A strange muffled roar came to our ears, but we didn't think anything of it.

We were grabbed by unseen hands of iron from the depths. The depths wrenched at us, but on the surface was a layer of fast water which practically boiled against the sides, a thrill shooting from one end of the canoe to the other.

"Paddle!" I screamed to Bud, both of us realizing that forward motion will help to overcome almost any obstacle. Then, suddenly, the water on one side of us was going one way while the water on the other side of us was going just as fast in the other! I took a quick side look, hardly believing my eyes. Something was wrong here. As the cliff fell back in a turn, we found ourselves on the very brink of the three hundred-foot, backlashing whirlpool which resided like a monster beneath it.

There was nothing to do but point her straight ahead downstream and hope for the best. And ahead, as we rounded the bend pell-mell and came out into the full blow of the upstream wind, were running whitecaps. We headed into them. But for the wave splitter Bud had installed on our prow, we would have been swamped in an instant. Bud was drenched from head to heels, as the tops of the waves rolled across his chest.

After ten frightened minutes we had ridden safely through the danger, just at the edge of the rip, and avoiding the worst of the running whitecaps. Had not the wind dropped somewhat with the sun, had we not paused to go hunting but had started through the gap an hour sooner, I hesitate to say what might have happened. We never forgot the lesson of Bishop Mountain. Whole boats larger than ours, powered boats carrying half a dozen people, have been known in instances to disappear completely on the Yukon, with never a trace found. We wondered why nobody had ever spoken to us of Bishop Mountain. Perhaps the reason is that the people on the river, as trader, missionary, and teacher staying close to their stations, do not travel about much and do not know all of their piece of river.

High head winds obliged us literally to fight our way from wave to rolling wave, along the edge of the shore, all the way to Koyukuk. We passed many excellent goose flats, Bud futilely cursing the .410, which was not like him, and I endeavoring to be patient and comforting. Bud could hardly stand without swaying; still he seemed obsessed with the desire to stop at a thousand likely places to wait for geese, though I discouraged him at every one, and finally refused to let him ashore. Bud was irritably positive that if we could get just one good meal of delicious fat goose meat under the belt, the whole country would look entirely different to us and that there need be no foolish fight against adverse circumstances to get immediately to town. I was sure that our best bet was to keep going as fast as possible towards Koyukuk, and not prolong the agony by useless hunting. I kept stubbornly paddling on.

Indeed, during this stage of the trip, the country did not look so good, even to enthusiasts. In our ebbing strength we saw the Yukon as stretching endlessly along the base of its unnamed northern hills, with which we had been well acquainted for several hundred miles, and which harbored never a sign of human life.

At last we began to look anxiously for the big Koyukuk River to come in and for the town of Koyukuk.

"I wish we had inquired what side of the river the town is on," Bud said. "We should always remember to inquire about the town below."

He was right. It would not be impossible to miss whole towns entirely on the lower Yukon.

Driving winds and rains met us full in the face, kicking up the tops of the choppy waves before us and drenching us with river water as well. We were crowding the extreme right bank, when at last it dropped away, and we saw ourselves entering water of another color. There was no doubt in our minds as to what it was. The tremendous mouth of the Koyukuk was drifted over with blinding sheets of rain, turning the surface of the black water white, under the even glare of a leaden sky. As the current and the efforts of our paddles moved us slowly into Koyukuk water, we realized that this was a dangerous place to linger. It would not do to be caught in the mouth of the big river in such an upstream williwaw. Through gusts that were sudden and ferocious we plied our paddles doggedly across the bad open spot, being met in the middle, for the first time, by large rolling swells, almost as though we were out at sea.

"Now where is the town of Koyukuk?" we wailed dejectedly. We hoped, how we hoped, that we had not missed it. If it lay somewhere on the far opposite side of the river, we were goners. At last, through the rain we believed we saw what might be the town, huddled beneath some cliffs in the distance. At least there was something white. It was a hope.

But it was only a fish camp, probably deserted. Our disappointment engulfed us. Where was the town that should be here? That couldn't be it. There was not possibly room for a town at the base of these frowning cliffs upon which we perceived that the waves were pounding. Riding like a cork the rolling swells which were now ten feet high and growing stronger, we knew that we were stopped. We could not get around the cliffs. What we had come so far to reach, approaching with agonizing slowness, an inch at a time, was simply the white tent, gleaming like a beacon through the storm, of a fish camp belonging to natives. But the camp was occupied!

"Come ashore. Come ashore." The Indian waved his hand expressively, and it took no imagination to read the concern on his face. Brown, willing hands reached down to help us. The very trees were lashing upon the cliff.

We grasped the brown hands eagerly. Other hands, the hands of children, fastened our canoe securely to the lee side of the family's large scow, where it bobbed with more decorum and less wildness. "Hands," I thought idiotically. "My hands are getting rough this summer. I should do something about it. But—if you could see the hands I've seen this summer—"

"That old *Queen Beaver* gets some pretty wild notions, doesn't she?" Bud remarked to me cheerily. To my surprise, while everyone waited for me, I could not step out of the canoe. My legs were no good for a minute. So, on hands and knees, in a totally undignified position, I crawled out on the makeshift rails which composed the dock, and there clung like a starfish. I gained my feet tremblingly and we progressed to the tent. Bud was holding my hand.

"Water is rough today," the Indian father laughed conversationally through the storm. To this we fervently agreed.

Thus, because we came to them in need of food and shelter, we became acquainted with the Cooneys, a splendid primitive family group which we could never have known so well otherwise, and whose name may conceivably be traced from the

Hawaiian kooney, which means "woman." In the old days when as many as 140 whalers were known to ply the arctic coasts in a single season, their world-wide sea jargon was introduced into the North, so that today traces of the South Seas and other distant places may be found in some of the local terms and names which the uninitiated may take for pure Eskimo or Indian.

The Cooneys were different from any of the other Interior Indians we had met this summer. The great tribes of the Interior Indians of Northern America, stretching from the vicinity of Great Slave Lake in Canada westward almost to the mouth of the Yukon, are largely related, according to E. L. Keithahn, curator of the Alaska Historical Museum in Juneau. They are Tinneh, D<§n£, Athabascan, Atena, Tahltan, Taniana, Ingalik, Koyukon, Nabesna, Kutchin and Han, all speaking the Athabascan language. Probably of the Koyukon branch, these people were different because they came from two hundred miles north on the Koyukuk and were relatively untouched by the white man, or perhaps I should say by the degrading influences of town life. This spot was the farthest south they had ever been. It was also just about the farthest north we had ever been. The Koyukuk gold camps in the arctic just north of here have been termed, incidentally, the most northern in the world. From Koyukuk the Yukon River starts to turn south, and it will never get this far north again before reaching the sea. We were in fact in the same latitude with and not far from isolated Nome, whose port is visited by steamboats but four times a year during the brief summer and which is a place that relatively few travelers these days see. These interior Indians are entirely different from their neighbors, the Nome Eskimos, however; they are of a different country, a different race, and a different economy. It is doubtful if many of them today know much of the existence of Nome, although conceivably their wandering ancestors were familiar with the coasts. Some authorities have gone so far as to prognosticate that there will be no pure, full-blooded Eskimos left in Alaska by the middle of this century, but there are, fortunately for the sake of the Eskimo stock that ethnologists would like to preserve, actually great natural barriers in the way of distance and location, not to mention cultural barriers, which tend to prevent crossbreeding perhaps as much today as in the old days when the two races were enemies. The Indians remain inland. There is probably more likelihood of both races breeding with the white, as time goes on.

There is the case of the town of Beaver on the upper Yukon in Alaska which is a remarkable example of the ways of crossbreeding and adaptation. It has been pointed out to river tourists as an amazing example of the migration of a whole people in our world today—which it is. The town of Beaver is Eskimo, was founded by Eskimos, who are now of course marrying with the Interior peoples. It came to its present location forty years ago by this migration all the way across the trackless wilderness from Point Barrow. The reason for the migration is given that the people were so far in debt to the Barrow trader of that time that they felt they could never be free. Therefore, with a Japanese by the name of Frank Yasuda, they set out upon their three-year march, men, women, and children, and doubtless no one will ever know the details of that mysterious wandering. One also should be acquainted with the difficulties of tundra travel in summer to imagine it. The little colony was headed for the Chandalar country and gold, but they missed it. Today they are living a peaceful life of hunting and trapping on the Yukon fairly near by. Frank Yasuda was their trader and he had taken an Eskimo wife. He was sent, along with his two lovely, college-educated, half Eskimo daughters, to a concentration camp to stay during the war with Japan. The Barrow trader is not known to have collected.

As we took our seats on the familiar packing boxes inside the Indian's tent, the wind shrieked outside, and we huddled gratefully once again at the side of a tiny Yukon stove.

"Are hungry?" the woman asked softly. We nodded without hesitancy. She put down the shuttle with which she was making a fishnet, and I realized that this trick of making fishnets must be Scandinavian in origin.

It was a truly handsome face and figure that bent over the preparation of our food now with a smile. Her black hair fell in braids upon her ample bosom, and her brow was elevated with a native dignity. Her skin was golden, with faint roses in her cheeks.

Like a mother hen she moved among her brood of tumbling children, uttering a word which sounded to our ears like "Cut! Cut!" which means in Athabascan, "Get out of the way."

"My wife, she say, 'Cut! Cut!' all the time, all day," the father explained earnestly.

The children, soon losing their shyness, climbed all over us with sparkling eyes and breaths like cats. The baby, a three- or four-year-old boy, was mouthing with well-developed teeth a large smoked fish fin.

Our meal consisted of coffee, sourdough bread, and chee fish, and was subsequently repeated in the evening with all of the family. Our table was a piece of cloth laid on the spruce-strewn floor, and it was set with knives, forks, spoons, and tin plates and cups.

The preparation of the fish held our eyes in some fascination.

Incidentally, much has been written about the eating of raw fish by primitives. We never saw anybody eating any raw fish on our trip and attribute it to the fact that the native people know that the white man laughs at this custom, and therefore do not do it in his presence. Furthermore, no raw or "green" fish is eaten in any quantities at any time; it is a legend. Green fish will make dogs sick with dysentery and it is our belief that it will also make human beings sick if the diet is not plentifully relieved with cooked fish as well.

As to our fish, a fine, twenty-five-pound chee was placed upon the chopping block and the woman took after it with an Eskimo fish knife or skinning knife, making the scales fly. This knife has a blade shaped like a half-moon, which is rolled over the fish by means of a short stout handle projecting at right angles from the middle. Carefully washing the slices of fish, our hostess next placed them in the skillet to fry. But the fish had been sliced, not as a white person would do it, but along the sides vertically, leaving the large fins on each piece, to stick up four inches high as they roasted in the frying pan. Were those for us? Didn't she forget something? Perhaps she made a mistake.

But it was evident that the Indians appreciated the fins of the fish and had left them on with this in mind—one for Bud and one for me. We put plenty of pepper on them and took them in our fingers doubtfully and greasily, thinking that so recently this fish had been swimming with these very fins. They weren't bad to nibble on, a bit fishy to our uninitiated taste perhaps, but no doubt better for you than candy.

The woman understood little English, the children none, for these children had never seen the inside of a school. We later learned that the woman was born of a white Scandinavian father, one of the adventurers for gold who wandered far into the Koyukuk. Half white, she had been raised entirely by the natives and in keeping with native traditions. She had seldom seen a white person of her own race; she knew no other life than this. Now, at the age of around thirty-six or less, she had borne unknown numbers of children (the trader guessed about fifteen), half of whom, like the seeds of wild nature itself, never reached maturity. Although she seemed happy enough and intelligent enough, if one can risk a judgment by a glance, her mind was destined by environment never to develop further.

We of course wanted to know what was to be known about Bishop

Mountain, above, where we might have lost our lives. It was Sam Cooney who told us the name of the place. He listened with lined, impassive face, then shook his head seriously. Yes, he knew the place well. It was a very bad place. "Many strangers drown there," he at last remarked candidly. We had gathered before now that the Indians hold the Yukon River in large respect at all times and are pretty discreet in their ventures on it.

Where was Koyukuk? Koyukuk was down just four miles from here, on the right-hand side. But one wouldn't venture to pass the cliffs today. Perhaps tomorrow.

Koyukuk was the only town the family from the north knew. It was the source of everything they needed and used, the supplies being bartered from the trader with their furs and skins. Apparently, they never wondered much just where the trader himself got these things, or perhaps they were shy in revealing their ignorance by asking questions of white people. Very often the white men will give evasive replies to serious questions or tell untruths just to make a coarse joke at the expense of someone less sophisticated. The grubstake for this prosperous family, which ranged over a wide area of good fur country, was $1100 yearly, Sam told us. Bud tried to explain to Sam about gasoline pumps at the service stations Outside, and about how automobiles travel on roads to connect every point. It was hard to tell for sure how much was being understood or if Bud was being entirely believed. Sam merely nodded and smiled politely in acquiescence. Sam had traveled quite a bit, however. He had at some time actually traveled all the way up the river by steamboat to Nenana, where he had seen cars and had ridden in one once when he was conveyed to the hospital of Bishop Bentley's Episcopal Mission. He described this ride to us with a childish wonder and delight. Deathly ill, he had nonetheless experienced the ride for all it was worth. At Nenana he had seen the railroad but was surprised to learn from Bud that the train ran on the tracks to other places from there. It had simply existed at one place for him. Speaking of the great engine, he said: "He makes big noise! Have you seen him, too?"

We nodded. Then he asked, "Is he In Fairbanks, too?" We explained that not only is he in Fairbanks, but he is in Seward where the big boats from the ocean Outside come. We illustrated on our map, but again it was difficult to know if the congenial family actually understood.

The family had never seen a horse or a cow, which Bud tried to describe as a sort of tame moose. Their butter in the can they thought of as "cow grease," rendered out by frying as they rendered the grease out of animals they got themselves.

Bud's and Sam's scientific discussions extended into the night. One tale was of a tragedy wherein a little five-year-old boy on the river had picked up the .22 rifle one day and accidentally shot and killed his little sister, age three. The grieved Indian parent threw the gun into the Yukon, but not altogether for the same reasons that a white man might have done so. Sam explained, "That man, he think something is wrong with gun. He never use him more."

Bud learned from Sam how to give the "fighting call" to call a moose. Our friend Dick on the Tolovana had given similar instructions, only Dick had perfected the Indian method by training his little dog to work with him by growling softly in warning when the moose arrived. For giving the fighting call is a dangerous pastime during the rutting season. All our informers attested to that emphatically. The call is made by rubbing a stick between two dead birches, or it can even be made with a canoe paddle or oar on the side of one's boat as one drifts along a river. This call brings only the big moose, because the little ones are afraid and hide. Approaching as softly as a ghost, the nearsighted mighty bull slides through the brush, never treading on so much as a twig or a dry leaf that will crack and betray his presence.

"Why doesn't he get his horns caught in that stuff?" I have asked. Nobody seems to know the answer to this.

The purpose of the bull moose is to surprise and charge his adversary off guard. The hunter must keep alert to see his quarry before his quarry sees him. Sam said that it was advisable to have a tree to climb right at hand. He knew a man who was picked up on the antlers of a bull moose and carried away into the forest. Sam explained: "He was long time dead."

An interesting insight was here gained into Indian psychology, however, which slightly shocked us. Sam and his partner were out hunting moose in the snow in the early spring. "We hit him here" (touching his forearm), "and here" (touching his shoulder), "and here" (touching his hip). "Moose go on. Never stop."

"What kind of rifle?"

"A .30-30." We weren't surprised at this. Aside from the .30-30, the .22 rifle is practically the only rifle the Alaska natives know. "It's a shame for the traders to sell those .30-30's to the natives, from the standpoint of the game," Bud had previously told me. "They're really too small for these moose and bear, and walrus; they make too many cripples in the hands of an Indian—in the hands of most white men, too."

"Snow is all red. Blood everywhere, red," continued the Indian, spreading his hands. "Follow moose long ways. Only one bullet in gun." His voice dropped.

"What did you do?" we asked. "You only had one bullet left in your gun?"

"Go back home, then/1

"What?" I cried, amazed.

"Save bullet. Maybe, find other moose sometime," was the philosophical answer.

As I undressed hurriedly inside the *Queen Beaver* that night, to fall asleep before I had a chance to get seasick, my mind hummed with the fact of our encounter with this family from the north.

How I should like to adopt this family and introduce them myself to the civilization pressing in upon them, yet of which they were completely unaware and oblivious. How interesting it would be to have the chance to observe the impact of our civilization upon them, if introduced in an advantageous way, by a friend I What would they think of it?

As we lay on the bouncing waves snugly haltered to the natives' boat, I had a dream. I dreamed that I returned to the States, not with one little Eskimo child, but with the whole of the Sam Cooney family with me, of all ages and sexes. The perfect family, certainly. They all had clinical examinations, vitamin pills, new twentieth-century clothes for travel, individual attention and care. There was a bugaboo about the wind in Alaska that no native can live Outside because of a tendency toward tuberculosis in the warmer climate and the change to a sedentary occupation, but certainly that couldn't be any more hazardous than the infectious conditions to which these people were already subjected, with the known disastrous results! And as for outdoor exercise—well, they could get that too, in the States, if they must have it. Yet they were only to be "led" in their adventures Outside, never forced or frightened into making any decision that they did not care to make for themselves. Would they go with me right now if I asked them, I wondered?

The children of the Cooney family, after some time of intensive tutoring, we would place in their grades in American public schools. That is usually the thing that is done. Of course, as a child I had hated school and the whole system of artificial grown-up life with my whole heart. If I had been allowed to take this same canoe trip on the Yukon with all of its glories at the age of twelve or thirteen, for instance, instead of delaying it for years, I would have been quite as capable actually, with the same judgments, of estimating physical phenomena and would have had somewhat more strength and animal vigor for the enjoyment of it than at the present time; I would have been a happier child. When nature was dearest to me it was withheld as entirely as possible that I might be "safe."

Well, now that I was grown-up, I knew that children had to go to school for thousands of hours or for around fifteen years continuously for the first part of their early developmental life. Or did they?

I perceived then the great difference between civilized children and the children of the wild: our children spend a great deal of time learning to do things which are useless, things not associated with survival or earning one's living at all. These things are a part of our culture. Wilderness children introduced to these activities have a hard time to understand the point of them at first. We would call them underprivileged because they have never learned to play, as we understand it. Little children hunt moose or break trail for the dogs at forty below zero in the North, with the nearest other human being miles away; wilderness children, like our own farm children, especially in former days, are needed for work, and the things that a little child can do are such as would exhaust the resources and capacities of many of our civilized men.

First the husband and father of the transplanted family must have a job if this transplanted family is to be "civilized." The father would have to punch the time clock, of course. I have an idea he wouldn't like it, because most of us don't. How would that compare with his old pride in outwitting his animal friends on his trap line and his pride in his fine furry dogs?

The mother would be another problem. She would not like to have her husband and her children away from her all day, because people do not like what they are not used to. Was this not an abnormal way of life, this separation of the once-vital family group? Was it not the unity of this primitive family which had attracted me in the first place? What did our educated white women do with themselves under the modern situation? Of course, that is a little problem in world society that we have never altogether solved satisfactorily during the transition period of the last fifty years; whole books are written upon it, the disorganization and displacement of family groups.

Then, keep the parents in Alaska. They were too old to change. It had been expecting too much, of course. The new generation, the children, are always the hope of reformers. But what about the tragedy of the separated family group, even when children are adopted alone in the first place? Perhaps the only thing is to take Alaska orphans, which would indeed be a great service, and one which, it is hoped, will come more into vogue in the future.

Like most people who stop to think intensively on such complicated subjects, in the dark of the night, I doubted at last the absolute wisdom of this system which I proposed to enforce upon the native, to change his life and make it go my way. It brought so much misery and so many problems that wasn't it better simply to let him alone? There are thousands who, becoming skeptical of the reforms which have never worked out as they were supposed to work out, have swung over to this opinion. Why can't we just mind our own business? To many practical-minded Alaskans today the incoming missionaries of different religious faiths and systems, for instance, are frankly a great plague which grips the land in darkness. But looking at it from an unbiased viewpoint, we must realize that the resultant confusion is no one person's fault or even society's fault altogether, but simply inevitable with the growing process, wherein there are "growing pains."

I came to realize in my reverie (and I was rapidly becoming seasick, for I had not gone to sleep) that our civilization, where it may not be right in all things, at least offers a human being such a wide variety of choices for living as has never been offered before by any culture at any time, and one simply cannot turn his back. Dismissing with a shrug all the world has to offer simply isn't done. Most people think their bondage is worth it, at least for the experience. If the simple native has not at least had the chance to make his choice from this great carnival, then he is really missing something. Even if it be peaceful, a near-animal existence is not enough I A few thousand years ago the human mind commenced to think, and now it cannot go back. We were given human minds with which to think. We all deserve that chance. One cannot even begin to know what his choices are until he becomes educated enough to have some basis from which to choose. Furthermore, the world is becoming so small that very soon now there will be no escape. The Outside can be pushed back but little longer by people living in obscure places in the world, for no place is obscure. This does not mean that these people cannot retain workable parts of their own identifying culture, but that they must add on the new. Natives in the Alaska of today must feel this, in a vague way at least, for they know that pressures are being exerted upon them. It is either adapt to the higher culture and survive or fail to adapt and die. Many are dying, giving up their lives like rabbits. They don't like to ask questions of the white men as to just where the gasoline comes from and why. They are afraid to ask, afraid to know; they are filled with feelings of insecurity, which they bolster up by periodic use of the white man's liquor, which makes them forget. There are psychological reasons for the Indian's illness and death rate as well as purely physical ones.

"You're a funny one," said Bud, when we were walking up to the Cooney tent the next morning for breakfast. "By your letters you would like to bring everybody you know to Alaska to educate them, and then you want to take all the Alaska natives that belong here and ship them Outside. Now I ask you, is that reasonable?"

"I wonder what will happen to our friends," I only mused, still engrossed. "You know, there's not much danger of our ideal family ever going Outside, but I am afraid the Outside is going to come to them, whether we like it or not."

❦

AT KOYUKUK WE SAT DRINKING a small glass of red wine and nibbling crackers and rare cheese with the hospitable trader of the trading post, who had heard of our coming.

It was raining softly on the faded windowpanes. Outside was another of the so many cold gray days which we had experienced on the river. Inside were the warmth, the food, and the cheer which had been awaiting us at the end of the trail to Koyukuk.

How many and varied were the personalities to be found along the hundreds of miles of this wandering Yukon River! The trader was a naturalized Italian, born in Italy. How had he ever ended up here? He was a very astute trader. He was just now opening a branch store at the new Army post. His oldest boy, born and raised here at this far northern point, was flying out next week to begin his fall term at a private military academy in Washington. His talented, half-Athabascan wife, who had been educated Outside, now joined us, bearing a platter of smoked sliced salmon strips, a big bundle of which we had just bought, and an open guest box of chocolate creams, nuts, and fruits. "I know you'll enjoy these," she said. How we did!

In the adjoining social lounge of the post, which had also become partially a roadhouse, an Army flying officer and an Army doctor were drinking quietly and reminiscing of college days and the wives they had left at home. The conversation was that of men sadly homesick.

These two, one of whom Bud had met before, now introduced themselves. They had been curious about us, they said. They 'could not imagine anyone taking the trip we were taking just for fun. "Seriously, what do you get out of it?" they asked. That was too much even to begin to explain to someone with such a divergent view. Perhaps it's a matter of temperament.

What we wanted to know, out of curiosity and also out of an annoying conscience, was if the stranded party, including the girl, had ever been rescued. We learned with relief that they had been; however, the experience had been very hard on the girl, who was ill for some days.

We further learned that at the Army post the natives working on construction were running wild with money and liquor. The streets were filled with dogs and children. Fights of whole factions took place on occasion. There was frequently no one to take care of the children, because their parents were drunk and the children were obliged to take care of them, or in some cases get drunk themselves.

While we were at Koyukuk we saw Sam Cooney's children in a similar situation. Our ideal family, on hitting town to buy supplies just before going out for the winter season, were lying happily with some of the town Indians, in their tent on a big drunk.

13

The Yukon Trader

O ur next run, down to Nulato, was a short one because we had full stomachs. We should never have such a consistently skimpy diet again; the worst had passed in that regard. At Koyukuk Bud had traded the combination .410 shotgun and one of the beautiful .22 pistols for that most priceless instrument to the hunter during a good fall on the lower Yukon: a twelve-gauge pump shotgun with a goodly supply of heavy shells, loaded with number-two shot. Shells, however, were hard to get since the war. We were able to get but one dozen eggs that were spared from the trader's own larder. Only one steamboat had come this far down the Yukon during the whole summer and only one more was yet expected for the year. As the government order to cease gold-mining operations would soon come, there would be but a handful of civilian whites left in the Interior during this war.

Indians along the river were picking up floating hundred- gallon cans of high-grade aviation gasoline and wondering where they were coming from. They were coming from big rafts which were being pushed down the river by a man who was being paid sixty dollars a day by the United States Army for his services and his boat. He had his troubles, however. He had to employ helpers, and the rafts were always getting onto bars from which it was virtually impossible to remove them. The high- grade aviation gasoline, unknown to the unthinking natives, was bound for a base or bases of strategic importance on the strange and lonely Bering Sea coast.

"I think we're approaching the suburbs of Nulato," Bud said as we passed five fish wheels in a row. (The commissioner's family's fish wheels.) The robber ravens were perched on the cliff watching the slow wheels turn; they were our only observers. Then—we rounded a bend, and there it was, the town. As Nulato is a good-sized town as river towns go, it supported

three traders. Nulato is one of the oldest settlements on the Yukon River, having been founded by the Russians in 1838, and before that being an Indian camp.

A man can make a very fine living at trading, or could in these areas in the past. Traders are recruited from all ranks. One trader who has a Bachelor of Science degree told us that he only works every other year, taking one year off for vacation Outside with his wife while his brother and the brother's wife take their turn at the post, alternating. There are some men who have been known to set up a number of fish wheels (made in a day or two of labor) and rent them out to the Indians for half of all the Indians catch in a four months' season—and that's a big profit for the investment of a few sticks of wood and a bundle of wire mesh. Fliers in Alaska, much too busy carrying passengers to bother with trade as a rule, or to bother getting off the main airways, can make a very profitable living from native trade alone. The Alaska natives find that trips out to distant camps are just as cheap by airplane as they are by dog team, because it costs so much to feed dogs, and is also expensive in time. Besides, they enjoy the airplane. A flier used to service the lower Yukon with reindeer meat from the Eskimo village of Unalakleet on the Bering Sea coast, and the demand was for more meat than he could possibly handle. The meat sells for five cents a pound at the place of butchering, for ten cents a pound at Kaltag, for fifteen cents a pound at Nulato, for twenty- five cents a pound at Ruby, and so on up, increasing in price as the distance increases. The enterprising young man, according to the story as we heard it, cleared $75,000 one year not long ago for hauling nothing but reindeer meat this way in his plane. But unfortunately, before he could spend the money this adventurer cracked up and was killed. The Army at the time we were on the Yukon would take all the reindeer meat from local sources that it could get, but there were no fliers to fly it in on a commercial basis.

Uncle Fred's saying rang in my mind, "When you've seen one you've seen them all," as we wended our way up paths made slimy by natives and dogs alike at the waterfront. Nulato's banks weren't as dangerous to navigate, nor as dangerously undercut by the river, as Koyukuk's had been; however, it is small wonder that any trader looking out over this same depressing view day after day from the window of his frame house on the boardwalk would become, out of self-defense, hardened and embittered toward the native and the native way of life. Close about the trader's house, the post office, and the building which housed the Signal Corps boys (Nulato being a stopover on Pan-American's experimental Nome-Asiatic route) huddled the small log houses of the Indians, with green fish, hanging unsmoked and putrefying, on the ends of dirty strings let down from the roofs—food for human consumption.

As we climbed up to the boardwalk with interest and headed into the first trader's building which we noticed, we were given at first to believe that Nulato was the most unfriendly town we had yet seen. Although we lingered at the trader's counter sociably, nibbling candy bars and drinking a bottle of soda pop, sent on its one-way voyage from Nenana in a barrel of sawdust, and retailed at thirty-five cents the bottle, no move was made toward us. The Signal Corps boys had already reported to the traders on our coming, on the fact that we were vacationers and honeymooners, taking a canoe trip, and the fact—of interest to the Army—that the pictures we were taking were not harmful in nature. Incidentally, word had drifted back up the river to the people we had passed that the Army had halted the canoe trip and had sent us out, but this was not so. We were allowed to proceed, and one might say that each town knew more about us now as we approached than we knew about ourselves.

Outside the trader's, walking the boardwalk again, we were met by sour looks from all sides. An elderly white woman in a dashing red shawl and with a gardening trowel in her hand passed us by, as though we had met on the sidewalks of a big city; although we waited for her to say hello, she didn't. The aging commissioner, alert to anything new and eyeing us with a curiosity he could hardly contain, obligingly looked for mail for us, although we knew full well that there would be none. All our mail was being held for us at Seward, pending our uncertain return.

Knowing now that it was customary to show interest in and to visit the town's graveyard, its chief pride and its only esthetic contribution, we now asked to see the graveyard. The commissioner took us.

Indeed, Nulato certainly has one of the best specimens of graveyards of this type on the river. "Look inside one of the houses," suggested the commissioner daringly, although he had never done so himself. We slipped the latch on one of the little curtained windows. The inside of the cottage over the grave was papered with wallpaper and the "floor" was laid with colored oilcloth. There were some partly eaten pink trader's cookies on the floor!

"Well, that beats me," said the commissioner. "I've heard of that," and he explained that the cookies and cakes are bought by the natives from the trader and then placed inside the windows of the house at intervals as gifts to the deceased. But the children, being always hungry for such things, cannot resist them for long, after the delicious gifts are entombed. The cookies disappear all right, but it is doubtful if the spirits eat them!

Standing surrounded by the grave houses in the tall grass overlooking the peaceful Yukon, we were silent for a few moments as people curiously are in a graveyard. A few obscure white people had also found their final resting spot here; we wondered what their lives had been. One of the most outstanding phenomena of Nulato's graveyard is a very fine three-by-five-foot plate-glass mirror erected over one of the graves. This gift, magnificent on the Yukon, was no doubt so that the spirits could enjoy looking at themselves—something that living native people do not often get to do.

"I have heard that there are a couple of white women in town," I offered the commissioner, knowing full well that there were. But I had said the wrong thing this time, for his wife was not one of them. Thinking then that I was not interested in any other than white women the commissioner apologized that his wife and daughters were busy cleaning house on Saturday and hesitated to ask us over. It was not for some time that we realized there was more here than met the eye. Although the Yukon as a whole is democratic in these respects, we had found a town where the whites live on one side of the railroad track, so to speak, and the natives on the other. We had also landed right in the middle of a town throbbing with bitter feuds and suspicions, an introverted town, with a considerably down-in-the-mouth expression.

Each side was waiting to see what the other faction was going to do and what we were going to do before offering friendship!

An old-time acquaintance of our Uncle Fred's was located at Nulato; that is, Fred knew him through conveying messages back and forth over Alaska, although for the last twelve years he had been strictly at Nulato. We found him and said our little greeting. The large fat man had been out cutting steamboat wood between his telegraph duties. He was at this time in the process of moving his woodpile for the fifth time this season, higher up the bank as the river followed. Uncle Fred had told us that it was sometimes difficult, in past years, to make a contact with Nulato as our friend was out with his woodpile and forgot to get back with exact promptness for schedules.

We went back into the first trader's store again. We still wanted to see more of this river town and the people in it. The youngish fellow at this store had appealed to us more than the others we had seen. He had sandy hair and a little sandy mustache, and in addition to his duties as trader he took weather observations, making reports by radio telephone on exact and confining hourly schedules by a code carefully composed of meaningless words, such as "love, George, king," and many others, nonsensical to the stranger's ears.

"We were wondering," said Bud, "if you people have had any fresh meat lately. We have a large goose in the canoe we would like to have you have. We know how it is here."

The young man raised his tired pale blue eyes with interest. "You bet," he said. "How much do you want for it?"

"Nothing. It's a gift, of course. I wouldn't sell geese anyway, for sentimental reasons. We shot it for you. We get chances for lots of them on the river, you know."

"Yes, I suppose you do," the young man said wistfully.

At that his slender wife came in, and we all introduced ourselves. The Busks were from Chicago, and both of them had worked practically all their lives at desks as bookkeepers before coming here. The quiet conservative Busks came all the way to the Yukon once, to visit their uncle, who was a trader, and they remained! They, too, had had an Alaskan sourdough uncle. We were invited to stay for a goose dinner, and we subsequently remained a whole week at Nulato, enjoying unprecedented hospitality and warmth of friendship.

During the week we were gone three nights on a goose-hunting expedition, traveling about two hundred miles over, around and about the Yukon by motorboat, and motorboating on the Yukon was indeed exhilarating sport. Forest, one of the Signal Corps boys, took his annual wartime leave of three days while we were at Nulato to do this. Back up past dangerous Bishop Mountain the three of us went. Bishop Mountain was equally dangerous or more so in a motorboat, we found; our nine-horse motor could hardly pull against the current but allowed us for a time to remain in one place, being sucked steadily and ominously towards the red walls of the cliffs again. And one felt even more helpless just sitting there in a motorboat, unable to do a thing.

The excursion was principally for a lark and secondly to get some geese for a portion of the white population of Nulato, who, confined at their posts, had no opportunity to enjoy them. Forest, who was an anxious and enthusiastic novice, fired fusillades of shots; I shot a great deal myself. Neither Forest nor I got results. The afternoon of the second day Bud was just about to walk out and cheerfully pick up his goose (he had been negligently shooting only those few which flew overland and dropped at his feet), when we heard Forest give an ecstatic shout, "I've got one!" And Forest walked out and picked up Bud's goose, triumphantly retrieving it. So, Forest got one goose, I got no geese, and Bud got the rest. We hadn't the heart to tell Forest about his goose, because he was certainly an ardent sportsman if not a successful shot.

Birds that Forest and I aimed at simply shook their feathers and traveled on. We protested that something must be the matter with our guns. We had shot forty or fifty times and believed that our bullets must be loaded only with powder. To prove that nothing was at fault but ourselves Bud handed us in turn his own twelve-gauge pump gun and continued himself at intervals to bring down geese easily with a light twenty- gauge! "You've got to lead them about fifteen feet sometimes, depending on how high they are. And you guys are shooting at them out of range. They should be close enough so that you can see their eyes. Never shoot at a goose coming towards you but wait until he passes so the shot can go between the feathers. You'll get onto it all of a sudden after a bit." But no revelation came. At Bud's remark that he supposed a person could shoot two hundred or five hundred geese right on this spot if he wanted to during the next two days by just steadily shooting, Forest and I simply looked at each other. Could he?

These days were clear and golden, the air like wine, our hearts jubilant. Mr. Busk had promised us a whole fall of such weather. "Fall is the only season I really like on the Yukon," he had said, but we thought that was putting it mildly. It was like heaven, and we wished that Busk could have got out to enjoy such paradise. Since Bud and Forest alone had been caught out all night in the rain once during our sojourn at Nulato, we built little houses of branches with their yellow and brown fall leaves attached and slept in them like creatures of the woods. With the wind blowing cold, in the early morning light we would slip from our sleeping bags, and before we could dress the wild call of the geese resounded, Windy cold days kept the geese on the move, and that's exactly what we wanted. The clarion calls of the wild geese on the wind just sounded like traveling, and the calls made us want to travel too.

The Nulato and Koyukuk liquor situation with respect to the native population and native trade presented two real-life examples of the problem which we had often heard discussed since coming to Alaska. Many persons in Alaska believe that liquor should be prohibited from the natives by law, as has been the policy in Canada and the States, but of course, even so, it is highly probable that a large bootleg trade would be developed. On the other hand, many of the natives themselves do not want liquor in the village, except that they cannot resist it. Nulato had voted not to sell liquor to natives, and the natives themselves had voted not to buy it or have anything to do with it. Nulato was thus supposedly a dry village and had received much praise in several publications. The actual result, however, was that instead of putting on one or two big drunks a year, the Nulato natives were encouraged to live in town all the time so that they could distill homebrew in their town houses. This brew is made from prunes and beans, from the process of sourdough bread, from potato peelings, from berries, from anything available. With liquor forbidden them locally, the Nulato natives traveled up to Koyukuk, which sold liquor over the counter gladly, or bought vanilla and other alcoholic extracts not for flavoring cakes, but for drinking.

At Koyukuk the genial Italian trader, who incidentally was friendly with many natives and was well liked by them, sold liquor. It was a large part of his trade. He had even been known in the past to charter an airplane for two weeks each spring for the purpose of distributing the liquor out into the "camps/* As his wife was half-Athabascan and from this village herself, wherein she knew every inhabitant intimately, her conscience sometimes bothered her at educating her own children Outside by this money, but with the terrible example of near-by Nulato staring her in the face, she felt that there was some excuse. As traders she and her husband were simply there to give the natives what they wanted and satisfy the demand, because if they didn't, someone else would. Nulato and Koyukuk were about equally besot with sins.

On the day we left Nulato, we heard a thrilling clarion call, like the voices of angels, filling the sky from zenith to horizon. The sandhill cranes were going south! We looked up, straining our eyes, and circling over Nulato at great altitudes, some so high that field glasses must be used to see them, were the great birds rising up from the inland lakes on the air currents—three gigantic fans of them, comprising perhaps three thousand birds in all. The white inhabitants rushed from their houses to witness the sight. These birds were the last of their kind to be seen in the world. But only yesterday a native had walked down the main street of Nulato dragging one of these cranes which he had shot for food; it was regarded by natives and whites alike as a prize to get one. To some they are still known here as "the Alaskan turkey." Only the student who reads the bird books or who has access to such information would realize what the sight really meant. The ignorant do not know and do not wish to know, but think only of killing, or of a fine roast in the oven.

The cranes, with their long necks outstretched, were marked by the sunlight against the deep blue of the sky. They were singing, singing such beautiful songs as I had never heard before, drifting in heavenly circles. "You know how they make that sound," offered Bud—"they have a windpipe seven feet long all coiled up in their throat."

"Shhh," I told him. "Just listen."

14

The Yukon Teacher

Down the river forty miles we went to our next stop of Kaltag. We had learned that an Indian Service teacher who was all alone there would be very glad to see us, and word was telephoned ahead.

At Kaltag we saw a small cub airplane moored on the water's edge, which had imprinted on its side "Alaska Dental Association." We had heard of the Territorial dentists who must fly to their clients at such outposts, where even electricity is sometimes not available and the hand drill must be "pumped" by a boy standing by.

However, this was not one of the flying dentists. The young fellow had just bought the plane when its too confident owner- dentist had unwisely landed on the Fairbanks Army field in a drunken condition. The plane and its young red-headed owner- pilot had been chartered for several weeks to "work out of Kaltag" by a gentleman whose business he did not state.

As Bud and I had a bite of lunch with the flier, the old trader, and the mysterious gentleman working out of Kaltag, weather for flying was the topic which was discussed. The weather, although it looked clear to me and the sun was shining, had held these people bound on the ground here for days, while the valuable time passed. It would soon be winter. These were the clearest days of the year. Yet the cloud banks still hung at a few thousand feet on the unnamed coast mountain range which separates Kaltag by but sixty miles from the isolated Eskimo village of Unalakleet on the Bering Sea coast. How we wished that we might step into that little plane and see Unalakleet! We had a little money ahead now, but the plane was not for hire nor the young pilot for bribery.

We asked the stranger, as we had been asking everybody, about the portage at Russian Mission. That was worrying us not a

little. What would happen to us if we got down here on the lower Yukon almost to the Bering Sea, and for some reason found that we could not get over the portage? How far in distance actually was the portage to the Kuskokwim River and what was it like? People had told us it was just a little way, but they didn't know. Some thought there was a road between the two rivers in these modern days where a canoe could be trucked across—we had heard that one in Fairbanks, and how wrong it was! The Game Commission had no recent reports of anyone taking the portage and couldn't tell us much about it except that the big bold line on all the maps, connecting the rivers, looked encouraging. It would seem to indicate that there was some sort of trail. One old trader on the Yukon informed us that he had heard of new developments on the portage, such as a tramway or something, but he didn't mention that that news was twenty-six years old. The best and most accurate information was given to us by Miss Emma Lambert, Indian Service Nurse, whose collection of Eskimo and Indian relics gathered in her travels is on display at the University of Alaska. She once went over or through the portage herself several years past. Her trip, as described to us, was discouraging. It was a wilderness of some sort. You simply had to have guides. It took them three or four days to get to the next river. She cautioned us not to plunge into it until we knew what we were getting into, as "it was very easy to get lost in there when I was there." She counseled us to make no move without first securing the advice of old Chris Betsch, the famous trader at Russian Mission, "who knows the portage better than anybody else."

The lone stranger with whom we had dinner had in his possession the only detailed maps of this country we have seen, and these he put at our disposal. They were sacred Road Commission maps in sections. They showed no trail between the Yukon and Kuskokwim Rivers, but a dotted and highly irregular path through a series of lakes, and the rivers themselves were far between by this tortuous route! The maps, best available in existence to date, were highly imperfect even at that, as the stranger and these two wandering canoeists could attest. To be exact, there were three different portages lying in this vicinity, any one of which we might take were we native to the country and familiar with the difficulties. They were devious and tricky, but the Indians knew them, had known them for generations. However, our outfit was too heavy to travel in the places where the Indians could go with their muskrat canoes, as I could barely lift my end of the canoe from the ground, let alone carry it any distance.

In case it was impossible for us to portage to the Kuskokwim we could as a last resort proceed sixty-five miles down below Russian Mission to the town of Marshall on the Yukon, and at this last outpost get a plane out, for there was a landing field there. But how we hated to do that. We wanted to cross over onto the Kuskokwim yet, for we knew that we would see Eskimos in kayaks on that great exciting western river, which is the second largest river in Alaska. "We must get across one of those portages somehow" was our only thought as we lifted the spread- out maps from the trader's floor and gave them back to our friend.

"I wonder what he's doing down here," I mused as we wended our way down the boardwalk of this new river town. "Did he ever say?"

"No, he didn't say. But I know what he's doing, I think. He's shooting angles for gun emplacements on those coast mountains and, well, kind of sizing up the country for the Army."

"Think so?" I asked excitedly.

"Yep. I pretty well know so."

While Bud went back to converse with the trader, I headed for the Indian Service School. The bell for afternoon classes had rung shortly before, and I hated to interrupt, but then considered that a slight break in the monotony of the classroom might be acceptable under the circumstances. I knocked timidly, but my knocking was not heard. I could hear the steady drone of the teacher's voice through the partly open door. Pushing the door farther open, I stuck my head in, and the teacher turned, looking me full in the face, with an expression of complete and astounded surprise.

Mrs. Wilson was one of those people who, met in such circumstances, can never be forgotten. There was something about her, although she was definitely of this generation, that reminded me of what we have been taught about the valiant days of old. She had been born and raised on an Iowa farm; so was her husband—they had known each other's "folks" since childhood. He was the boy on the farm next door, so to speak. She knew how to plant and can, milk and sew, rear baby chickens. She could also plow and drive a tractor, and she loved farm life with the bubbling independence of an Irish spirit. Life had never been particularly easy for her. It had been largely composed of hard work, with few of the things most young girls expect nowadays in the way of pretty clothes and fun. She thought just as a man thinks; that is, there had never been room in her busy life for excess emotionalism about the nonessentials. This was fortunate, or she could never have survived long in her present environment, for this brave farm girl had, in farm words, a hard row to hoe. She was alone just now, as her husband had joined the Army.

Introducing myself, I asked briefly if I might sit at a desk in the back of the class and watch her teach school.

"I could let school out for this special occasion," she replied, then, at my remonstrance, "We'll just let them out a little early today. How long are you going to stay? There are so many questions I'd like to ask you—"

"Just a couple of hours." I had walked down the narrow aisle, my heavy boots clumping. I had a large burn on one side of my breeches where I had got too close to the fire on some cool night of late; my face was worn and perspiry. The teacher in her cotton print dress was sadly out of style. Yet I think each felt at once that two kindred spirits were looking each other in the eye here in this Yukon classroom.

My gaze was drawn to the small round Indian faces (round, as a characteristic of their malnutrition) which looked up at us from the rows. Although my visit caused some excitement in school the appearance of my clothes, as of the teacher's faded dress, was not noticed; there was nothing strange in our appearance to them, for this was what they were used to.

"Could I help you teach school today?" I asked impulsively.

"You could," she said quickly, with happiness.

Consequently, I taught school for the afternoon before I learned any of the facts about the interesting teacher. For the first time I had opportunity to be in the classroom and watch an Alaskan schoolteacher. I noticed that she was an angel of patience with her pupils, repeating things over and over, and enunciating slowly and clearly in a calm voice. This is necessary not only because the pupils are learning in a language which is different from the language they speak in their homes, but also because the pupils do not get enough to eat at home. "It is pretty hard to teach a child who has an empty stomach," as Mrs. Wilson put it later.

"Do you mean to say that they don't have anything to eat?" I asked.

"I'm afraid that's true sometimes. We had measles here all summer during the salmon run and not much fish was put up this year. It's going to be a hard winter, too. They still have time to put up quite a lot of fish, but they won't."

"How many did you have die here?"

"We buried nine."

At the end of school Mrs. Wilson decided to have a weighing day, and together we weighed the school, chalking the names up proudly on the board and calling each name off for all to hear. The children didn't know that this roll call was almost similar to a death knell for some of them. Some of these children would never see the spring, according to Mrs. Wilson. Yet here they were in class, expected to learn, little walking skeletons whose clothes hung on them like bags. I remember the smallest child attending school, age seven, weighed thirty-four and a half pounds.

"Do you see what I mean?" the teacher sighed, after they had all trooped gaily out.

A tall adolescent girl weighing ninety-two pounds now came in to see the teacher and ask if she could come to school. "Sure," I said. "School is lots of fun. You must come to school, Mabel." Mabel nodded happily. Mrs. Wilson gave me a hard kick under the desk.

"No, Mabel," she said firmly, "no school for you now. Perhaps later." Mabel's face fell. "You must gain a little weight. You must eat much food at home." Mrs. Wilson smiled encouragingly. The girl smiled wanly and went out.

"She's dying. Advanced stages of tuberculosis. I can't have her in class," Mrs. Wilson explained. "She had a hemorrhage in school the other day."

"Really, Mrs. Wilson," I said, thoroughly shocked, "sometimes this summer I've wondered if I exaggerated or imagined things."

"I don't think you could exaggerate their importance," Mrs. Wilson said simply. "It is historic that a strong bold peasantry is an index of a country's wealth. It is the real wealth, more priceless than gold. I think Secretary of the Interior Ickes when he visited Alaska said something of the same sort when he said he was most of all interested in Alaska's natives when he visioned the real wealth of the country."

Certain facts weren't apparent to the casual visitor or the untrained observer, I had come to see; it had taken me all summer to realize the implications of some of the things I saw. It was and is a veritable cesspool of infection all along the Yukon through which we naively traveled to "see the country." The high mortality from such usually mild diseases as measles is of course in accord with the universal experience of infections when introduced into primitive and unimmunized peoples, those who have not through long generations acquired a high resistance to the disease by incidence of infection. The tuberculosis death rate in Alaska has been estimated at 397 deaths per 100,000 population, against the national death rate of 44 deaths per 100,000 population throughout the forty-eight states.

Tuberculosis is, according to Miss Marcia Hayes, author of Some Problems of Health in Alaska, the chief cause of death with the Alaska natives, as with all Indian races. Tuberculosis of the bones and joints is responsible for most of the crippling conditions which are found, and circumstantial evidence seems to suggest that it is human in origin since it has been known to run in families, and as all the families are limited to canned milk in this country it is here not associated with the bovine type of tuberculosis with which it has generally been supposed to run. Miss Hayes lists economic status, the lack of facilities for either isolation or treatment, malnutrition, and constant exposure as the fundamental causes of its continued prevalence. Listing exposure as a cause when we know full well that Indians and Eskimos thrived on exposure before the coming of the white man may seem peculiar to us at first. Some people even believe that the native must continue to be "exposed" in order to survive. But we must get out of our heads the myth that he differs from "civilized" human beings by necessarily needing to be rained and snowed and blown on for his health. As an organism he is just the same as we are and has the same organic needs. Although he has established a certain immunity to the elements, as any white man may do within less than a quarter of a lifetime, this immunity has been much overestimated. And when he becomes ill he needs exactly the same kind of rest and care that any other human being needs.

There are sixty beds in the Territory definitely allocated for the care of tuberculosis patients, and perhaps twenty-five more are available in the general hospitals. The Office of Indian Affairs has a constant waiting list of approximately a hundred. The Office of Indian Affairs has eight hospitals scattered at strategic points: Barrow, Kotzebue, Tanana, Bethel, Kanatak, Unalaska, and Juneau, with a total bed capacity of 184. There are three field physicians in Alaska and each hospital physician makes some field trips. There are thirty field nursing positions. At the present time there are a few cases of bone tuberculosis under treatment, the expenses being borne by the Territory and by the Office of Indian Affairs. The present program is not preventive in scope but is merely one of correction of preventable deformities. Private rates for hospitalization are from five to ten dollars a day, depending on the locality, and public cases are charged from three to six dollars a day. Three tuberculosis sanitariums are to be built in Alaska by the federal government, it is to be hoped as soon as possible. The patients will be both native and white, without discrimination.

The known statistical figures on these points of public welfare give but little reality to the true facts behind the scenes as portrayed, for instance, in the life of one lone schoolteacher.

The cases which come to the hospitals are in the extreme advanced stages of disease because there are not enough hospital facilities to care for them and also because the Indians do not give themselves up for treatment except as a last resort and are difficult of contact. We ourselves have often heard them say, when asked about a child who is obviously unwell: "He is all right. He walk O.K. all right." To treat these patients by bed rest at home, much as they dread to leave home for the terrors of the hospital, where people die, would be and is impossible, even with the constant supervision of an attendant nurse. The unsanitary conditions in which the family lives with a tuberculous member, the using of the same drinking cups and towels, the spitting on the floor, the excitability and irritability of the patient when surrounded by his many relatives, seem to indicate that the only hope in such cases is to remove them entirely from home. In an Indian or Eskimo family such a thing as schedule or routine is unknown. We thought this a very relaxing way in which to live when we first saw it, and many explorers have praised this freedom of life wherein everyone eats simply when he is hungry, from the pot boiling constantly on the stove, or sleeps when he is sleepy, not closing his eyes for three days in summer. A child is never told to eat or is put to bed, incidentally, for an Indian or Eskimo child is never crossed. Although the system has its good points in its place, apparently turning out fine social, communistic, tribal citizens, you may be sure that it is the bane of Indian Service teachers and nurses entering the field today in hopes of improving the present conditions which are terrible from any standpoint. And as a treatment for persons who are ill, the conditions are impossible.

Malnutrition and respiratory infections are given as the other two major health problems. In the present generation of "preschoolers" one finds a high incidence of blackened pegs which bear but a faint resemblance to teeth. These are replaced by the permanent teeth, which soon decay, so that by the time the children reach the grades, the molars and often the incisors are mere shells. The gums are red and spongy, giving the appearance of a low-grade infection. This is another evidence of malnutrition.

With infants, according to the uncertain reports which trickle out, largely from the medically untrained teachers, there are few deaths caused by diarrhea and dysentery in Alaska, but one third of the infant deaths are surmised to be due to respiratory infections. Respiratory deaths among the older age groups are common. Influenza spreads in periodic waves throughout the Territory, despite isolation, and whooping cough, once started, takes a terrible toll. All of these diseases are intensified even among the white people in these areas, according to some with whom we talked. Almost epidemic waves of pneumonia, both lobar and bronchial, occasionally overcome nearly all the inhabitants of a village at once. Until recently serum has not been available and is not available now of course out in the camps where the people are scattered for most of the year. Little or no typing has been done, and the treatment is entirely symptomatic.

Three other diseases are worthy of mention as known to public-health authorities: poliomyelitis, cerebral spinal meningitis, and diphtheria. In one community on the Kuskokwim, there have been repeated outbreaks of epidemic meningitis. A study of the carrier rate in the village was made and found to be about 5 per cent, perhaps the only study of its kind to be made as yet, for here is practically an untouched field medically.

There are adequate and exceptional doctors in Alaska's larger cities and the conditions among white people in Alaska are probably up to par; it is the native situation which we are principally discussing. A Department of Public Health nurse with whom I talked was rather appalled on first becoming acquainted with the methods of sewage disposal. However, as with the Yukon River, a period of four to six months' freezing insures the killing of over 95 per cent of typhoid germs. The immensity of the country, with its sparseness of population and the long severe winters, probably accounts for the fact that typhoid epidemics have not in the past run rampant over Alaska.

When Bud came to the classroom to get me, Mrs. Wilson prevailed upon us to stay for supper with her, saying that the day was almost gone for travel anyway. Out in her garden the teacher picked lettuce for salads, and that vegetable which is Alaska's redeeming virtue, a large fresh cabbage; then she opened until the spring muskrat and beaver season in March. A day then comes once again when the children are restless in school. They have a curious impassive way of just smiling and saying nothing when asked a direct question. On the second day the teacher may be just in time to see the last dog team, stretched out to a magnificent fifty feet in length and the dogs yellow against the snow, go dashing with a flurry and yell past her schoolhouse window. This time the sleds carry the small Indian or "ratting" canoes to be used on the tundra ponds when the water starts forming around the ice.

Later in May, before the salmon begin to run in the Yukon, the people return once more, carrying sleds, dogs, and muskrat canoes, with their winter's catch, in the big boat. During the first part of the summer they are flush with money and this may be the time for drunkenness and indolence unless the trader has withheld a part of their credit, as he usually does, and extended it over into the fall. Conscientious teachers tend to arrange the school year around the migratory habits of their particular village, but even at best, native children do not have anything like the full year in school which their so-called "brighter" white contemporaries have.

It was eleven o'clock at night and pitch-dark when Bud and I flashlighted our way down the cold beach. Nothing in our canoe had been touched by the natives, although several hundred dollars' worth of equipment, including the most beautiful rifle a native had ever seen in his life, complete with telescope sight, reposed in it. We had learned in which towns to trust the natives. And one certainly cannot trust them in a town where "poor white ways" are at every hand.

All about us in the blacked-out northern village dogs lifted their muzzles, and slowly at first, then swelling, came the wail which we knew so well. It spoke of something unknown. The fringes of the dwarfed forest pushed closer from every side of the clearing. "Listen," said Bud. We listened, standing by the canoe, and for the first time during the whole summer saw starlight reflected on the water; there were stars now, and a pale sliver of moon near the horizon. Each must have had the same thought in mind, that suddenly it was going to be winter before we knew it. Here for a moment was the strange romantic Alaska of which we had read, revealing the adventure, the terror, and the heartbreak of its past.

"Look!" said Bud. "The northern lights! Across the Yukon!" Avoiding the moon, which was way over in one corner, a long green streamer commenced to serpentine in the sky, coming towards us and swelling as it came until it reached the dome of heaven. The dogs ceased abruptly, as with one throat. Now shafts of white light, as of distant searchlights, stabbed out from different angles of the rolling heavens, and walked solemnly about. It almost seemed as though one could hear them, but there was nothing for human ears to hear.

We waited for the dogs to begin their song again, but they didn't. The dogs and the northern lights had spoken of something very real which sleeps inside the race of man: some knowledge of coming events. Perhaps the dogs howled simply because they were hungry, and the coming winter urged every instinct within them to hunt. Perhaps they felt certain electrical changes now taking place in the atmosphere and water by the lowering of temperatures. This is something which even civilized man can feel in his skin, as measured by certain apparatus in psychology laboratories. How intensely then must half-wild dogs feel it!

It seemed to us that for a moment the North had shown itself to us. Concerning the winter to come, it seemed as though the dogs must somehow know. The one portent which impressed itself in white letters on my mind was: starvation. And it still comes to dogs, and to some humans, on the Yukon.

15

Wild Things

It was early September. The days now were clear and golden, with the sun circling ever lower on the horizon and reflected in a merciless glare on the serene autumn river. It was freezing hard at night. The muddy waters of the Yukon had clarified themselves at this season to a turbulent yellow-green, and from the mouths of the small creeks the grayling would soon come with the dropping of the first fall leaves upon their pools. They were taking no chances. They spent their winters in the Yukon under six feet of ice and snow.

Although the federal season for shooting wild geese is open along in November, it was now wild goose weather on the Yukon. November would find the Yukon shrouded with cold and darkness, and all of the goose flats, so radiant now, would be piled with barriers and ridges of the unevenly frozen ice pack. Needless to say, in November there would not be a single goose left in this northern part of the world.

As we paddled due south, paralleling the Bering Sea now, we realized that we had yet almost as far to go before freeze-up as from Seward to Fairbanks on the railroad. We would not be likely to see caribou crossing on the lower Yukon, and moose were getting scarcer at every mile. We would have liked to get a bull moose for the experience and would have given away or sold the meat at the next town in this case, as we could expect to eat but little of it ourselves and it would have to be disposed of quickly. A whole moose is worth about $180 on the Yukon market. It was now open season and we might by luck

yet see one because in the fall when they "run" they lose their quiet invisibility beneath the full-leaved trees of summer and move about the country with some boldness and bad temper, even swimming the mightiest of rivers to meet their lady loves. We drifted along mile after mile while Bud resoundingly
thumped at intervals with his paddle on the side of the canoe in hopes of getting a response from an angry or lovesick moose.

For almost a hundred and fifty miles along the edge of the interior Kaiyuh Mountains there was nothing, not even a vacated fish camp, to show that human beings had ever been here before. The trees were golden, the sky blue. Such a river as the Yukon does not bear the traces of former human beings long, for all are washed away.

The rosy dusk of sunset's autumn glow found our tall orange bonfire of piled driftwood burning each night on a different beach. We had potatoes to bake, cabbage, salmon strips, candy bars.

The rosy glow of each dawn found us sleeping, usually.

However, these were such beautiful mornings and it was such a rare opportunity for trying to shoot a goose that quite often the faintest light of dawn would find me all alone in my hiding place on the goose flats, searching the skies anxiously from behind the big twelve-gauge shotgun. Bud kept us well supplied with geese by day and slept of nights the sleep of the blissfully content. I was on the hunt twenty-four hours a day, for I was tired of sitting on a log down-wind and picking Bud's geese. I wanted a few of my own.

A person who can stalk a bank of wild geese on the flats has something to boast about. Geese are great travelers and the same geese one finds here are used to seeing the hunters of New York, and have flown right over Philadelphia and Washington, D. C. Geese are indeed sophisticated. While in the wilds they are used to watching for foxes and wolves, and the smallest creeping thing attracts their attention, as they are watching for legs on the ground first. Furthermore, they always keep together in a band while grazing, with lookouts on every side. And has a goose got eyes? We really learned the meaning of a "wild-goose chase."

The hunter usually arranges himself in a "blind" where he thinks the geese will come by, and they usually don't. Hunters in the United States wait hours and days for just one shot. Yukon Indians locate a flock of geese on the ground, crawl up on them, and get four or five in one shot, crippling several which escape; this is pothunting. Indians who saw geese fall from high altitudes in flight at the report of Bud's gun were amazed, and some of the less sophisticated would have given anything to have that gun, because a sportsman's tactics and proficiency are unknown to them.

The Indian Sam Cooney had taught Bud how to "call" geese. Traveling in the canoe we would keep close to the shelter of the banks; then, when the call of a flock of wild geese was brought to our ears, Bud would call back a few times, and sometimes they would veer our way, and sometimes Bud would be able to shoot one from the canoe as they passed.

Between Nulato and Kaltag we must have seen around 10,000 geese in an area that was untouched by either white man or brown, and here the geese were considerably tamer, perhaps because of some faith in the great numbers of their kind which here congregated. Surely, I must be able to shoot one goose out of these—"just one for my own," I reasoned.

I did. I at last got a splendid Canada honker on the wing, and, gaining confidence, two more like him in succession, while 2000 geese boiled around me on an island one day and the island itself practically got up and flew. Again, on another day I was fortunate in shooting three more in succession without a miss, and once I shot a great goose and kicked over the tea and fell off the log on my back to do it, and the goose plummeted right down in my lap. After that prodigious feat, Bud said I had graduated from amateur to sportsman's class. After that, too, I was no longer compelled by conscience to get up early in the morning. But we both began getting up early anyway and wandering far afield because both had entered the nature lovers' class by now.

During the late summer and fall we took black ducks, pintails, mallards, green-winged teal, redheads, blue geese, and Canada honkers. One goose we looked for and never saw is the rare and little-known emperor goose, which is by repute the most beautiful of all.

The greatest fun for us on our trip became our small amateur attempts to take pictures of our geese, and indeed we spent more time at it than we should have, lingering dangerously. We could not obtain the proper equipment for taking wild-life pictures, but the geese were here in numbers such as civilized man with the equipment doesn't see. As we crouched behind our screen of willow stakes, mosquito head nets down against the season's last deluge of gnats, allowing ourselves to be bitten rather than move an arm, we promised ourselves that we would come back some day. Yet we knew that youth and age alike say these words. The probability is that we never will.

There was a large island known as Eagle Island where we had hoped to go on a moose hunt with a kindly half-breed of whom we had been advised, but our friend was not home; his place was locked up tight. A cut-off slough to the tortuous Innoko River ran along for a hundred miles near the base of those strange, bare, sugarloaf mountains, and we might find moose there. Should we risk it? We might find another Dick . . . No, it was slow water, and this might be an early freeze-up. The river was parting in its vast sweep, like the hair on a woman's head. We made our decision just as the sweep began to divide: we had better stick to the main river now.

On the left side of the river were the goose flats, on the right side a low string of mountains from which icy springs poured. Daytimes we would be with the geese on the flats; nighttimes we would cross and crisscross the river in a quandary of excited and gesticulating indecision, torn between goose flats and possible grayling streams. On one or two occasions I have known Bud to be paddling in one direction while I was paddling in another, until some reconciliation was at length reached.

One night we had slept by one of these springs with a number of oven-ready geese hung up to drain and chill on sharp sticks driven into the ground. The *Queen Beaver* lay docilely between her stakes by the side of a rocky shore, and the inmates were asleep inside. The Yukon was as peaceful as a dream as the sun rose, dispelling the night mists in another dawn. Dawn didn't come until about 8:30 or 9:00 o'clock now.

Enter upon the stage a shiny-coated, hunting mink. Incidentally, mink are always hunting. They painstakingly hunt over every inch of their territory, following a trail invisible to human eyes, just as we walk down a street each day to work or to do

our marketing. This mink looks at the canoe and the dead campfire ashes for a moment with eyes like little coals, and, abruptly dismissing whatever thought comes to him, continues darting down the shoreline; he is looking for any dead fish that might have floated in, for there is a reasonably sure rule about the diet of wild things generally: that they eat pretty much just what they can get, and that they are remarkably versatile, too, incidentally. This mink's movements consist of a series of electrified jerks, as though he were on springs. Even to the act of turning his small sharp head, this is a perfect, bouncing mink.

Now to the geese. Who can say that he did not scent them from afar? Perhaps he has something on his mind other than the dead fish of which he is so fond. But the inmates of the boat are at this time beginning to stir restlessly; they are waking up.

The inmates of the boat throw back the canvas flap. "Just breathe that air," they say luxuriously from within. They will not get up yet but will lie lazily in bed for a while.

But the man has caught a glimpse of something moving on the bank. With a flying leap across the intervening channel of water, he hits the icy shore on bare feet, and he is quite awake. The mink won't mind if the young human being is in a decided state of undress, if in fact he is not dressed at all.

"A shiftless mink," comes the lament, "has eaten away the side of one of our geese. There are mink teeth here."

"Come back to bed."

"Brr! There's thin ice along the shore. The water in the canteen froze last night. All right. Let me in again."

A little later another animal of unknown denomination enters the stage. He, too, has been attracted by the camp. The leisurely conversation of the inmates is interrupted by the statement, "I hear noises. I hear the rustling of bushes and the crunching of teeth."

"You do?"

Peering out: "The bushes moved. It's not a mink this time, dear. It's some big animal."

"Oh!"

"Maybe a wolverine. Boy, if you get a shot at one of those clever devils, it's once in a lifetime."

The peering inmates allow their glance to relax for a few moments from the scene of the hillside at their hand. They dress silently while the scene becomes rapidly brightened with streamers of sunlight predicting a perfect day. The funny thing is that they think they are watching all the time.

Then—it was there; now it isn't. The goose! It's gone! The twelve-gauge shotgun is aimed, waiting. Why doesn't one reach for the camera instead of always the gun? There is a slight movement of waving bushes;

the sides of some animal are gliding by. One couldn't have gotten a picture anyway. The animal is carrying the goose. The vision of getting this largest of the weasel family, the crafty and little-known wolverine, is unfortunately too much for a boyish heart on this autumn Yukon morning. There is a crash. Before one knows it the deed is done. Bud leaps up the hill, thrusting his way through the bushes, reloading as he goes in, infallibly. But his judgment has already told him that the creature behind the bushes has dropped silently and now is lying still. The wild thing held up lifeless now by his great, beautiful bushy tail crowned by a white tip is—a red fox. His sharp teeth are bared in the grin of death, his slanted yellow eyes are closed to slits; they will not wake again. In death he has been found with the heavy goose slung over his shoulder.

Poor fox who tried to steal the goose and who paid for your act with death! Why did you not say it was you? Elegant professional thief—we feel very badly about this. And what use have we for a fox who sheds hairs, whose coat is not prime? The only thing for us to do is to hide our heads in shame. This one morning on the Yukon is spoiled.

With the golden sunlight sifting through the creaking trees I walk on your hill swinging a bucket and looking for cranberries which the frost has touched. I think of how you and Mr. Mink ate our goose right out from under our eyes without our seeing, in broad daylight. How clever and how beautiful are you children of the wild! And the interesting thing was that you each, after looking all the geese over with a practiced butcher's eye, chose the same goose—the fattest one. Mr. Mink here—he too had tried to carry that goose away, but it was anchored too hard for him. He left, but not because of sounds from us. He left because of your arrival.

But here was Mr. Mink now! I could hardly believe my eyes as my fanciful reverie was interrupted by the actual presence of the mink hitherto unseen by us in actuality, but only surmised. Hoppety-hop, he darted towards me down the hill, the sunlight undulating in warm patterns on his dark brown coat. I was amazed at the rapidity with which he was hunting. Or was it a marten? No, it was our mink. I had never seen either in my life alive before, and I held myself breathlessly as the animal advanced unseeing; he was watching the ground for little things and he never thought to look up. He hopped with both front feet hitting the ground equally at once, then brought up the hind part of his elongated body in the same way.

Abruptly the wild animal was but six feet away from me and about to go by. He paused, sensing my presence. I looked from the corners of my eyes unmoving, not daring to stare openly, and he approached me.

Goodness, did he think I was a tree? I controlled an impulse to do something as he made a motion as though to climb up my legs, standing on his hind feet to look up. I controlled an impulse then to reach down and pick him up, for he was, after all, a wild animal with teeth like knives. After he sniffed my legs to his satisfaction and my own spine-tingling, he went on hi$' way.

Doubtless he had never seen a human being before and did not know what I was, the practical-minded and more prosaic person would say. But to me the experience brought up that fundamental question which perplexes ever and again every intelligent person who has had occasion to live awhile in the wild: can it be, can it be by some strange miracle, that wild things in some way know when we are without trap and gun, but love them and mean them no harm?

We fished the last grayling stream of the summer just as it started to rain again, which was unusual at this time of year, but it was a good thing for us in a way, because as long as it rained there would be no freeze-up. It might, in fact, be a very late freeze-up this year, designed especially for us. We fished on, the rain pattering on our tight hoods, and for once we were getting our faces washed! We were in the canoe tied to a branch by the side of a beaver slide. In the still deep pool a saw-billed fish duck meandered back and forth gracefully. And down below them, fanning the water with powerful flukes, some large red creatures were swimming! We had not seen these before. This was my lucky day. I had scarcely thrown out the lure, when I felt a strike.

I thought I had hooked a grayling for a minute as I started to reel in. But this was no grayling! Out from the quiet water leapt a scarlet monster. His jaws, beneath a vicious hooked nose, and his gills, were of black-and-silver-plated armor. His lip alone was sharp enough to cut my dainty four-pound test "leader" on its rasping edge wherever it might rub against him. This fish's eyes were sunken and little, like those of the mighty king salmon, and his tail fin was broad and powerful, and along one of his sides stood out in bold relief the old white scars of a bear's striking claws, ripping from stem to stern.

My big consolation in holding the monster at all was the knowledge that in the water he didn't have much weight, which Bud had told me time and again. If I kept the proper spring in my rod I might eventually tire and bring to gaff almost any creature. Round and round the great fish darted, leaping out of the water four feet into the air, my rod flexing accordingly. He towed the canoe upstream as far as the branch to which we were tied would bend, and then back again the other way. We were having quite a ride, but I didn't have time to pay attention to that. At some length he was brought unwillingly into Bud's strong hand, and lifted by the gills into the boat. He was perfectly enormous gasping there, but already his colors were fading as he dried and it seemed almost like a dream.

He was a red sockeye salmon, not spawning and in perfectly robust condition. These fish are known to run late in the fall. Interestingly enough, analysis of the stomach contents showed absolutely no food that we could see. Bud set right to work for two days to catch one for himself, but that was another matter. Others told us they had never known one to take a lure before. This was my lucky day. I confess that I am in a picture, smiling, with my fish.

16

Mission Nurse

We heard of Miss Anderson, the missionary nurse, a long time before we met her. Everybody liked Miss Anderson, yet nobody could tell us what she was actually like. She must be a very practical person, we imagined, for everybody knows that sourdoughs typically have little use for frills. Every sourdough for the last fifty miles into Anvik (and not one of them was "religious") mentioned her. It was "Miss Anderson says this," and "Miss Anderson says that," and "When Miss Anderson was here last spring." Whenever Miss Anderson stopped it was obviously a red-letter day. All they would say in response to our question, "What is she like?" was, "She is the friendliest nurse we've had. She's just Miss Anderson."

She must be extraordinary, we thought, to be so well-known in a land which swarms with missionaries of a multitude of faiths from its southern-most tip practically to the North Pole. Their campaigns have been laid in an intricate network for centuries. Decrepit missionary women of pale complexions and bad livers are the real travelers of the world, and the adventurer will do well to see as many strange lands and peoples as they do. The missionaries have access to remarkable material in their observations of isolated cultures detached from the rest of the world for centuries, but they have not been trained in any way to do anything with this material and most frequently are not interested in it. If you heard a missionary describe a place and compared his descriptions with those of a scientist who has made an expedition to the same place you would not recognize it as the same locality.

Along with interior Africa, Alaska is considered as a foreign field, and to the religious-minded is viewed as a sort of pie out of which each faith wants its chunk. It is for this that the people back home have generously loaded the collection plate in past

days, and still do to some extent. In its pure form the desire to help and uplift suffering humanity is of course the most beautiful motive known. Actually, in the case of religion, because there are so many conflicting faiths, we find that there is a human amount of confusion in our methods and duplication of useless services. Even at that, however, we must say in all fairness that many of these faiths have done inestimable good in Alaska. Long before the Departments of Education and Indian Affairs stepped in, the missions had been caring for the ill, the aged, and the orphaned of Indians and Eskimos for generations, and, most of all, usually had been treating them as human beings.

A brief religious roundup of Alaska finds the Presbyterians, whose Sheldon Jackson brought in the reindeer from Siberia for the starving Eskimos, entrenched in the southeastern and coastal parts, Point Barrow and St. Lawrence Island. Point Barrow is a town of missionaries. The equally conservative and rational Methodists, co-operating closely with the Presbyterians, are strong from Unalaska to Seward to Point Barrow in several scattered missions. The Catholics and Episcopalians are to be found in the Interior. They are good at agriculture, accept the concepts of evolution, and have a good time wherever they are. A small faction of the Seventh Day Adventists, a little later than some of the others in getting a start in Alaska, have very recently taken over the Matanuska Valley Hospital on a new lease and staffed it with their own personnel from their own medical schools. The Baptists, recognized universally for their friendliness and homely virtues, have the mission field of Kodiac Island. The Moravians, who are Quaker-like in some ways and older than the Quakers, are dominating the western Alaska and Kuskokwim scene. They are very honest in matters pertaining to money, are industrious, self-sacrificing, and hygienically and immaculately clean. Christian Scientists and some small metaphysical cults flourish in a small degree among the white population, but have established no missions, nor do they particularly want to. One finds some rare philosophers among them.

Field missionaries are perhaps all alike in that they are the friendliest people in the world to the traveler who chances by their way if it is in an out-of-the-way place. And in themselves they are interesting people, an accepted part of the scene in any foreign country of the world. The disinterested traveler-adventurer will be exposed to and will take samples of many wares as he goes along, and in the end he will be convinced, if not of the religion itself, then of the intrepid individuals who perpetuate it.

To our minds the most discouraging obstacle of all which missionary endeavors must meet in the foreign fields is not the inertia or the wickedness of the people to be converted. Nor is it the heat and the cold, nor the unsanitary conditions, nor the hardships to be endured. Rather it is the encroachment of rival religious faiths upon one's own sacred ground after years of patient effort. None of the missionaries admitted this to us, but if we were in their place we would find a most discouraging element in our work in the fact that other perfectly honest, intelligent people, our contemporaries, who alone of all the world's people were willing to endure the same things we endured and who had the most in common with us of all people in the world, were at exact opposite poles in their interpretations and methods, and longed in the sincerity of their hearts to undo everything we did as soon as we had done it. Making conversions today has difficulties of a different nature from those the old-time missionaries faced. With the spreading of scientific and worldly knowledge there has come to be among the American people a decay of these orthodox religious structures from within, and probably a new type of spiritual growth which the old-time fundamentalists are slow to admit. Most of the young people of our age feel that way. It is not so much that they are pagans, but that they are not so quick to imitate as were their credulous elders. While expanding here in the field among the primitives it is probable that these faiths are tottering on shaky foundations among the younger generation at home, or else are in a process of great change and adaptation. The way religion is presented to the natives in the foreign field is at least fifty years behind the times, if not more, and leaves them utterly unprepared to deal with contemporary times as presented by the magazine and radio.

A compromise about the slices in the foreign pie is agreed on today by some of the stronger orthodox Protestant faiths in membership in an organization known as the Federation of United Churches of Christ in America. In Alaska, rival Protestant churches of the Federation do not build in the same town: as the white Alaska population is still transient, all Alaska churches are missions, supported from the States. Their upkeep is appallingly expensive.

Membership in the Federation works out fairly well for the members and increases their united strength in crowding out other faiths which have not joined them. The Catholics, who are extremely successful in making large numbers of conversions among primitives, are about the only other faction that can find a place in Alaska aside from the members of the Federation. They go where they please and their attitude is believed by some to be that the end justifies the means. Other smaller Protestant denominations believe this too, but they don't have much success in expanding because they lack power and facilities in support from home.

Today it seems that more missionary nondescripts are pouring into Alaska than ever before; even wars don't stop them. In fact, wars accelerate the missionaries as some spot like Alaska gains prominence in the world's eye. From the boats at Seward step people who call themselves Independents. They are not ordained ministers, but are evangelistic only by nature, and receive but scanty and irregular support from home. One has to admire them. Sometimes they have paid their own passage to get to Alaska and do the Lord's work, which, they will tell you doggedly, never has been easy. With the religious pie in its present state, how do they expect to be accepted seriously? But they are nice people.

Then there are the missionaries like the boy and girl twenty- one years old who have come from Oklahoma to spread their faith. They have come to abolish movies and dancing, and it is doubtful if they have ever been to a movie or dance in their lives, although there is nothing wrong in listening to radio skits. They have never read a book about Alaska and know little about conditions in their own part of the country, let alone a foreign field. The boy carries a pocket Bible as his support in all things, along with some pamphlets to be distributed; the girl characteristically suffers from night blindness. Both of them came from a family of ten children. She is a pretty girl, rather frightened. She hates this strange. country and would like to be back in Oklahoma right now were it not that she and her husband have placed themselves at the Lord's disposal. These kids have somehow got a Diesel-powered boat a thousand miles down the coast, by which they plan to travel on the Yukon next summer to make conversions. The boy knows nothing of boats or engines, and he doesn't know whether it is a river boat or an oceangoing boat with which the Church has supplied him, or where the money will come from to transport and run it, or where the two will spend the winter on the Yukon when winter comes. Missionaries of this type indeed lead an adventuresome life. One wonders just how they will be received by natives and whites alike should they actually get to the Yukon. But everything looks as though it were going to work out all right somehow and these two would remain to become the new Alaskans in today's growing population, for the Lord seems to indicate that they are going to raise a good Alaska family. But of all the various missionary types we met, Miss Anderson at Anvik stands out most vividly in our memory.

Anvik, located within the mouth of the Anvik River, is blocked from view by an island, but we managed to find it. Back on green lawns sat the graceful mission living house, with its attendant classrooms and medical dispensary. It was a welcome and refreshing sight. We went immediately to call.

A white-haired dignified lady opened the door at our knock, her eyes widening questioningly. We introduced ourselves. Could this be Miss Anderson? No, Miss Anderson was taking a nap, as she was out all night on a case the night before. This was Miss B., a Southern gentlewoman from South Carolina. Of much natural refinement, and far from all that she was originally used to, Miss B. was a person of unsuspected courage. She had been doing mission work in Alaska for twenty-nine years with an occasional furlough, which she spent in Charleston.

There was a thump on the stairs and bouncing into the room came this Miss Anderson of whom we had heard upriver. She didn't walk as other human beings do, or even glide, but literally bounced along. As she was five feet nine or ten in height and had very long perfect legs, this Norwegian girl always took the stairs at nothing less than about four or five at a time by the sound. She was twenty-nine, with long blond hair the color of gold, piled on her head, blue eyes, and a ravishing complexion and equally ravishing figure. Everybody on the Yukon who met her must have felt the same utter shock that we experienced for a moment in first meeting this kind of missionary here.

Miss B., who was somewhat on the conservative side and who was not easy to get acquainted with, watched Miss Anderson with a faint smile of pride which was hardly concealed as the introductions were made. The two women were obviously very fond of each other.

As soon as introductions were over, Miss Anderson came directly to the point, looked at or through Bud, who turned a fiery red, and said in a undertone, "A man with a beard!" It is doubtful if our good chaperon Miss B. heard it, but we did. I felt my eyebrows inwardly raise from the unexpectedness of it all, but a growing sense of humor suffused me. Apparently and coincidentally, Miss Anderson, alone in the solitude of a manless mission on the Yukon, had dreamed of men with beards, just that. Few men happened down this way. Outside of one priest who was rather nice-looking we saw no young eligible men on the Yukon, and one could hardly count the priest.

Reverend Henry Chapman and his wife, who were in charge of this Anvik mission, were on furlough and the two ladies were entirely alone. Mr. Chapman had been born and brought up here at this post, going Outside only long enough to be educated and choose a wife, whom he brought back with him to continue the work which his father before him had established. Now their own children were born here. His father had been a great man in the work, and had compiled the only existing Athabascan-English dictionary, among other accomplishments.

We were shown to the guest room and were prevailed upon to stay a couple of days in all, enjoying the hospitality of the mission with its two lone white women. My diary entry thoughtfully and practically begins: "What good meals, what food!"

I washed underwear in the plentiful rain water caught at this season from the roofs of all such establishments on the Yukon. The drinking water was hauled by boat from up the Anvik River. We made a sail for our canoe, because it was vital that we travel very much faster from now on. The missionary ladies greatly enjoyed the geese and grouse with which we supplied them. Miss Anderson was amazed at my capacity for food. "How can you do it without getting fat?" she asked, as we went on to buy a whole box of candy bars from the trader across the way. 1 was too ashamed to tell her that even if there had been no danger of getting fat during the greater part of our trip, Bud and I together on the river with Forest had been known to put down a two-pound can of butter in three days, for instance, just eating it spread on graham crackers, goose wings, and such. The women watched us eat in a sort of fascination and plied us with more food to see what we would do next. In one day they became very fond of Bud, who was so handy at fixing everything about the house which had needed fixing for months, and besides, he had his admirable beard. I am sure they would have kept him forever as a part of the institution could they have done so. "I think they would keep me just to look at, even," he reflected conceitedly.

"These old sourdoughs in this neighborhood certainly think the world of you, do you know that, Miss Anderson?" we told that young lady.

"They're a case, aren't they?" she agreed, exhibiting a fondness for them. She told us a good story on one of them whom we had met. He had developed a psychosis over the mosquitoes and believed that he had the solution to wiping them out of this section, if not all of Alaska. The way he told Miss Anderson he did it was this: he and his family got into bed beneath the mosquito nets, leaving the door wide-open every night during the summer. This lured the mosquitoes in. (We could follow this far.) In the morning they arose and closed the door and trapped the mosquitoes, whereupon they delightedly took after them with fumes and swatters. The mosquitoes which entered this house every summer really got it: he collected the bodies in gallon jars. Miss Anderson said he believed that a few summers of repeating this method would substantially deplete the mosquito population in this vicinity until they were all wiped out and the pest would be ended.

"Where were you before you came to Alaska?" we asked her later.

"Liberia. Doing nursing, the same."

"Liberia. Where's that?"

"The central, west coast of Africa. Right next to the Ivory Coast and the Gold Coast."

"Africa 1" we breathed. "Were you in Africa? In missionary work, I suppose?"

"Yes, we worked with leprosy and yaws. And other things. I got fever and had to come home. Some of those people in the interior have never seen a white woman," she reminisced dreamily. "They simply can't understand what you are."

"You like to work with native peoples then?" I asked stupidly.

"Yes," she said. "But I don't think of them as natives." (How often we heard this from people in these occupations!) "They're just the same, really. The same hopes and the same fears. They're so frightened when their children are ill. These people here with tuberculosis—it must be a terrible feeling to look down and see your life's blood gushing forth, don't you think? I've supported them many a time in bed, while they coughed blood in my face, and then they would die sometimes, just like that. They are so frightened, so alone then."

Then she told us how she had given away as many as ten pairs of her own fur mittens during the past year for the burial of natives. "I just can't seem to keep any," she laughed. "You know they believe the dead will need warm things to keep from being cold in heaven, and of course they want them to have the best. You have to respect their views. I've become used to seeing perfectly good furs wasted by being buried in the ground. Stick around here long enough, and you'll get that way."

There was a tuberculosis funeral while we were at the mission. Miss B. and Miss Anderson climbed the steep hill in procession behind the coffin to the graveyard and did the honors beneath a sodden sky.

That night there followed a dance in the recreation hall, attended by the whole village. We all dressed as carefully for the dance as though we were attending a great social function, I myself exchanging my clumsy shoepacks for neat leather boots and putting on some of Miss B.'s lipstick which she loaned me with a dignified gesture. I had lost my shoes overboard in the Tanana River and had traded my lipstick, along with creams, soaps, nail polish and remover, to Yukon Indian women for beadwork souvenirs. The Indians got much the best of the bargain, as I later realized.

Miss Anderson and Miss B. acted as chaperons for the dance, as we did ourselves in a measure. Tea and mission cookies were the refreshments, served at the end, at the respectable hour of eleven o'clock. The whole affair seemed to work out extraordinarily well. We danced to two creaking and repetitive phonograph records—both with each other and with the natives. All the Indians seemed to take their dancing seriously, and every single one was as good a dancer as one would find among a comparable group of whites. Although they sometimes still had their native ceremonial dances, which were not especially prevented by the Church, they took to white man's dancing as a duck takes to water.

It was a strange sight to me for a moment to see Miss B. and Miss Anderson whirling among the dancers, all of whom were Indian but ourselves. "We too have to have a little amusement here," as they put it, indicating that the evening was no trial. But beneath the mere fact of dancing was something important here, and I regretted that all religious missions to the natives did not allow the same. More than school activities, more than sermons, more than any other single thing, little community "parties" shared by both natives and whites alike taught a cohesive unity, promoted mutual love and respect, and taught by example friendly, correct, social behavior.

Our presence at the mission inspired Miss Anderson to one of the practical stunts which characterized her, one which was not without its humor. She told special people privately—those who were inclined to drink at all—that we were really secret government agents who were here to find out which natives used liquor. And if we caught anyone, we would probably take him away to jail for no one knew how long. It worked admirably and had a deterrent effect for some weeks after our passing through.

The next morning after breakfast we got down on our knees and prayed with the two missionary women. It was hard to tell what a person like Miss Anderson really believed, I thought, as she arose with her usual energetic bounce, her mind already snapped back to present realities. She who rode by boat in summer and by dog team in winter out among the people—when she lectured on furloughs church members often wept for one so young. She was conscious of the fact that she didn't make much of a salary but was just compassionate enough to feel sorry for the inhibited lives of the weepers. Of course, she wouldn't have changed places with them for anything. And she was religious in the finer sense of the word, in a way that probably nothing would ever touch.

The two handsome missionary ladies walked down to the water with us when we set sail. The last river boat had come and gone back on its way upstream beyond recall. Even at that, it was taking a chance on being caught in sudden unexpected ice. We had passed up our chance once and for all to ride back on that boat, as Bud had diffidently suggested we could do if we wanted, and we too were now taking a chance with the ice. It promised to be an exciting race from now on.

Miss Anderson, her waist-length golden hair piled on her head and her winsome face serious, shook hands with us in farewell, raising eyes of a startling blue, so much like Bud's own that they might have been tall brother and sister of the same Norwegian family.

It wasn't until we were around the bend into the great Yukon again, and the mission was out of sight, that I breathed a sigh of relief. "The most dangerous moments I ever put in on this trip, in case anyone ever asks me," I told Bud, "were spent with a missionary woman!"

17

Bud's Moose

S ailing ships used to ply the Yukon at one time. Although this generation of Indians has not seen them, all trading and traveling was formerly carried on under power of great sailing barges. But sailing on a river, even a wide river, is difficult because the river is always turning, and this calls for constant trimming of the sails. Moreover, there are many precious summer days when there are no winds, and there are many times when the wind is blocked temporarily from the river by a hill or comes in veering and capricious gusts.

The Yukon had turned color. With the approach of winter, it was positively blue. High cirrus clouds at approximately seven thousand feet scudded in the sky above the river. I was doing the sailing, learning by doing once again, as neither of us had ever sailed before or had any lessons in it.

Fortunately for us, our *Queen Beaver* was an exceptionally stable river canoe, for we had no keel to speak of under this big sail. Canoe sailing can be extremely dangerous.

We found it just about impossible to tack with a head wind, because our spanking breeze would invariably turn into a gale when we rounded a sudden bend, and we might be caught in vicious seas far from shore before we knew it. Moreover, you can't tack without a keel. The wind blows you sideslipping out of your course.

Sailing close to the shore was what I loved, watching the land slide soundlessly by. I got so I could just cut by the snags and sweepers by a narrow margin and still be in perfect control. A single knot held the sail rope tied to my seat so that I could loose it with my knees in an instant; with both hands I bore down on the paddle that was our rudder. When head winds stopped us, instead of wasting our strength in fighting them by paddle as we once did, we took the day off and went hunting the

spruce chickens which in countless thousands now strutted the beaches eating gravel after a summer spent in subsisting on soft berries inland.

On landing we took the sail down, folded it up on its mast, and laid it on the shore while we slept. Lowering floods had left so much driftwood on the banks that sometimes there was no place to pull ashore. Logs were piled like matchsticks. One night we retired to what we thought was going to be a peaceful sleep after a peaceful and perfect day. An hour after the sun went down, the Yukon became the wildest we have ever known it. Bud rose, put on his hip boots and went out to pound stakes so that we would not be blown off the face of the earth. An icy rain was driving, it was pitch-dark, and the flashlight had been left at Nulato. Bud returned to bed, but the canoe continued to pitch with increasing violence, spilling spray down onto the top of the sleeping bag. I was so sound asleep and cozy within our little nest that I hardly cared what went on outside. Like a worm in a cocoon I thought I would be safe if I just remained asleep. An hour more and Bud decided he must get up again and haul us up onto the beach beyond harm. We were being thrown this way and that, and how easy it would be for the canvas canoe to rub, unknown to us, back and forth against just one small invisible snag. So, Bud crawled out again, disrobing to face the elements and save his clothes from getting wet, and in hip boots he set to work. He removed the fallen trees and debris, and while I slumbered he lifted us inch by inch to safety. In my pleasant dreams the sounds of the dashing waves grew distant, and presently there was beached beneath me once again solid land. Canoe's contents and me: at least four hundred pounds. "How did you ever do it, dear?" I asked in wonder the next morning. That had been one time at least when I was a camper who did not volunteer for work.

We sailed up exuberantly the next day to a native fish camp, for the express purpose of making gifts of our used clothing which we had begun to get rid of. Bud by now had lost his original reluctance in dealing with natives; in fact, he dealt with them magnificently, much as Columbus must have done. By his very modesty and their modesty, they had a great deal in common. He seemed to know how to get along with them by instinct. "We should have taken out a peddler's license and brought a bargeful of stuff," Bud would say laughingly to me as the people clustered around for the gifts which we distributed. Our first-aid triangular bandages ended up in a strange capacity, grabbed daringly by a playful older woman who delightedly wound them around her head.

To our surprise the Indians responded immediately by giving us a gift: bear meat, shot the day before back in the hills. The Indians cut their meat in side strips and chunks so that it has hardly the delectable tenderness that it might have, but Bud and I had sound teeth and in fact relished tough meat. How we wolfed it down!

The Indians along the Yukon we found live in great fear of the wandering grizzly bears, and they hunt only the black bears for food; nothing can induce them to go far from the river into the hill country of the browns. Ask them about the brown bear and they will shake their heads ominously and say: "He very bad."

One old-timer who was bothered by natives infringing on what he considered his own private beaver creek solved his trap-line problem in an interesting way. All he did was to carve out two great wooden claws at home, as of some monstrous, prehistoric type of bear. With these fastened on his feet, he then walked along this beach in the vicinity of the beaver houses and left those tracks. The old-timer told us that he never had native trouble any more after that.

My great elephant rifle was one of the greatest boosts to our prestige among the Indians of anything we could have had on earth. As stated before, they use only .30-30's, and had never seen a rifle as large as mine. A rifle was something they could understand the need of; it was something which played a prominent part in their own lives as an estimate of a man's worth. To see a white woman, own, possess, and fire such a rifle Bud thought would make the Indians admire me beyond words. The occasion seemed to call for some kind of dramatic spectacle: I must shoot for the Indians.

I was a little shy about this, for I am one of those who secretly wonder if they will hit the mark. Moreover, I hadn't much desire to impress anybody. But Bud got out the rifle, emptied it of shells, and passed it around to the men of the family by way of introducing ourselves. Bud didn't say much but waited for them to do the talking. A low deep guttural "ahhhh" sounded from the old woman at my side, as she avidly felt the great chunky bullets, but she refused to touch the rifle. Only the father and the oldest boy dared to pick it up. Perhaps I should say "dared" in the social sense more than in the physical sense, however, as these people are modest. Interestingly enough, we learned that the other, older boy of the family had recently been taken by the draft.

"Would you like to shoot it?" Bud asked the man of the family. The old man demurred, hardly concealing his delight. To shoot that gun would be the greatest thing that ever happened to him in his life. Bud indicated a small stick in the river at which to aim (Indians are not used to shooting at small targets), threw a shell into the chamber, and the man squinted bashfully along the sights. I put my fingers in my ears and all of the women and children followed suit. If the rifle cost us fifteen cents every time the thing went off, that scarcely mattered. This was what it was for, wasn't it?

The men were greatly impressed by the thunder of the report and by the recoil which sent them reeling back dizzily; they widely missed their target. Bud looked their rifles over then, cleaned them with solvent, oiled them, and then shot for the Indians himself. "No, you shoot for the people, dear," I had told him. Bud's pleasurable pride in me as a huntress and my own pride in aiding in the emancipating of women, if any, would have been of little matter during these happy fireworks: the Indians thought that I was a man.

When a day of very favorable traveling conditions followed in the form of a wind directly from behind us, we clipped off most of the forty miles which lie between Anvik and Holy Cross, making the first half of the distance practically within the first hour. We were only stopped when, the wind driving us inch by inch into the treacherous snags on one side of the river, the *Queen Beaver* shipping water with every wave, I myself leaning all my weight on the rudder and Bud gallantly holding up the mast, we crashed broadside into a soft mud bank, and thus ended our traveling for the day. Only a short way from Holy Cross, we could go no farther. It rained, and Bud stood in the middle of a mud pie on shore boiling tea. The tea water largely evaporated before it finally came to a boil with the rain pouring down in it and onto his smoldering little fire. Then at last he came to me inside the boat with a pint of tea—wet, cold, weary. We had a tea party with candy bars, inside the boat, lying on our elbows.

We saw Holy Cross in the rain and did not remain long. Holy Cross was first established as a military post. It is now a trading center and Jesuit mission, founded in 1886. Lying across from where the famous Iditarod River comes in, it is located behind a narrow spit of land wherein lies a shallow lagoon. The spacious lawns and gardens, as well as the white graceful buildings, are to be seen for a long way from down river. Holy Cross keeps the only beef and dairy cattle on the Yukon and puts up hay and tons of vegetables.

We called on Jesuit Father Superior Speels immediately and presented him with a goose and two ducks; in return he gave us garden vegetables. Besides several priests and three lay brothers with shorn heads, who are pledged to do all of the laborious and dirty work to which they are assigned, in strictest obedience and with no thought of material gain, nine Sisters of Saint Anne make their residence at Holy Cross under the Mother Superior, whom we met.

The entire community of Holy Cross is dominated by the industrious Jesuit monks, who have sworn vows of poverty, chastity, and obedience. With the Jesuits an especial emphasis is laid on obedience; they never know where they will be sent into foreign fields or when recalled, as they relinquish all choice, even in the matter of their work. Wearing long dark gowns over their trousers, the Jesuits possess but sparse clothing, of which they take immaculate care, and endeavor indoors, and outdoors at suitable seasons, always to affect if possible this costume of Biblical times. As this is difficult to do on the Yukon, however, the gowns are conveniently made so that they can be slipped out of easily for active work or travel or may be trussed up and tied beneath a raincoat or parka out of the way of mud and snow. None of the Jesuits are very young men. All have gone through a long and arduous initiation period comprising several years before being allowed to enter the stern, unchanging, ancient order.

"We wonder if you would care to take some mail down the river as you go?" we were asked at Holy Cross. Therefore, we continued now carrying about fifteen pounds of letters with us. This was the first time but not the last. We carried the U. S. Mail from Holy Cross to Paimiut and again from Paimiut to Russian Mission, and on the Kuskokwim carried a thousand dollars in cash from an Eskimo village to Bethel, with the mail.

Sailing, precarious as it was, made the miles seem like nothing. Our hearts were as free as the winds with which we now rode. Seeing two little Indian boys hunting with their .22 rifles on the beach, we shouted to them to ask where Paimiut was. It was just around the bend, as it developed. We had dashed off thirty miles like nothing. But the little boys had a tale to tell when they reached the village. They told the people that two terrible white men on the river had pointed guns at them and threatened to kill them.

Such a tale might conceivably be common to boys the world over. But it served to remind us that among native peoples the weirdest ideas about one can easily arise and gain credence; hence one should always be very careful about his actions in dealing with them because they do not think about things in the same way that we do. Rather than shouting to the boys from the river as we might have at white boys, we should have taken the trouble to drop sail, paddle to shore, and speak with them quietly so that there could be no misunderstanding.

At Paimiut for the first time we saw the high cheekbones and flat faces which indicated Eskimo blood among the Indians; this was especially noticeable with some young children and babies. The new blood seemed to make some improvement in adding to general attractiveness of appearance. These younger children were as heavy as little chunks if you tried to pick them up.

Paimiut marks the turning point at which thousands of small lamprey eels come in from the ocean by winter. They are caught by native ice-fishing methods in hand nets, an Eskimo trait. No one knows why the eels are never found farther up the river than this point.

We found Paimiut just in time to be invited to a fine bear-roast dinner with the Indian Service family stationed there. We brought geese and grouse with us, but our friends had little use for them as they had plenty of their own at this season, the man of the family being an outdoors enthusiast. Extra game was distributed in the village.

If there was anything pleasing to Bud, it was to find a man companion who liked to hunt and fish as well as he did; he and Mr. H. went out the following day to have just one day of bird shooting and fishing before we went on. It was a gorgeous warm day which broke for their excursion. I longed secretly to be out with the men instead of assigned to woman's dreary task of staying home in the house. I had met a lot of Alaska wives whose only pleasure or activity seemed to be housework and the care of small children in this land where every person must do things for himself, without assistance. Although loving service, within limits, is never to be despised as such, mother, too, deserves a vacation once in a while—with pay. But try and get it. To be kind to this fine wife I decided that one day, at least, of sharing her lot wouldn't hurt me. She herself was invited to go on the jaunt, but in the general excitement which prevailed her refusal of the invitation was scarcely heard; apparently it was habitual on her part. She was always tired. It was too much to go, to manage the toddling child, to come home and have meals ready for hungry people all in one, she explained to me. I suggested that we all share in the work so that this might be a holiday for her too. But this suggestion did not go over. The husband was not in the habit of assisting her in such matters, and no move was made on his part.

"Well, let them go," I thought. They went happily, with a beautifully packed lunch, and a native boy to run the boat for them. "Bloated plutocrats!" I thought, and then threw myself into the activities of our day. I could have gone had I wanted to.

It was on this day, of all days, when I was not along, that the only moose of the entire trip jumped up before the boat in which Bud and Mr. H. rode effortlessly along on one of the many Yukon sloughs in the country of the portages. Such is hunters' luck. The natives of the village had been hunting moose for a month now, with never a sign of one.

The native boy was slow in stopping the boat for a shot. By the time he stopped the motor, the moose had disappeared into the forest. But presently he ran out along the bank again, followed by a cow and a calf. The good shot had been muffed, but here was a long running shot at three hundred yards. Mr. H. with a .30-30 and Bud with my .405 shot several times. Bud and I used to practice shooting under unfavorable lighting conditions from bouncing cars and recently from boats in anticipation of just such contingencies as this. At his fourth shot Bud heard his bullet "smack" as it plowed through bone and flesh. The moose disappeared into the forest, not visibly wounded, but Bud knew that he had made a hit on the big bull.

When our men came back from their hunt with this tale, I was really jealous. One cannot follow a wounded moose in the woods after dark, so tomorrow at dawn the hunt would begin again. Moreover, from experience with big game the hunters knew that a wounded animal pursued may go for miles, but one that is not pursued will soon lie down and get stiff from his wounds so that he can easily be located the next morning.

Mr. H., never having killed a moose himself and most anxious, as we all were, to recover the wounded animal, decided that it would be best if several of the best native hunters and trackers from the village came along the next day. Bud preferred strongly to hunt down his own moose alone, taking only me with him, but we were overruled by the advice and fears of our hosts, not to mention a sense of fairness to them. There was no proving that H. himself had not scored a hit, and it might yet be his animal as well as ours.

Mrs. H. packed us a lunch and said good-by to the excited crowd again. I wondered if she was really suffering from not going as much as I would have had I been in her place. I just couldn't bear to stay home and affect an interest in the limited, so-called feminine world myself today, selfish as I was. If there was a wounded moose afoot in those woods, I too wanted to see if I could put in my shot before the Indians got him. And as for that—I knew Bud would need all of my help were we to claim the honor of getting the moose before the rest did.

As I looked at that crew of five Indian hunters who accompanied us, I hoped for the best. We knew of at least one Indian Service teacher who came so close to being shot by one of his guides on a similar moose hunt that his jacket was partially blown off him and his rifle was shot into in his hands below the bolt. Although Mr. H. had great faith in his hunters, we wanted double reassurance on that score because we had known some Indians to be excitable and wave guns around like banana leaves in the wind.

When we reached the spot on the slough where our quarry was last seen, we all jumped out of the boat and began casting around like hound dogs for the trail. "Watch out for those Indians," Bud whispered as we started. "Remember no moose is worth it."

Bud was a little slow in getting started, as he was working the ground over carefully, and obviously did not like to be hurried. It was eleven o'clock in the morning rather than dawn, we had all eaten too much, and another unexpected guest, a white man, had been included in the party.

Seeing the Indians forge ahead I ducked under and kept in front of them and took the lead myself. I had never followed a trail before, but no one could miss this; hoofprints larger than those of a cow cut deeply into the soft earth, with spots of blood everywhere to be seen. I was really sure that our moose, when we found him, would be dead.

Presently we found a depression in the grass where the animal had lain down. The men felt it with their hands, and then laid their cheeks against the earth. They said the bed was still warm, although I could detect nothing. From here we scattered out in twos and singly to pick up the track again, but after forty-five minutes were again brought back to the bed. Apparently, we had lost the track; it was confused by something else. "Other moose come here," remarked the oldest hunter, pointing.

The tracks of the cow now joined our bull; she had been waiting for him here; never leaving him, she must have hidden the calf nearby, and now she confused the trail.

With his face close to the ground, Bud selected one of the hoofprints and slowly began to scrape the leaves away from it with his hand; he did this with another track and then another, without interest, while we all waited. Bud was showing a depressed outlook which I had never known him to have before on a hunt. I knew that he was not having a good time, that the hunt for him was spoiled when there was a crowd. "It's here," he said at last, and we were on the trail again. There was blood, and suddenly strings of red tissue were seen hanging from a bush, and everybody knew the animal had been hit somewhere in the right flank.

The Indians had scattered out in a fan; that moose was close by. The last Indian to get ahead of me had charged by, letting a bush fly back, which caught me in the eye.

From one side suddenly came shots. "There it is," I thought, and with Mr. H. ran as fast as I could through the forest. By the time we arrived it was all over. The oldest hunter had jumped the moose at close range, fired three times and missed, and fired the fourth time, catching the moose broadside in the heart. The mighty animal, weighing close to a thousand pounds, lay dead with the last twitch shuddering down his great shoulders. The expressive eyes were wide-open, but unseeing. Even at that we were wise enough not to touch the animal until we were sure that it was dead, for these moments are some of the most dangerous in big-game hunting, as I well knew.

We all stood staring down at the animal for a few minutes, grouped around, hardly knowing what to say now that it was all over. Some of the Indians now went back to the boat for the ax, which all had forgotten in the confusion, although we had guns to spare. To kill a moose without an ax in one's possession and a truck or a barge nearby to pick it up is useless. We could do nothing about carrying it out until the ax arrived.

"You want to take picture of me now?" asked the oldest hunter proudly, seeing my camera. Patiently I took his picture. He couldn't know his prowess had spoiled the hunt for Bud.

"You shoot moose now," the Indians suggested to me in great good spirits, desiring that I shoot into the dead animal with my big rifle, as it lay on the ground.

"No," I told them kindly, "when I shoot a moose he is going to be a real live one, not a dead one."

It took the combined strength of all the party to roll the animal over to a position where its intestines, its large white stomach filled with leaf pulp (the moose being a browser rather than a grazer), and the other organs could be removed. The abdominal cavity was filled with a black, tarry substance in great clots and strings, which I believed at first glance must be the liver. I was wrong in that. The substance was an unbelievable quantity of clotted blood from internal hemorrhages caused by Bud's single shot which had plowed through six feet of moose from end to end, until it was stopped by the vertebrae of the neck. "What never fails to strike me in cases of this sort," Bud said musingly, his arms red to the shoulders, "is the tenacity of life in all things."

But life, if it had been extinguished by us, was now going on and being converted into some other life. As we watched quietly without staring, the Indians, who had restrained themselves for a long time while the white men peeled back the thick clean creamy fat which encased the intestines, now were reaching with little ecstatic chuckles and gathering handfuls of this fat and stuffing it into their mouths. "That's the part they prize the most highly," Mr. H. explained from the side of his mouth. But he need hardly have worried about their hearing; the Indians were far gone and absorbed.

And as for Bud: I was glad that he was a hunter. Some women

do not like to have their husbands hunt. They think it is cruel to animals, and they think that the instinct to kill is beastly. When this subject comes up in polite drawing-room conversation among people who "just love the out-of-doors," but who know nothing about it, someone should in all fairness say a word for the hunters as well as against them. It is the hunters belonging to sportsmen's clubs who love nature, the out-of-doors, and wild life more than anyone else, for they are the only ones who have taken any action to preserve it, while the drawing-room conversationalists really aren't interested enough, if the truth be known. Many women regret that their husbands are just beastly enough to enjoy going off on a hunt rather than sitting of an evening and listening to concert music with them or reading poetry. The explorer Stefansson, who originally studied to be a poet and who ended up living off the country with the Eskimos, found what he has termed a "poetry of action" in life. I believe that the "poetry of action" is what a great many of us theorists miss out on, and our poetry is bad and our lives hypocritical.

As we wanted the animal quartered white-man style rather than haggled native style, it was up to us to carry out the butchering, which nobody knew how to do but Bud. Taking the ax Bud split the backbone, a feat which calls for some precision, and then we packed out during the rest of the day. I carried Bud's rifle, my rifle, and the wet liver. Nobody wanted the sixty-inch spread of antlers. The natives had no use for them and we ourselves were faced with the uncertainties of a hazardous portage ahead, close onto freeze-up time. The antlers were left in the forest.

Leaving three fourths of the moose at Paimiut we took the best hind quarter as our share, maneuvered it into the canoe, and headed downstream towards our last and final stop on the Yukon: Russian Mission.

18

Russian Mission

Sailing down the Yukon with the hind leg of a moose and the U. S. mail in the canoe, we were approaching the beginnings of a country that was new in our experience—the tundra. For could we have seen the landscape from the air we would have seen, except for a fringe of tree line along the meandering course of the Yukon River, the barren, treeless, true tundra stretching out level and empty on all sides of us.

Tundra is a word which we should be careful about using. Visiting writers to Alaska frequently call everything they see tundra, even the forest which they find stretching along the railroad from Seward to Fairbanks. True tundra looks much like the flat American desert or the rolling prairies of the Midwest at first glance; arctic prairie is really what tundra is, which in Alaska may stretch out endlessly and treeless to an occasional distant mountain range. Beneath its carpet of flowers and grasses the tundra is in summer a quaking slimy bog interspersed with thousands of arctic lakes, ponds, and streams, and it hums with mosquitoes numbering into the billions. Although the Eskimos today herd reindeer on the frozen tundra in winter and mush their dog teams over it from point to point, not even an Eskimo or Indian ventures far into the tundra from the coast or from a main river in summertime.

Packs of wolves live on the tundra, following the wild caribou and the domestic reindeer herds and the ptarmigan. In some sections of Alaska, the reindeer are not thriving, supposedly because of the enormous take of the wolves, but we have heard local people give their opinion that human wolves may be the real cause behind the reindeer decline, meaning that the Eskimos have killed off their own herds indiscriminately. Men have tried hunting the caribou and reindeer wolves by airplane in recent days, but this method collects only the bounty and not the pelt,

which cuts one's profits in half, and more than that, airplanes are much too scarce in Alaska generally to waste on such pastimes. Even in winter, because of the frozen vegetation and uneven hummocks, it is impossible for an airplane landing to be made in most places on the tundra, although landings are made, at one's risk, on frozen lakes. Flying near the ground on the tundra is dangerous because the sameness of land and sky, the lack of objects by which to make comparisons, makes it difficult to gauge height and distances.

We camped at the base of strange Dogfish Mountain which reared up suddenly out of nowhere from the cold blue seas lapping at its base. At night we cut our own T-bone steaks and downed quantities of juicy moose meat, which, prejudiced as we perhaps were, we deemed the most tender that we had ever eaten. Just as we had once found a town on the river which did not exist on our map, so now we read on our map a town which did not exist at all: Dogfish Village is gone from beside Dogfish Mountain, in case anyone is interested in erasing it from the map. The natives have died or moved away from what was once a good-sized river town, and nothing is to be seen but a few sticks.

An icy spring gushed forth from Dogfish Mountain and there was a little log cabin five feet high which had been erected for the shelter of the traveler—just a hole to crawl into out of the storm, if need be.

An icy wind swept from Dogfish Mountain, which looked to our wondering eyes as if it should rightly be a mountain of iron or copper, it was so burnished. This desert mountain stood as a sentinel, and it was burned dry by the Bering Sea winds of ice. The gravel lying steeply on its polished slopes was about the last bit of rock of any description we would see until we flew back to Seward, for the tundra of the valleys of the lower Yukon and lower Kuskokwim has no rock. The rocks have been ground into gravel and the gravel into mud by the prehistoric ice sheet which once sliced across the western coast country here ages ago in its march to the sea.

In the morning as we ate our moose steaks a lone man in a small

Indian canoe appeared paddling through the great green- blue seas of the surging river. Charlie Wolf was his name. I think there must be several Charlie Wolfs because the name was not unfamiliar to me from reading and travel. He was a half- breed of magnificent stature, with the shoulders and neck of an ox, with dark-lashed blue eyes, a clean easy smile, and the speech of a white man. He bucked these seas in his little canoe, making a trip of several days in length with no food that I could see; only a rifle held lazily on his knees as he plied his two-bladed paddle. He was a very beautiful young man, half Indian, perhaps some Russian, part white.

When we sailed up to Russian Mission a day later the moose leg, after we had eaten off it for some days, still weighed 280 pounds. Keeping out twenty pounds of sirloin, we sold the rest to Chris Betsch at twenty-five cents a pound.

People had said: "Russian Mission is not what it used to be, from what I hear, but guess old Chris Betsch is still there." Chris is. He has been at Russian Mission for well onto fifty years. He is the landmark of the country just as is Dogfish Mountain. For years he has been the only white man there, except that recently another old fellow has drifted in to become the postmaster and take for a wife one of the very young native girls of the village. Although Chris is not married, some people have said that he may be grandfather to the present generation of the village. This is open to question.

Eighty years old now and quite deaf, he believes he is the last man alive to have sailed on *Old Ironsides*. His little private museum above his store at Russian Mission houses everything from polar-bear rugs (for which there is a large market could he but get the supply) to souvenirs from the Livingston expedition in Africa. One wedding cowl of Indian-wrought beads interested me because Chris explained it was a native adaptation of the wedding headdress taught the Indians by the early Russians of Russian Mission, who have long been gone. Except for one other like it, which he had given to the Fairbanks museum, Chris believed this one to be the last of its kind.

One of the articles Chris gets from the north for the Yukon Interior Indians is white whaleskin; another is black and white calfskin from United States cows, used for "trim." We saw several examples of this native tendency to import. On the lower Kuskokwim, for instance, the traders import wolverine fur from Wisconsin for Eskimo parka hoods, it being cheaper to get from the States than from other parts of Alaska. Even lynx and wolf capes are brought in to Alaska from Outside. Probably one state in the United States exports more fur, incidentally, than does the whole of Alaska.

Chris as a typical trader had made few if any changes in the living conditions of the natives but accepted them as they were and furnished them as nearly as possible with what they wanted, be it soda pop or hair tonic. Asked if it wouldn't be a good idea to encourage the people in drinking canned fruit juices rather than soda pop, which costs just as much in freightage to ship in and has no vitamins, Chris replied that actually the natives do drink quite a few canned juices from the store when they are "flush" with money for entertainment. They drink them right at the counter, from the can, and the cans are thrown into an empty barrel to be dumped. But it is not often that such novelties are afforded, and the traders keep but a small stock of juices.

By all appearances, after fifty years of dealing with them, Chris must have known the natives well. He knew just how much credit to allow and no more, and what seasons would be slack and what seasons would be good. This applied, too, to the fur market Outside, as well as local conditions. Take muskrats, for instance. Natives will come in with ragged pelts, shot all to pieces. They expect just as much for one skin as for another, and differences pointed out to them make friction. The experienced trader accepts the skins at a standard rate, good, bad, and indifferent. He knows there is no use in entering into the argument concerning the merits of each skin. Incidentally the Indians are sly at slipping over inferior skins and placing them in the bottom of the bundle so that they are not easily noticed. The trader takes a chance on how these skins are going to be received Outside. To compensate inferior skins and to balance the books, which must indeed be a complicated process, the trader simply charges the natives more on the articles they want from the store, and thus makes up his own losses. However, since the trader is competing with other Yukon traders he must be tactful enough to keep his natives satisfied or they may all simply leave and he will find that he has no trading post at all. Some traders in some years have been obliged to take a loss in order to keep their natives and stay in the game.

Chris Betsch, who had a noble and enterprising gleam in his

ancient blue eyes, reminded us that in the old days no holds were barred.

"Chris," we asked the old man, "can we get across the portage into the Kuskokwim? We are bound for Bethel."

"Young man," replied Chris, eyeing Bud, "you ask for my advice and I shall give it to you as best I know how. I have lived on this river for years, as you know, and I have yet to see anybody start across the portage this late in the season. If it was jist two weeks earlier you might try it, with somebody for guide. But this late in the season, it would be very foolish to take the lady in there."

I as the "lady" referred to sat open-mouthed and anxious while Chris elaborated. "This is the latest freeze-up I seen in twenty years. Should of froze up three weeks ago. Any night now it may turn forty below zero overnight, and I see you ain't dressed for it. You haven't no business being on the river this late in the season with a lady," he admonished poor Bud seriously. "But since you are, and you ask my advice, I say go on straight down the river to Marshall, fifty-five miles, and there you get a plane out. There's a landing field there and good accommodations for ladies."

It was plain that chivalrous Chris had my welfare seriously at heart and had made it his concern. Chris also knew that a "lady," myself not excluded, is of no help in jams. "I've been across that portage twenty-three different times myself," he told us, "and I wouldn't want to go in at this time. There's nothing you can do: you can't paddle out and you can't walk out. It's all tundra. There's no wood nor nothin' to burn. One time I was in there pretty late and we had to drag our boat through shale ice in Mud River, wading for six miles the last piece, and the boat—three-quarter-inch plank—was just cut to pieces in no time at all."

After a disdainful look at our canvas canoe, Chris was even more pronounced in his opinions. "Besides, who would take you?" he asked. "None of these people here have been across for years. They don't know the way. Oh, they'll say they do, but they don't. Five years ago, in the summer a dentist came down this way and hired some Indians to guide him across. This was late in the season, too. Well, the guides got in there and got lost, see? That dentist was almost froze to death before he got out of there; he was sure mad about it. Oh, one of the guides did get drowned under the ice, too, in the lake, before they got through."

"We were led to believe all along the river that it was pretty easy to get across the portage," I said, still hoping. "How far is it, Chris?"

"Game Department says 105 miles. I say 130 miles is closer, the way you have to go by water. By air it's only around forty. It's pretty easy to get across if the water's high. A couple or three strong, skookum fellows, now that's one thing. But not with a lady," Chris said definitely.

By this time, I was thoroughly disgusted with being a "lady," but I knew full well that Chris was being honest and that he was right; I simply didn't have the strength to lift and transport my end of the canoe across unknown distances in the swamps. In case of trouble, Bud would be left alone to solve everything. A guide would cost fifty dollars plus his grub for the trip and back again, in case we got one. All along I had been playing with the idea of the two of us getting through by ourselves, because we had decided from the outset that our policy was not going to be to start hiring guides if it could possibly be avoided; one can have so much more fun taking things slowly and figuring them out for himself, and then he really knows those things, too!

Chris put us up for meals, giving me the run of his own house and kitchen; he wouldn't think of charging white people. We would remain overnight and then continue down the Yukon the next day. My disappointment knew no bounds. This was not as I had wanted it at all. We wanted to see the Kuskokwim. We had learned that if we once got to the Kuskokwim our trip could be further extended not only by seeing new sights and new peoples, but in the matter of time. The Kuskokwim freezes usually two or three weeks later than does the Yukon.

While we were waiting out the evening around the trading post the teen-aged Indian girl who was married to the old postmaster came to me and asked me if I would look at a sick baby in the village.

I followed her swiftly along the boardwalk. Although an Indian Service teacher held school at Russian Mission in some past days, and the people of the village have had some medical treatment certainly in the past, Russian Mission has so decreased in population during recent years that it is no longer given attention.

Of course, I couldn't help the baby. I knew nothing about babies and little about medicine. All I could do was go and look at it and regret that I did not have the training by which to know what to do, nor anything to do it with.

Abruptly my friend led me to the door of one of the little log cabins of the village, where she paused and knocked, and we slipped in. In the dark and airless inner regions my eyes presently made out the form of a woman squatting on a low stool with a baby in her arms. She was quite a pretty woman, certainly under thirty. I wondered if she might have Russian blood in her veins because her complexion was fair.

The woman spoke no English, but my girl guide was an admirable interpreter. A rubber suction disk used as a breast pump was displayed, and it was explained to me that the mother could get but little milk: the trouble with the baby then was with the mother. The baby was probably starved for food and moisture. I asked the mother through the interpreter if she had felt any hard lumps in her breasts. Could she have cancer? No, she didn't. But the baby vomited. I was quite positive the prescription wouldn't be followed, but I tried: the baby should have a milk formula. Was the one I gave right? I hoped so but wasn't too sure. I remembered Karo syrup is used in these formulas for carbohydrate content. Since the trader had no syrup other than maple syrup, I thought the mother should make her own syrup out of brown sugar and water.

The baby should be bathed all over—I stressed the "all over"—with soap and water. Soap and water is good for babies to be washed in once in a while. Babies should be kept clean. Babies should have raw egg yolks and orange juice from the can, every day, and they should not be given sourdough bread, pancakes, coffee, fish, and the list of things which I should write down. None of my audience could read, but the old white man, the postmaster, could read the directions and interpret them when desired to the interpreter, who would see that the native woman carried them out. Babies should also have clothes of their own, I explained. Reaching out my arms for the child with more confidence than I felt, I was startled to find how stiffly bound was its form. So rigid was the baby that she could scarcely move hand or foot, swathed in blankets round and round, as tightly as a mummy. I felt terribly sorry as the eyes of the small imprisoned creature blinked up at me—just four months old, helpless, bound like a mummy! But she couldn't be released until she had some clothes. What I should have done was to contrive some sort of clothes and make the milk formula for the baby right on the spot, showing how it was done by example. But I had never been around babies a great deal, and I was shy and awkward. I went away merely leaving directions, to realize later that my presence as an overnight visitor at Russian Mission would have but little effect after I left, and that the baby would soon be dead in all probability.

I told Chris and the other old fellow about the baby quite earnestly in hopes that my directions might do some good. Of another generation which had different standards than ours and which accepted sights which would astound us today, Chris replied genially: "Yes, that woman always loses her babies. She hasn't raised one yet that I know of, although sometimes they git to be two or three years old. The people in the village say she abuses them. Neglects them and doesn't feed them, you know. Confidentially I think that's where the real trouble lays. I don't pay no attention.

"But I think I've got an idea about you folks," he said, scratching his head. "You still want to go across the portage, don't you?"

We nodded excitedly at this sudden hope of reprieve.

"Well, I just happened to think. There's a native here that's been wanting to go across. He knows the way, and I can vouch for him as a good man and trustworthy. But he's got no boat, see?"

We saw. "Then he can guide us, and we can take him in our canoe?" Our minds were now at once turned to the subject of our own salvation. "Do get him to come here quickly. If we're going to go, we haven't a moment to lose. I'm ready to leave here right now myself."

"Hold on. Not so fast. This is just an idea, see? This man is their priest here. We'll have to work slow. You can't hurry these people. He was born and raised here at this spot. It will take him some time to say good-by. If he goes he will have to make holy candles and holy water and hold a mass first. I'll tell you what we'll do. If Changsak wants to go under this here arrangement, we'll just leave it up to him if it's safe at this time. You know I've lived on the Yukon half my life, but I still can't hold a candle to what these people know, only they usually won't tell you. Changsak is a good man, though. We'll leave it up to what he says."

Wasile Changsak was his name. We had been looking for native priests of the Russian Greek Orthodox Church from having witnessed their trail ever since the first mysterious graveyard on the Tanana. Perhaps there is some literature telling how many of these native priests are in existence today, perhaps not. One can make a good guess that, like the wild whistling swan that nests in the arctic, they are rare to the point of being a practically extinct species.

Wasile Changsak was an altar boy under a Russian bishop located at Russian Mission in this century, in fact a little over twenty years ago. In 1919 after a change in the Russian regime, the bishop, lacking funds for the support of his missionary work, returned to Russia, although some of the Alaskan bishops did not. In his place this man appointed young Wasile as a sort of makeshift priest, that the faith might not be forgotten by the people. Wasile Changsak has been that leader ever since. Educated to read and write in English, Changsak's altar ceremonies are conducted in Russian in the old manner of centuries past, so that the chants are almost meaningless to the people they are supposed to reach, but still very impressive. The flag which drapes its folds inside his church is the flag of old Russia—the Russia now gone.

Changsak bears himself very well, in all ways affecting the manner which becomes a wise and noble priest. He is celibate, he has taken no wife, he bears his trust well. He buries the dead, counsels with the living, visits the sick. His people support him faithfully and in reverence, and his influence among them is great in all things. Several times he has visited the Eskimo Kuskokwim and Stony and even North Fork region from his home mission on the Yukon; Chris said the Eskimos, who incidentally lie largely within supposed Moravian territory, had been trying for months to charter a plane by which to convey Changsak over to their country for the winter, where housing and hospitality would be awaiting him in plenty; but because of the war conditions no planes could be found doing such small jobs off the regular air routes. The Eskimos, however, had the money for the ride ready and were anxiously awaiting the time.

Knowing all this, Changsak may have been just as anxious himself, but if so, he did not betray it. With iron-gray hair, smooth, ageless complexion, dark, alert, foreign eyes, and agile yet dignified carriage, he had the most noble Indian countenance I have ever seen, bar none. He was a truly handsome man, outstanding among his people. In another day he would have been a great chief or shaman, I am sure. Or in still another day he might have become a great Alaska statesman. The man had natural talent; the Russian bishop had picked his man well.

He was called to the trading post and he took his time about arriving. Fixing us with his intelligent eye, he permitted us to tell our tale and make our proposition.

"All right," he agreed. "We will go tomorrow."

I was so overjoyed at this wonderful turn of events that I could hardly contain myself. "Let's go early," I suggested, as casually as I could.

It was agreed upon that we would all be ready by 7:00 A.M. Changsak neglected to say that by seven o'clock he meant sun time rather than our time, and that actually ten o'clock was what he had in mind. However, that was all right. When we found that out later in the day, it was too late then to regret that we had got up early. We waited in dignified impatience as the hours ticked by, in Chris's trading post by the side of the elephant-ear plant, watching for Changsak to come to us, for having spoken once Bud regarded it as bad policy to go to him. For myself, I should have liked to nag him a little to hurry him up. "I have never known anybody to have as good luck as you folks," Chris kept encouraging us during this time. "You are mighty lucky people to get Changsak, and right off the bat like that."

We weren't getting Changsak right off the bat, though, because hours passed and still he did not come. "He'll come, all right, when he can git away," Chris explained. "Why don't you go over and look at the Mission while you're waiting?"

To look at the Mission we had come many miles. This was our opportunity.

The village takes its name from Russian Mission, the old original church of unpainted hand-hewn logs (with no celebrated dome) which the Russians built and furnished here long ago with art objects brought across Siberia many thousands of miles. The old Mission building itself has fallen into decay, and the accouterments of its interior have been removed to a new wooden building much like it which acts as the new and present-day church. This was erected by the people, and no effort has been made to preserve the old church.

We timidly approached the door of the more recent church, and this was opened for us by Wasile Changsak, who was alone inside blessing holy water at the time. Bud had the camera. We were going to ask if we could take a few pictures of the art of the interior, and if the favor should be granted Bud was prepared to act immediately with fast black-and-white film before anybody should change his mind. Pictures of holy places, we were sure, were the exception rather than the rule.

Our favor was granted, perhaps because Changsak was on the point of leaving himself, perhaps because we were to be his traveling companions for a time, perhaps because the palm was crossed with silver, perhaps because he had no antipathy towards cameras.

The interior presented a carnival of colored paper streamers and flowers which bedecked the statues of otherwise elegant saints and hung from the ceiling in general. Through the streamers looked down upon us original Russian icons and priceless life-sized oils of winged saints. Beyond a little gateway within a bower wherein no woman may enter reposed the Bible, which no woman may touch. It was enthroned upon gold leaf and velvet. Wading through the flowers and tinsel, I gazed and Bud shot angles, realizing that while these treasures belonged to America and are a part of our great country, few persons have yet seen them.

I asked Changsak to explain to me as many of the masterpieces as he could or would. The explanations were naturally hushed, brief, and scanty, and he presently withdrew, maintaining a dignified aloofness, leaving me to my own meditations. I had an idea that he was not used to much of this type of questioning on the part of his people, modest as I endeavored to make it, and perhaps did not know all of the answers.

Although I knew nothing about art, I saw that in painting the figures of the Holy Family, the artist, like all artists, had painted his own nationality into his work. The Christ which beamed down upon us with outspread hands and marvelous skin tones and supplicating eyes was a Russian as was the Virgin Mary holding the little doll of the Christ Child in her arms. All the disciples were Russians. Yet all had straight long noses and small rosebud mouths of a delicate pink—the Greek influence. These noses and mouths are of course a tradition of the early Greek Catholic Church at Constantinople, whose missionaries and whose corrupted alphabet came to Russia in the days even before Belisarius and his generals. In the elaborate scrolls and curlicues on the frames of the pictures, in the halos of the ornate icons, appeared the Oriental influence, I guessed.

Institutions and some private individuals both inside and outside Alaska have been aware of the historic pieces of art reposing at Sitka, at Kodiak, at Russian Mission, and a few places in the Aleutians.

Many have had their try at it. But the pictures just aren't for sale at any price. The well-known Alaskan artist Eustace P. Zeigler, speaking in Anchorage, urged the public to attempt to do something about the art of Russian Mission, which he feared would be rained on through the leaky roof or burned up by the candles, and which he longs to preserve for posterity. He claimed that the art should be housed where it would be safe.

I urged this idea upon Bud after seeing the art myself, but found him not so receptive as I.

"The pictures belong to these people," he stated simply. "Haven't you the slightest respect for that fact? To legislate to take it from them at any price would be nothing less than robbing them."

"But look at their filth, their poverty, their disease, then- dying babies! Do you think they are exactly in the stage of culture to appreciate great art?" I turned on him savagely, but he stood his ground.

"That's a matter of opinion. They worship those pictures more than any person seeing them in a museum would. They would probably give their lives for them—if that's appreciation."

And so, the art remains at Russian Mission in care of Chris Betsch, Changsak, and the dying natives. To my surprise Father answered my letter by saying that he agreed with Bud. It is all that a dying people have left of their own, and they do not relinquish it. As to whether they will keep it safe from the elements, I think they probably will.

Later, Chris Betsch wrote us a long letter, which we prize very highly. Like many older people, Chris remembers his early days before he came to the Yukon more clearly than he does the later days, and his letter told us little about Russian Mission, but did tell us something about the man who has lived there for half a century, and who should not be forgotten.

～

WE STOOD ON THE BANK of the Yukon at Russian Mission with Chris and the other old gentleman, who was "not much company now, being a family man," and watched the entire village one by one kiss their priest good-by, while he gave each in turn his final blessing, marking on their breasts the sign of the cross.

"I've seen that a lot of times," said Chris. It was three-thirty in the afternoon.

A large, impressive, twenty-five-foot, green and white houseboat was drawn up before Russian Mission, and we perceived now that we were to go for the first forty miles in that, after which the houseboat would be obliged to turn back to the Yukon. This houseboat had apparently been bought and kept by the village for their priest, but it was too large a boat to take him all the way through the swamps to the Kuskokwim; one needs a very small boat for that, so Changsak would have to leave his boat behind. Seven Indians had apparently decided to accompany the priest, but whether they would go all the way with us to the Kuskokwim or not we didn't know. We didn't dare ask at this point. We knew the story about our being dangerous characters as told by the young boys upriver had reached Russian Mission by the grapevine system, and it occurred to us that perhaps the people were thinking all sorts of things about us and thus were going to protect their priest with a double escort.

Behind their houseboat the Indians were prepared to tow not only our canoe and us, but a small one-man wooden kayak (the first kayak we had seen) and a flat-bottomed rowboat equipped with a three-horse motor. Altogether the natives were much better equipped than we were in our thin, tattered clothing.

It was good-by to the old Yukon River. The Yukon, formerly classed by writers as the fifth largest river of the North American continent, has recently been moved up to the third largest river, along with the Mackenzie and the Mississippi, as the world has at last begun to realize its true size.

We left the Yukon just as we found it, with nothing much changed. Who could change the Yukon? It is still there, waiting for the next adventurer to come along.

19

Portage

The portage between the Yukon near Russian Mission and the Kuskokwim near Kaltag is an old mail route fallen into decay. Over twenty-four years ago the government spent $60,000, some say largely as a result of the efforts of Chris Betsch, on this route. It built three separate tramways with handcars running on them over the swamps to connect points of water; the trams were equipped at each end with windlass and cables to lift and move loads. The government dug out the smaller shallow lakes and connected them with each other and with the larger lakes by means of narrow artificial canals, so that a single small boat, the government boat, could carry the mail.

A man by the name of Oscar Samuelson carried mail between the Yukon and Kuskokwim for about fifteen years, by dog team in winter and by boat in summer. The Indians we traveled with showed us the lake where they laughingly told us the mailman had once thrown all the mail overboard to save his life. The waves can get pretty rough on some of the lakes on the portage.

After the route was equipped with mechanical devices and fine wooden signboards, complete with arrows and directions along the way, mail-carrying by dog and boat between the two rivers was discontinued. The airplane took over the mail, landing on the river at all of the little villages down the Yukon, whether there were landing fields or not, and there usually aren't. There are still dog-team mail routes in Alaska numbering into the hundreds of miles.

There is little mail for Russian Mission and its sister villages compared to what there might have been if only the white man's diseases had not taken a toll that practically depopulated the formerly bustling and prosperous North. Since the white man has come and there is now no going back to the old days, it is to be hoped that these people, as the Eskimos seem to have done,

will in time develop their own natural immunity and yet survive.

The old trader, Chris Betsch, and his dying village are virtually forgotten in the era of transition from the old to the new for which we hope. Russian Mission was Chris's pet find. He loves the place fiercely, and sticks, although he could live any place he wanted to in the world. Despite his professed illiteracy and lack of education he is worth all of $200,000, people say. If so, he did all right for an uneducated man.

The old mail trail to the Kuskokwim has been used occasionally by the wandering natives during past years. The tramways are rusted, and the cross ties sagging so that a man must brace his shoulders and hold the railway up, as it were, while his helpers push the car over the bad place. The canals are overgrown with vegetation and are filled in with mud. The signs telling the directions have long ago been burned up by the natives in campfires for fuel.

As we chugged through the still green waters of the first big slough, we watched a lynx gallop along beside us for a distance. Presently he turned on powerful hind feet and high-tailed it into the brush. On the other side of us a red fox sat like a flame among the autumn foliage. The Indians were intent upon making coffee inside the houseboat; they did not see the animals, and I was glad. I was sure they would have shot them if they could. Bud smiled out of the open back of the houseboat where he was making himself sociable with our crew, and I, being towed behind, met his grin knowingly. We were entering the country of the unknown, a new adventure, a new river now.

A porcupine that looked as big as a bear was presently aroused on the bank. As he waddled along in plain sight I knew that our companions couldn't miss him! Poor old fellow. He meant no one any harm. The boat stopped, and before he knew it a .22 bullet was put into his brain, and the corpse was thrown into the houseboat and taken along with us. It would make a delicious morsel for the returning section of our party to take back to Russian Mission. Porcupine to Indians is like ice cream to city dwellers.

The fact is that one can see more animals from a power boat within a short time than one can see from a canoe all summer. The animals are apparently not alarmed by the sound of the motor, perhaps because the element of surprise finds them in a temporary state of indecision, but a stealthy approach on foot or by silent canoe is often another matter. However, it is against the law to shoot animals from powered craft, just as it is from cars.

Nightfall found us still traveling. We were winding ever deeper and deeper into the swamps. Our route took us through small lakes and into new channels again, which were many forked and forty feet wide. Clouds of exhaust fumes drifting on the cold green water enveloped me in halos. The Indians had a good electric light on the front of their houseboat, but they did not use it. How could they know every treacherous snag rearing up in these channels? The answer is that I don't think they did. At any moment I expected to see a snag come right up through the bottom of the canoe.

But if only all of the portage were as easy as this! The miles were quickly being thrust behind us. I hoped that the Indians were well prepared to fend for themselves in the matter of food. We had about twenty pounds of moose, dried fish, candy, and one can of sweet brown bread of which I thought the world. Chris had suggested cold boiled potatoes and cold boiled fish as his own favorite diet for the crossing, but I couldn't see that. This fare was also much admired by our Uncle Fred, I recalled. Perhaps we had been born in the wrong generation of Alaskans.

When the throb of the houseboat motor at last ceased, we all were stiff and shivering in the cold which had descended upon us. The stars were bright and frosty and very distant, giving little light. The atmosphere was as clear as a bell; the glassy waters looked as though they were going to freeze solid around us at any moment. It was going to be cold before morning—how cold, none could tell.

There was no arctic summer orchestra now. The silence of the swamps shut down upon us instantly when the throb of the motor ceased. Our voices took on hushed notes. We were far off the beaten track of the big river now at a bad time of the year, and I think all of us felt it.

We had arrived at the beginning of the first tramway, the ancient wooden rails and rollers of which were revealed by flashlight beam to be ascending onto the land in a gradual incline and descending into the depths below. Our companions had found the right spot all right in the dark. Now all would sleep in our boats, there being no dry land, and the houseboat would turn back the next morning. How many of these boys were going to continue with us and Changsak, if any? We didn't ask.

Bud climbed from the rear of the houseboat into the canoe, we drank a little cold water, ate some dried fish and brown bread, and retired for the night. A few feet away from the Indians Bud had beached us upon floating grasses, out of which purple iris had at one time sprung.

When I awakened the next morning and looked timidly out upon the cold pink dawn, the sun was ringed with rime and a heavy frost was turning the earth into iron. All the grasses were encased in jeweled sheaths. However, navigation still appeared to be open.

The Indians had already eaten their breakfast in the houseboat as the aroma of coffee attested, and they were stirring about restlessly. The pale-yellow boy with the Chinese features had already rolled the two tramway cars over from the other end of the line a quarter of a mile away. We joined them immediately. While I had time to nibble on my dried fish Bud set to work with the men, loading first the "kicker" (the Indians' only name for motorboat) and then the canoe, so that no time might be lost.

On every side of us stretched the undulating, treeless tundra. We had back-tracked the Yukon to work this far inland; directly opposite us was distant Dogfish Mountain once again. We were leaving all wood behind us.

At the end of the tramway we slid down into the grasses which rimmed the first of a chain of small lakes. Beneath the grass was water. Bud carried me on his shoulders and deposited me in the canoe in open water. It was too shallow, even with the high waters of this year, to do more than pole. The three Indians who remained with us and the priest now led the way, poling their "kicker." We endeavored to keep directly behind them in the channel. Each plunge with our sharp paddle blades to shove us forward ensnared the paddles two feet deep in gray glacial mud, which, lying under the warm water, had not frozen. To pull our paddles out entailed such an effort as to pull the canoe backwards to the spot from which we started. The bottom of the canoe was barely scraping the bottom of the lake. The boats left a muddy channel behind, but we managed to jump them through every obstacle, one after another. We all had gloves, and one man had a reindeer-skin parka along, but the cold wind soon dried the mud on our bare hands. One can lift and pull objects best bare-handed.

Plunging into the grass at the opposite side of each lake, we unerringly found the almost hidden canals. The hot sun of midday melted the rims of ice. The canals became completely choked with mud and grasses as we progressed, and when the water gave out, we got out and dragged our loads over the raw earth. Sometimes when it was pure soup I would remain in the canoe paddling in mud and guiding as best I could while the Indians and Bud floundered alongside and dragged. The last few exhausting yards to Grass Lake accomplished, we next found a sign pointing towards what looked like open sea, for we could not see the other side. The sign hung on a tall pole and rattled in the lonely wind. It could have been seen for a long way when snow covered the tundra and the lakes were frozen. It was all like interpreting a maze on a treasure hunt to travel through here. From a few yards away Bud called casually, "Do you see the swans, dear?"

Retreating in the distance even as I looked were two pure- white whistling or trumpeter swans, floating on the waters of the large inland lake.

Bud saw the Indians almost visibly twitching as though they wanted to pick up their guns. "Don't try to nail one of those swans, boys," he told them genially, for the first and only time asserting his authority. Then he stressed the penalties for killing swans in a very serious voice indeed. The boys replied nothing but seemed to be impressed with the information expounded for their benefit. The rest of the time Bud got along with the Indians as one of them.

At Russian Mission the old postmaster had told us of seeing in his day whole sled loads of swans brought in early in the spring by the Indians. He hadn't known, as had none of the people down this way, that it is now against the law to kill swans. Even at that he seemed to miss the point, because he only said, "Well, swan ain't very good eatin' anyway. I always thought it was kind of tough," whereupon the conversation lapsed into the merits of swan meat.

The exact kind of swans which we saw was impossible to tell. The whistling swan has a yellow spot at the base of the bill in front of the eye and compared to the trumpeter swan is somewhat smaller in length, being four and a half feet as against the five feet of the other. The whistling swan also has somewhat less vertebrae in the neck, which incidentally is longer than his body. Whatever kind they were these two stragglers we knew were among the last of their kind in a wild existence, and as such were the very epitome of all that is beautiful in nature.

We sailed across Grass Lake under our own power, Bud taking opportunity to nibble fish for his breakfast. Canals, and an arduous portage composed of rollers, admitted us to Round Lake, which was on a slightly higher level. Here we left Yukon waters for the waters of the Kuskokwim. The water in some of the canals began to flow almost imperceptibly our way.

"What is the name of this creek, Changsak?" I asked.

He replied that it was Crooked Creek, twenty-eight miles of which we would now have to traverse single file except for intervals of small lakes. After that, we would pick up Johnson Creek.

Not more than fifteen feet at a time were straight in Crooked Creek; then it would turn back upon itself so sharply that one could barely make the turn. The motor could not be used because the creek and the small lakes were choked with grasses and water lilies. It was well into the late afternoon when we first began to traverse Crooked Creek, without a camping place in sight in this wilderness of ponds, creeks, and swamps. If night overtook us here the men would have to sleep upright in their open boat, or probably, more likely, we would continue somehow by flashlight until we got out of this country which was so treacherous to linger in at this time of year. The sight of the slightly flowing headwaters of Crooked Creek gave us some hope. These waters would not so quickly freeze. But many stagnant pools were still before us, which connected the links of the creek like the links in a puzzle. We weren't by the worst yet.

Then the "kicker," just when things were going nicely and we thought we might begin using it without risk of shearing a "pin," took it into its mind to stall. Futilely, over and over again, the Indian who owned the motor whipped it with his rope starter. I was holding my breath each time, while the valuable moments passed, praying that it would go, but it didn't. As the sun circled and settled lower, the Indian commenced meticulously to take every piece of the motor apart.

He laid the parts on the back seat, cleaning them with a rag as we progressed in train, rowing and paddling down the bends of Crooked Creek. "Oh, Lord," I said to Bud, "what would ever happen to us all if that fellow should lose one of those parts overboard? And will he ever be able to put them all together again?"

"That's just what I've been wondering myself."

"Well, dumbbell, why don't you help him? You could probably tell in an instant what's the matter with the thing."

Perhaps I made a mistake in calling Bud a dumbbell. This was his cue to shake his head stubbornly. "They'll handle it," was all he said.

Changsak now spoke up, as we drifted; he had the attentive ear of every one of our little party. "I think," he said softly, "we take other way, here."

"What does he mean?" I whispered to Bud.

"Your guess is as good as mine."

We came out upon a new little lake literally choked with water-lily plants in time to see about fifteen swans cross in labored flight, long necks outstretched, low against the water. Like the cranes and the geese at this season, fall, they called continuously as they flew. Their call was a bell-like exquisite tone different from anything I had ever heard, a sound that carried through the atmosphere, near and far. But we took just a moment from our paddling to see them as they disappeared into the low- hanging sun. We were in a spot, and our minds were on that.

"Crooked Creek is full of grass. Wind up motor anyway/' Changsak presently explained to me, as we all paddled slowly back into the lakes again. "It is very long ways on Crooked Creek. We have no time"—pointing at the sky. "We take short cut. Indian people know. I go there once, long ago."

"I don't like this, Bud," I whispered again as soon as I had a chance. "Look, not one of these Indians knows the short cut but Changsak. He looks very serious, too, don't you think?" Changsak was standing up in the boat, waving his hand expressively at intervals, and speaking with his companions in a low voice in Athabascan, interspersed with what sounded like Russian words. "Suppose we get into these lakes and can't get out to Crooked Creek again. I don't see how Changsak can possibly remember the channel. I'd rather keep in flowing water. These terrible swamp lakes look like the worst place to be, if you ask me."

Bud of course was thinking all these things himself, but

characteristically did not express them. We both knew that should our party be caught in the swamps after freeze-up, there would be no way of getting back to the Yukon across the larger lakes, which would not freeze for a month. Neither could we get to the Kuskokwim, as scores of large, deep, winding creeks crisscrossed the whole area, blocking the way. The only thing we could do was to pray that Changsak's memory might be refreshed, that he might receive at the proper intervals the right inspirations to guide our travel and that not a day might be lost.

While the man tinkered with the parts of the motor, another Indian methodically rowed the heavy boat in which his companions rode and which we followed at a distance of four feet. He had a long, narrow, mournful face. Although older than any of the others, we noted that he and only he rowed all the way across the portage as long as rowing was to be done. Apparently, it never occurred to any of the others to take shifts and offer the poor old fellow relief. He was Changsak's brother.

Changsak himself, dressed in modern sportsman's shoepacks, jacket, and breeches, as we all were, observed the situation with a glittering eye. He was carrying on his person either as a charm or as a sort of novelty purse a little packet made indisputably, according to Bud, from the webbed skin of a wild swan's foot, the toenails still intact. At one time he had it around his neck, at another time in his hand, as we progressed. Yet it was hard to believe that Changsak or his people would practice magic in any way. They had motorboats and flashlights, were dressed better than we ourselves, and one of them wore a fountain pen clipped into the pocket of his jacket.

Changsak took one channel and then another, all of them overgrown and hidden so that we must push aside the willows to enter. Each channel admitted us to a new lake. Just once Changsak became confused, and we all stopped while he thought it out. Then, speaking quietly to his men in Athabascan again, he motioned us to go back and retrace our way; this one was the wrong lake. It was the other lake we wanted, for this one would have been the thing that I had been fearing all along—a blind alley.

Once we wound our way through a lake of pure mud in order to find passage through to the next lake. Here I lost the channel. Our guides had got too far ahead for me to remember the exact track they had taken. Out in the middle of the mudhole we got stuck: no way to paddle and no way to walk, it seemed. We couldn't get out. The more we stirred up the bottom in our efforts, the worse our plight became. Our guides, who were powerless to help us anyway, were around the next bend, and couldn't be seen. In a sort of desperation to catch up with them we sat down in our seats, lunged forward in unison, and jumped the canoe through in lurches. I was relieved indeed when we caught up with the Indians.

The sky had now become overcast very suddenly and a cold wind swept warningly across the tundra, bringing with it the first wisps of snow. The sun had gone out. The man who had his parka with him put it on. Suddenly winter had come in one day, or rather, in one hour.

Two large coveys of ptarmigan, just half dressed in their winter coats of white, and perfectly speckled to match their background, were seen on the bank beside us, backs against the wind and their plumage ruffled up. Ptarmigan are perhaps the most important food and game birds of the northern latitudes, for they are not migratory but stay in the North all the year. In summer they are brown, or nearly so, to match the earth; in winter they turn snow white to match the drifts into which they can plummet without making a track that a fox or a mink or a weasel can trace. They walk, when they do, on feathered feet which are snowshoes of the most improved type, without danger of sinking in. Ptarmigan inhabit barren grounds generally, rather than forest country, and are of three types: rock ptarmigan or frog ptarmigan locally (they growl like frogs), inhabiting the steep slopes of bare mountains above timber line, which in Alaska seldom extends above three thousand feet; willow ptarmigan inhabiting a lower altitude and being somewhat larger; and the white-tailed ptarmigan known to more southern latitudes, such as Colorado. The meat is rather between a dark and a white meat and is delicious in flavor.

It is interesting that the Indians were not impressed by these ptarmigan. Bud said, "Wait a minute. I think I'll have to shoot a couple of these ptarmigan, but the Indians paid no attention and continued as though they did not hear. They did not say not to stop and hunt them; they simply continued traveling. Bud had hopped out and clambered along the muddy bank in hip boots almost before the words were out of his mouth. He did in fact come back with just two ptarmigan, which he had shot on the wing by stamping the ground and shouting to scare them up. The other ptarmigan just sat staring and watching, uttering their peculiar croaks and growls, and would not move. They didn't know what it was all about and were not frightened by the shotgun. I also watched from the canoe, but I had an eye, too, on what the snow clouds were doing and on what the Indians were doing. "For heaven's sake, Bud," I called, not for the first time, "don't go hunting now."

Bud jumped into the canoe, and once again we somehow caught up with the Indians. "You see, they were waiting for us all the time," said Bud, but I wasn't entirely sure of that.

I think we all breathed a sigh of relief when Changsak at last waved his hand and triumphantly presented us with Crooked Creek again. He commented, "I go this way once very long time ago when I was a boy. We save ourself many mile. I am not sure I can remember. But I remember O. K., eh?"

"O. K.," we told him. "Lead on."

For the second time the Indian who attended the motor had taken it apart and put it together again. "Indians," Bud generalized, "don't seem to reason from cause to effect, do they? Now instead of taking the whole thing apart, a person who knew anything about motors, or a person who reasoned it out the way we do, would simply check the two systems to find the trouble: the trouble is bound to be in the ignition system or the fuel system. I can tell you what it is: the engine is not getting gas from the way she sounds to me, and that means the feed line was clogged. But the Indians think it's the whole motor. See what I mean?"

Bud may have been right about the Alaska Indians in this, but certainly not about the Eskimos, who are very clever mechanically.

But this time—I could hardly believe it—when the Indian got his propeller in the water and had a try at it again, the motor purred off like a kitten, and away we went, being towed. It was a relief indeed to rest my paddle arm, although I ruddered to assist on the turns. An hour later found us in the late twilight just about out of danger. We were in the valley of the Kuskokwim, very close, in fact, to the big river, and we were down among the timber once more. The creek continued doubling and twisting in indescribable contortions, but was growing larger and swifter, and each bend presented solid banks with admirable camping places for wood and fuel. This was good, for we knew that the canals which we had thrust behind us on this day were closing as we passed, not to be traversed again by boat until the next summer. We had just made it by the skin of our teeth. We found the mouth of

Johnson Creek in the dark and made camp at the fork. "Water will not freeze here. We are O. K. now," Changsak told us with a grin.

At the mouth of Johnson Creek, we built a fire on solid land for the first time in two days, hovering around it gratefully. Since it was a small fire, I was as polite as the others and did not crowd too close. The Indians built it very quickly with peculiar shavings sliced from kindling made of packing boxes. I later learned the Eskimo had been using this type of shaving for thousands of years. The shavings are used in place of towels to wipe greasy hands or sweaty bodies in the kashima (club bath house) and were invented long before the white man brought his towels.

We offered the men warmed-over moose steaks, of which they ate a Dutch oven full. Our raw moose was frozen hard, yet we did not greatly feel the cold, as from living outdoors all summer we had gradually become used to it as fall progressed. All of us drank much tea, which the Indians called chi (from the Russian chaiyu), and ate many crackers of sorts, and candy. How our friends could possibly have spent a very good night, four men lightly dressed and without cover or sleeping bag other than a small strip of canvas, I don't know. I don't imagine they did.

"Why do we have to go up Johnson Creek?" I asked Changsak. "Where does Crooked Creek go? It looks as though it leads right on down to the river to me."

"Crooked Creek is very long," Changsak said. "Go many miles, come out far below Bethel."

I later ascertained by the Kroll Map of Alaska, which even the National Geographic Society offers none better, that parts of Crooked Creek, if one should continue on it, would be a mighty bad place to be at any time. If one took the wrong channels he would be led into that country marked simply on the maps as "Tundra and many lakes." The creeks, like Crooked Creek, are countless, and practically unknown of course, except for their probable channels where a person has to fill in the map to make it look as it ought to. No outlet into the Bering Sea is plotted for Crooked Creek's other channels leading into the tundra, and there may not be any outlet. This would be a good illustration of the country I have mentioned where even the natives do not go.

The next day we continued up Johnson Creek, the motor towing us along for the most part without any trouble. Johnson Creek was exactly like this lower branch of Crooked Creek. It was so winding that no person could think of crossing this hummocky country on foot, unless prepared to swim the deep icy channels countless times. Sunk down between high grassy banks, we could now see nothing but a few feet ahead at a time to the next bend. The diversion of watching Changsak in front potting away at the hundreds of ducks which rode the waters of the creek at every bend engrossed us, and the time passed. Changsak was not a very good shot. He shot at over a hundred different ducks at close range with the .22 rifle, and finally winged one, which his companions retrieved. The Indians who thus carelessly and laughingly squandered their ammunition in passing the time did not know that the winter would find them unable to obtain a single .22 bullet in the country, because the war had necessitated a halt in their manufacture. We mentioned it, but the fact didn't seem to make much impression.

Two hours up Johnson Creek brought us up to the third and last portage tramway. It was now snowing dismally, and several inches of wet slush covered the ground on all sides and drifted at the edges of the water. By the lee side of a little shelter cabin we built a fire and warmed up on more hot chi and moose steaks.

We noticed that Changsak would eat no steaks, although his men did.

"How do you expect to be strong, Changsak," we asked him good-humoredly, "if you do not eat meat?"

"Crackers make a man very strong," he replied, but I thought that a strange reply even at the time. But then I remembered. It was Friday, of course! Therefore, even when traveling with great exposure and exertion across this dangerous country, going for hours without food, Changsak would eat no meat, and that was about all the food there was, too! But his men ate meat on Friday, and in front of their priest. Why was that?

The only solution I have to offer refers to something one of the Jesuit priests at Holy Cross told me, and I believe this could conceivably be the answer. In Roman Catholicism, I learned, a bishop can at any time, by word of very ancient church law, relax the maxim of meatless Friday throughout the diocese for which he is responsible. Meatless Friday has in past history been abolished in certain areas and during certain times of wars, famines, or other emergencies, for the Catholic Church is practical. If it is considered necessary that a man eat meat in order to engage in arduous work or undertaking, it is also decreed by the Church that his wife and children too shall be allowed at all times to eat meat in the home when he does; this law has especially been applied to the peasants, and this I had not known before.

Bud used the rusted crane to haul our boats out from the deep-sunken creek and onto the railway cars. I wondered at every moment if the equipment was going to break, but it didn't. I ran ahead to spot the bad places and found some that were bad indeed.

"When tram was new, we run cars, fast along here!" one of the men told me, his eyes sparkling. No doubt they had! The natives of the country had used the tramway as children use a new toy. They had aided nature in tearing it down.

The tramway rode eight feet high across a marsh, and as I stepped across the open spots from tie to railroad tie, I could see far out over the tundra, and at last knew which direction was which. The snow clouds parted, the sun streamed warmly through for a moment, and far to the north appeared a new huge mountain range I had never seen before. Snow-shrouded, and appearing as a vision between the parted mists, it beckoned as I knew all the mountains of Alaska would forever beckon me or anybody who had any love of adventure left in his heart.

But my legs were very unsteady. They were trembling with weakness, for the portage and its exertions had been almost too much for me; trying to walk the high railroad ties was a good test of drunkenness. I became dizzy and short of breath and was obliged to sit down to keep from tottering into the swamp. If one of the railroad cars should crash overboard here, I reflected, we would never get it with the boats back onto the tracks again, for with only rusted and decrepit cables to work with, we would be in*a bad situation. Those cables wouldn't hold enough to lift an iron railway car.

The railroad tottered, but it held as the men pushed our loads over. How glad I was that Bud and I had not attempted this alone. This would have been a little too much. It took the utmost efforts of five men to work the equipment.

The end of the tramway brought us to the banks of Mud River, sunken deep in a straggling spruce forest growing out of the swamp. Mud River was known to be extremely shallow, and there was no telling if the Yukon's season of high waters had at the same time been a season of high waters for the Kuskokwim drainage area. It was but six miles from here, however, down to the Kuskokwim itself—and the water was high I Down Mud River we sped grandly. I was so tired that I didn't know what I was doing. Once we rounded a turn and I neglected to change sides with the paddle and rudder just this one time, and the canoe crashed into a tree growing out of the bank, and sprang back like a steel spring, in a shower of leaves and twigs. Presently, wide daylight sifted through the narrow aisle of the forest, Mud River was framed for a moment in arboreal splendor, and before our eyes rushed the swift, strange waters of the Kuskokwim!

20

Kuskokwim River

B y crossing over from the Yukon to the Kuskokwim we had
entered Eskimo country, and Bud and I had never yet seen a
real Eskimo for all our stay in Alaska; I should say that quite a
few Alaskans haven't.

Eskimos in Alaska do not live particularly in snow houses, and
igloo-building is practically a forgotten culture trait, if it was ever
learned in the first place. East of Point Barrow on the coast of the
Arctic Ocean we understand that they have learned from the Canada
Eskimos or with the Canada Eskimos to build snow houses when on
the trail overnight in some localities, and I talked at Bethel with an
Eskimo girl from Point Barrow who was a high school graduate and
of a completely American personality who told me she remembered as
a little girl camping in such houses. However, this was only camping.
Eskimos, like anyone else, seem to prefer to build their permanent
houses with rock or wood, if they can get it, rather than snow, and
incidentally the Alaska Eskimos are much more permanent and less
migratory in nature today than they once were. If an Alaskan should
ever see a real snow igloo in his travels it would be such a rarity as
happens once in a lifetime, and he would have to travel a long way
from the so-called beaten track.

On the Kuskokwim, as at Point Barrow and on Saint Lawrence
Island and most other places, the Eskimos of today live in floored
log cabins erected white-man style with straight rather than leaning

walls, around the white man's trading or missionary or teaching post. Their tents to a canoeist on the lower Kuskokwim would show white among the trees at the fish camps of summer, just as do those of the Yukon Indians. In winter these tents, although inferior to the original skins which were once used, may be used for camping, erected behind windbreaks of snow.

The Eskimo camps are just the same, complete with dogs, except that the dogs are better fed, and there are no fish wheels; it is too near the sea on the lower Kuskokwim for fish wheels to be used, for the law prevents their use in areas affected by tides. The people use nets, and live principally on fish, because game, especially big game, aside from the reindeer herds, is even scarcer here than on the Yukon. Where we entered the Kuskokwim, one must go two hundred miles to find a moose. Except for the fringe of spruce and willows which follows the course of the river, all is tundra on every side. Thousands of ptarmigan are blown in off the tundra in droves at this season and will often wing their way across the river before a canoe. The Eskimos, who were essentially a coast or water people in the first place, have adapted here to trapping and reindeer herding. They have been driven up the mouth of the large river in past days for lack of food. Their habitation of the lower Kuskokwim must be very old.

It was in 1884 that white men first penetrated the Kuskokwim country, and these were Moravian missionaries, coming largely from around Bethlehem, Pennsylvania. The country had apparently been largely overlooked by the Russians.

Although sanitary conditions by summer are appalling, sewage disposal being via river as in the case of the Yukon towns, the Eskimos are thriving and are on the increase. They seem to have less trouble than do the Indians, according to the opinion of many, in adapting themselves to the white man's ways, which might indicate to the eugenicists that their ancient Oriental blood is responsible for their quickness in grasping things. Another possible explanation for their obvious superiority to the Interior Indian as a whole is that they had already evolved a very sophisticated and intricate culture of their own long before the white man came, which made it the easier to add the new layer of culture onto what they already knew.

If one can generalize about a whole race, we found the Eskimos a wonderful people—lovable, affectionate, demonstrative, and so jolly in their appearance that we truly lost our hearts to them. We wouldn't have missed this part of the trip for anything in the world. The little babies with their great fat cheeks and slits for eyes make the traveler want to wrap them up in packages and send them home to friends for Alaska souvenirs! Perhaps it is fortunate for the Eskimo babies that no tourists come to the Kuskokwim.

There are two native foods with which we came in contact on the Kuskokwim; these are not unknown to the Interior Indians, for that matter. One of them is agootuk or "Eskimo ice cream." It is a mixture of blueberries, snow, and seal oil. As seal oil is secured largely by trade, it is not always available, so one can use substitutes in making this food, and today the substitutes are perhaps more usual than the real thing. Kuskokwim Eskimos commonly use blueberries, snow, whitefish and fat. Canned lards are popularly used today in agootuk.

The other food of which we had learned during the summer and which we found on the Kuskokwim also is *tipnuk*. This is a very ancient food, in that its likeness goes back to the beginning of human times. First you catch salmon or other fish. Then you bury them, heads, fins, scales, entrails, and all, in a fine deep pit dug in the riverbank, covering them with leaves and earth. To be good, *tipnuk* should remain over one summer and all the next winter before it is exhumed to be eaten. In appearance the flesh of the fish, if salmon, becomes very red, and it is clean and so soft that it falls to pieces. The natives love it, eaten raw. No other preparation is needed. Like sauerkraut or processed cheeses, it has a strong odor, one which civilized man has been trained to abhor, but nutritionally it seems to be a good food when it turns out such beautiful faces and bodies as those of the Eskimos. Fish which has putrefied underground has different qualities from fish which has been hung out of doors on the houses to putrefy in the open air. The latter is considered by white people dangerous for natives to use, and its use is highly discouraged, although *tipnuk* is tolerated by those who have been long in the country.

Our little party of the portage, led by Changsak, reached the Kuskokwim on the afternoon of our third day of traveling. The Kuskokwim looked small to us although it is classed as a large river. It is much smaller than is the lower Tanana, which is a mere tributary of the Yukon. With the Colville of the North, the Kuskokwim vies in being Alaska's second largest river, although little is known of the

Colville. Even the Yukon has never been but half surveyed, for that matter.

However, we had been prepared to see much more water here. There was not a great deal of water but we could see at once that it was a treacherous river, with a very swift current and many bars, and therefore a river to watch out for. Navigation with barges must be difficult, we thought. Navigation of the Kuskokwim is open for eight hundred miles up as far as the town of McGrath and above, where the Kuskokwim forks into several branches coming from the mountains. One branch of the river is the Stony, of gold-mining fame. The mountainous regions of the upper Kuskokwim are a true big-game paradise, and one of the least accessible and least known regions in southern Alaska.

No sooner had we hit the waters of the Kuskokwim than we saw a little man with a rifle seated in a little kayak floating quietly at the edge of the shore. It seemed exactly as though he were waiting for us. But I don't see how he could have known we were coming, for there are of course no communications across the old portage.

As we drew near, his creased and leathery face smiled all over from ear to ear, exposing large white square teeth. He picked up a cigarette and hung it between his lips; then he picked up his two-bladed paddle. The paddle threshed like a windmill through the water, only soundlessly and with seemingly no effort at all; it was controlled entirely by wrist motion.

Our Indian friends had cut their motor. It was apparent that the men recognized each other at once.

"I wonder what they're going to do," Bud whispered. It was entirely forgotten by our companions that we were being towed right behind, and drifted on the water with them. We were glad to be forgotten and have the opportunity to witness at close range this interesting meeting in mid-river.

Did the priest speak to the stranger in Athabascan or in Innuit? How did they understand each other? As much at home on the water as on land, the little man arose gracefully on one toe from his narrow twelve-foot shell, and stepped lightly into the motorboat with our Indians, all of us drifting along meanwhile on a five-mile current.

Our friend Changsak clasped him eagerly, kissed him on each cheek and on the mouth, and made the sign of the cross. Smiles of delight lit up each face, and rapid-fire conversation flew back and forth. Scarcely controlling his excitement, the little man now stepped lightly back into his kayak and, sitting with his short legs curled toe to knee, paddled swiftly away. Our party followed his lead, and Bud and I followed them as a matter of course. At the next bend of the river dogs were barking and Eskimos were shouting on the bank.

"We really got in with the right crowd to be popular, didn't we?" Bud observed. So, this was the Kuskokwim.

Changsak, blessing babies and children upon the way, was escorted by crowds up the bank to where a log cabin nestled among the trees. Excitement and happiness were in the air, so much that we felt them, too. We had beaten the freeze-up to the Kuskokwim, and the Kuskokwim had new visitors from another land. And let it never be said that Eskimos are unsociable or do not like to visit or have visitors.

Presently Changsak recalled that we were with him, and we were invited to come up to the house for hot coffee and a share of the reflected glory. Climbing up steps cut in the raw earth of the slimy, caving bank, we trailed into the small house with a dozen or so of our first real Eskimos all about us. The interior of the house was as hot and moist as the tropics, for what with their furs and the heat of their houses, travelers before us have said truly that Eskimos live in a tropical environment the year round. Incidentally, students have written that the sexual maturity of Eskimos is very early and corresponds with that of the supposedly tropical native peoples inhabiting equatorial climates.

There were no blubber lamps in this house, which is something we doubt if any contemporary Alaskan has seen in action, but there were kerosene lamps. The stove was of sheet iron, the fuel, wood. All the furniture was very low. The three-legged stools upon which we sat were certainly not more than six inches above the floor. Three tiny squealing husky pups quarreled for the warmest place on the floor by the stove. I reached down and took them onto my lap, stroking their large square heads and balancing my coffee on the other knee.

Everything smelled of dogs and fish, and the women's faces and hair were slick and oily. I tremendously admired the women's hair, as I had all summer. I had observed that native people, no matter how dirty they may appear to us, never have dandruff or diseases of the scalp, and for them to wash their hair is unknown. By necessity I had not washed my hair for some months. The first month of going unwashed was the hardest because of the breaking of lifetime habits, but after that I had noticed no particular difference, and later a hairdresser, when I got back to town, assured me that my hair was in splendid condition and was not offensive in any way, and that the dandruff with which I had at one time felt myself troubled had completely disappeared on the Yukon trip. As I looked at these women's glossy hair for the thousandth time it occurred to me that the white person's constant irritation of the scalp by washing and by permanent waves may have something to do with our nation's chronic scalp troubles.

I noticed that my feet sprawling out from my stool in their boots looked positively immense compared to the small feet of the natives. I tried to tuck them under me, but it was no good. They must think of white women as being awfully big and awkward and good for nothing, I decided. I knew this from what I had been told by Indian Service teachers during the summer. The native people respect the teacher in a certain way, with the kind of respect or awe which we hold for nobility or a society matron, but in another way, it is hard for them to understand what use she is if she never does any work. "I teach school, Lena. That is my work," one teacher tried to explain. "You do not work," Lena stated irrefutably. "Why, you do not chop wood." And Lena smiled at the teacher as one would indulgently at a child.

On the portage I recalled that Changsak had been extremely kind and considerate to me, asking me all the time if I were tired, and endeavoring to answer any question I asked about the country. He had learned I was from Seward, and he said once: "Winter is coming soon at Yukon. It is hard for white woman. You should go back to Seward."

What did Changsak really think of me? He certainly hadn't read books or seen movies to prompt his chivalrous leanings. He wasn't brought up on chivalrous fare as we were, and little had come his way surely to show him how gentlemen behave with white ladies. Yet he had struck the right note and behaved towards me in all ways as a considerate and self-respecting gentleman behaves towards a lady in my own society. Did he do it by charitable instinct to be kind to one who is weaker and over whom one feels protection? Did he feel that I was an important personage to be so traveling? As the Greek Orthodox Church does not hold women's place in the social structure as being equal to that of the men, I could not believe that Christianity had particularly taught him reverence toward white "ladies." But we seemed to understand each other, irrespective of differences in creeds, and there was no embarrassment between us.

Bud said to Changsak, "What can I give you for the portage?"

Wasile Changsak was embarrassed, although there was nobody but ourselves to listen behind the house. I realized now once and for all that the intelligent glitter in his dark eyes was truly kindly and thoughtful. "Nothing," he said. "That is all right."

I think we had convinced our friends that we were really poor. And we were poor, too, from our standpoint, although possibly from theirs we were rich. Money cannot buy the most interesting and precious experiences of life, of which this had been one. Now, however, Bud pressed a ten-dollar bill into Changsak's hand for his brother's gasoline, and for their trouble. "We may be poor, Changsak, but we want you to take this," I told him. He nodded sympathetically and accepted the ten dollars.

We had been gone from Changsak less than twenty-four hours on the Kuskokwim when we awoke in the morning to find our canoe and the ground all about us almost obliterated beneath a heavy fall of snow. Bud arose first, stamped into his shoepacks, scraped a little hole down in the snow, and built a fire laid carefully on spruce logs; we had a breakfast of moose steaks and tea, which had become our usual subsistence. Altogether we were traveling pretty light now. But that breakfast in the snow was never completed. Out of the silent gray sky and low over the willows towards us stringed a great V of five hundred wild snow geese. They were coming down from the north. Every twig was ridged with snow. Held for just an instant, with the white lacy forest twigs against their solid gray background of winter sky, the fast-coming snow geese should have been impaled upon an artist's canvas. But since wild geese average forty-five miles an hour in flight when there is no wind, the artist would have had little time in the fast, real-life action which followed. Bud grabbed his shotgun, shaking snow from the bush by his side, and shot twice.

"Well, it looks as though you missed this time," I chanted.

"Nope, I got one. If we can find him. Come on."

And so, there we were, down on the Kuskokwim, snow covering everything, still cheerfully continuing our summer's canoe trip. Dousing the tea into the snow, we picked up the Dutch oven still sizzling with its steaks, plunked duffel pell-mell into the boat, and with the sail rolled around its mast and balanced precariously on the roof of our house canoe shoved off again on the run. For a half hour we paddled with all possible haste downstream in the direction the geese had gone, using the glasses at intervals to pick up the straggler which we knew must be floating in the water here somewhere if we could but find him. Which way exactly did the current tend? The island on which we had camped had disappeared into all the other countless islands.

But Bud found the geese, two of them, floating on the silent water a couple of hundred yards apart in midstream. They looked so like chunks of ice or floating pieces of wood covered with the night's fall of snow that it was a miracle they were found. Both, in falling behind the flock, were dead when they hit the water far beyond our sight. Thus, do many geese die that the hunter has no conception he hit unless he looks carefully for as long as he can observe the flock.

These first and only snow geese we saw were pure white except for black-tipped wings and black eyes. Their bills, scalloped with jet-black fringes, and their feet, were of an indescribable, exotic shade of shell pink. I should say that they were really not entirely pure white: to be exact, they were as white as angels every place that they could clean themselves with their bills. But there was one place they could not reach. Their upper necks and faces were as dirty as any dirty faces I have ever seen in close-up, wearing all the dust of every storm they had ever come through, including no doubt some soil from Siberia across the way, and perhaps China.

Towns are much closer together on the Kuskokwim than they are on the Yukon; the whole plan is in miniature. At nightfall of that day we arrived at an extremely smelly camp, where we asked the distance to the next town, Tuluksak at the mouth of the Tuluksak River. Up the Tuluksak River is the N.Y.A.C. or New York-Alaska Company, a large and luxuriously equipped mining concern which would have been of interest for us to visit had it been midsummer rather than winter. In the camp we found one Eskimo sitting alone in his tent, and he said he was just going in to Tuluksak in his motorboat. It was the only inboard motor we had seen, and it traveled all of eight miles an hour. He would give us a tow.

That tow was the longest and coldest ride I have ever lived through, I think. Once we ceased paddling and exercising we realized that the country was beginning to cool off considerably, for persons dressed in light clothing. I have heard people say since that just sitting still and riding in an open boat at this time of year in Alaska is the very coldest occupation they know of. Dog team or other travel in really cold weather isn't so bad because then one is dressed for it. Daylight dimmed into twilight and twilight into pitch-black night as we traveled behind this Eskimo who was taking us up to the nearest white person at an Indian Service outpost.

The village, when we reached it, was veiled in darkness without a single light showing from the windows of its low little cabins. Only the barking and wailing of the huskies made its presence known in the night. But about a thousand miles from the Japanese-invaded islands of Kiska and Attu, these villages of the Interior wilderness were not concerned with wartime blackouts; finding them would be perhaps more difficult than finding a needle in a haystack if one wanted to look. It was simply nine o'clock at night and time to be asleep.

Bud untied our canoe from the lead boat with stiffened hands and carried me on his back to the shore. Once again, we climbed the familiar banks of a native town, slippery with ice, now. Its being a new river didn't make much difference. Only I had a hard time to navigate it. I fell down five times in getting to the Indian Service teacher's door, because it was hard for me to get my land legs once again after that cramped, nightmarish ride.

It wasn't a very proper hour to make a call. We could have anchored and gone to bed in our canoe comfortably, really. When she opened the door, we felt apologetic because of the lateness of the hour and what must have been, we felt, our perfectly awful appearance. It had been too cold for me to comb my hair without freezing my hands, so I left it uncombed under my trapper's cap.

She was very surprised when she came down in her night clothes and opened the door, a slim, almost fragile-appearing girl with glasses. "One of your Eskimos brought us here. We just got over from the Yukon," we told her. She was sleepy and didn't seem to understand that at first. I guess the Yukon psychologically is as far removed from the Kuskokwim as is Africa, and we must have been equally far removed from her thoughts. I continued, feeling ridiculous, and knowing that I was swaying back and forth like a drunk's lamppost where I stood: "It's a little late, but we came to call." She didn't say anything, so I added, "You're the first white person we've seen on the Kuskokwim."

I was not yet sure if in the dim light of the warm sitting room she realized that we were white people. But white or brown or yellow or black, it would have made small difference to Janet. She was on call to her village twenty-four hours out of the day, and her sitting room was habitually crowded with Eskimos who came to visit, or more frequently, as is their way, just to sit. We met teachers who kept regular schedules conscientiously but had no desire to see their pupils or their village during the rest of the day, which they reserved to themselves. Janet was of the other sort: she liked to see them all the time, for they never wore on her nerves. I have never seen a person so saint like in her pure desire simply to serve humanity in any way that circumstances might offer.

"I am not here to analyze the Eskimos under a microscope. I am not here to live on one side of the river and have them live on the other," she said. "You've seen villages like that? I don't want to set up the white man's pattern of oppression in any way. I do not desire to make a name for myself off them. I don't want to write a book. My purpose is just to live with the Eskimos for a while because they're people— human beings—and a very wonderful, interesting, different people I only hope I can learn a little something from them/'

"You are an idealist, aren't you?" I asked her on the second day when I was roasting the snow geese. She was not a good cook, as she had never had to cook for herself before, incidentally.

"Well, I guess I am," she replied to my remark. "Everybody on the river may call me that, but to look at life according to ideals is after all getting at the real truth of life."

We had fallen in love with this little slip of a husbandless girl who stayed here all by herself in an Eskimo village. Janet left us with the peculiar feeling that we had known her all our life. Her life was worth the lives of a thousand Eskimos any day, I thought impulsively and undemocratically.

"How long is it since you've seen any other white people to talk to, Janet?"

"Oh, several weeks, or months, I guess. I don't know. But I'm not lonely. That's what I like. I don't miss other white people, really. I enjoy being alone. That's why I stipulated an Eskimo outpost wherein I would be the only white person in the village. We get along fine, I think, if I do say so. There is no outside interference or quarreling in our village. The terrible world war and its repercussions are far away. We have perfect peace here. I sometimes miss intellectual companionship, but I am never lonely."

Janet had been a girl of refinement. Anyone could see that by the way she walked and talked, but especially by her naive inexperience concerning a world of practical things, a world, incidentally, which it had been difficult for her to master, although she longed to conquer it. She had belonged to a social sorority throughout college and had taken some of the student tours to Europe, but even throughout the former world depression, her life, with those of her best friends, had remained relatively sheltered and secure. For some years she had worked with the National Birth Control League and other organizations and reforms and had twice owned and operated a bookstore which netted her many friendships with mutual book lovers but consistently lost her money; apparently, she had no heart or head for finance.

"Last spring, we had some interesting visitors from the Outside/" she told us, as she went on with her descriptions of life in a modern Eskimo village. "A dozen soldier boys came up from Bethel and camped several days right by the village. They were looking for one of their companions who fell off one of the barges and drowned in the river, so our people helped them look, too; they never got him. Anyway, our people here were very interested in hearing about how people live in other places and how the war is coming along, of course. None of the boys had ever seen a real native Eskimo village before, so it was an educational experience for all of us, I think. We had a community dance for them, and they promised to come back and see us again."

"Weren't you a little worried about the dangers of community disorganization? We mean, ah, the dance, and your Eskimo girls and all?" we asked the idealist, with a practical thought in mind.

"No, everything worked out just grand," she said. "Of course, a wide-open town like Bethel is a bedlam as soon as the Army arrives in large numbers. But these chaps, when it was explained to them that these people have seen very few whites and would like to know them better, really put on their company manners and showed the best that was in them. I was really proud of the white race, for once. The boys enjoyed dancing with the Eskimo girls immensely and found them good dancers, except that they didn't smell like white people do. The reason for this I am positive is not that there is any peculiar odor to an Eskimo's or an Indian's skin—that's a superstition—but it's the food they eat and what they have been around, you see. Any of us would smell the same way if we lived on fish or spent our time scraping bearskins. That fixed idea of how natives smell is hard to shake from many Alaskans, incidentally, and I believe that it may be the main reason behind many people's revulsion toward them, if you got to the bottom of it."

At Tuluksak I taught school again for half a day, enjoying myself immensely, except that I could never get any of the first grade to so much as tell me their names. These little monkeys had me stumped. They would watch my face attentively as we turned the pages of a magazine and pointed out objects in the pictures, but never a word would they say—only stared at me with unblinking eyes, while I talked to myself. Possibly they were too interested in gazing at the new teacher. Janet told me that it had taken her some time to find out their names and learn to know which was which, for Eskimos use the father's given name as the last name for the children, so that it is hard for the new teacher to perceive family relationships. When a teacher makes the mistake of calling somebody by the wrong name, she may well go for months and years never knowing the difference, for nobody in the village will tell her. The Eskimos are a very polite people and a very subtle people in some ways.

I made a terrible faux pas at Tuluksak for which I never forgave myself. We went calling at several houses, although Janet would not allow us to take pictures. I peeked into what was cooking on the stove; it was some sort of bloody meat in water with what looked to me like white maggots floating in it. I should have known better than to refer in someone's house to what he eats when I do not know whether he eats it or not. I should have known that it was not the season for maggots. But I thought the food was for the dog team and I referred to it as such to the people. It turned out that it was their own supper cooking. The meat was rabbit, which is not wasted on dogs. The white things were rice. I had jumped to my conclusion simply because the Eskimos had not washed off all the blood as white people do but were saving it in the cooking.

"We think they have little intelligence sometimes, but it is certain that they also must think the same of us according to their view. I'll tell you one on me," Janet soothed. "My roof was leaking upstairs, so I asked my Eskimo helper to put some wash- tubs beneath the holes. They don't seem to be capable of fixing such a thing as a roof, in the way that we would do it, I mean—so I was only going to use a preventive measure for the time being. Do you know what he did? He got a brace and bit from the tool shop and went up there with the tubs and drilled holes in the roof and placed the tubs beneath them. You see, what he thought I wanted was to catch rain water. Now what kind of intelligence could he think I possess to want to catch the water inside the house rather than outside? I sometimes wonder what these people must think of us."

One of the cutest things I ever saw in my life was Janet's little Eskimo boys and girls doing folk-dancing at school recess.

Fur mukluks on their small feet, the little boys in jeans, and the little girls in bright cotton prints with hair ribbons flashing in their hair—when they danced they were a rollicking crew of pirates! Stamping these steps and clapping their hands in unison to the tune of this same old phonograph record was something they never grew tired of; their animal vigor was unsurpassed. Unlike white children and also unlike Indian children, they were all about the same height, solid little chunks who simply widened out as they grew older, and who as adults would still all be about of a uniform height. Incidentally they have been described as a small people, and in comparison to us who are large they do seem small, as the tallest of the men are but five feet eight inches. In this, however, it is too easy to forget that the average height of our own men is just five feet eight, so that after all Eskimos should not be described by the word "small" so much as by the word "uniform." This uniformity of face and figure, as with all races foreign to us, grows less as we grow used to them and can see their individual differences. But the fact that the Eskimos, along with many other native peoples, have had a communistic form of community life has tended to eliminate the great individual differences in outlook and manner which we expect in our actually highly individualized society. The communistic type of culture in primitive societies as studied by sociologists is supposed to be peculiarly unproductive of genius and invention, but if so is similarly unproductive of crime, perversion, and insanity. Life in an Eskimo village, I thought, as I watched the children dance, must certainly be one of the most happy, carefree lives in the world, where each has his own place in society and is a part of the integrated whole.

Now whenever we think of an Eskimo village we think of Tuluksak and Janet, and her rollicking crew of dancing children, with their dark twinkling eyes and great round red cheeks.

21

Eskimo Land

We were frozen in down on the Kuskokwim. Actually, the freeze-up came within a week instead of the two weeks we had allowed ourselves. And because of the freeze-up we were stuck in this country and obliged to stay awhile. And because we were stuck we had some rare experiences knowing the inhabitants of the lower Kuskokwim in a way that no mere passer-by could. Actually, it was December first before we arrived home in Seward from our summer's canoe trip.

We had sailed down to the town of Akiak under full sail in a fine wind. The native half of the town with its Indian Service teacher station and the only sawmill since Ruby on the Yukon a thousand miles away was located on one side of the river, and the "white" town was located on the other side. We hesitated in a kind of indecision as to which part of the town to approach. The wind decided it for us. The wind was so strong that it blew us unavoidably over to the native side of the river, so we went to call there. Thus, it was this wind which changed our entire fortunes. For if the wind had not blown us to the native side of the town, we would not have called on the Harts and had Sunday dinner with them, and if we had not called on the Harts we would not have met a young Moravian missionary worker who also was at the dinner and who invited us to come with him to visit him and his wife overnight at the Moravian orphanage for Eskimo children down the river.

We were delighted at the unexpected invitation to visit the orphanage. As the orphanage lies, not on the main Kuskokwim itself, but on the Kwethluk River which in turn flows into the Kuskokwak Slough and thence into the Kuskokwim again, it is a place we should never have seen or perhaps even known the existence of had we not chanced to meet friendly Jake. When Jake towed us to the orphanage for an overnight's stay, we got a

day's run (for us) off the main river. This was bad at this time of year because the smaller sloughs and side streams freeze first.

When we awoke the next morning the small Kwethluk River was running ice. We lingered for goose dinner with our new friends, then set sail belatedly downstream, never realizing that we should soon be seeing the orphanage again and quite a bit of it. We only got three miles. The floating ice, one-half inch in thickness, came down closer and closer in big pans, while we deftly sailed full speed between them, watching for the open spots before they could close again. Three miles below the orphanage we chanced onto the village of Kwethluk, which I myself hadn't realized was there, as Bud had got the directions from Jake. I was certainly glad to see that village. All the ice had closed in around us like a living thing, hissing and grinding as the pans slid over each other at the turns of the stream, until there was only a narrow channel of open water left. Could we have progressed through this channel a few feet farther down to the opening into the larger Kuskokwim Slough, we might yet have got to Bethel, but the day had almost ended. We were afraid of being caught by ice jams which might span the whole river between us and our destination and leave us really stranded without shelter. It takes weeks for the ice to freeze solid enough to walk on, inclement winds and thawings being the rule, and the country is of course so cut by sloughs and side streams coming into the main river that it is impossible to walk to town along the banks at this season. We were stopped—with Bethel just twenty miles away!

A few feet from us, also pulling their wooden boat out on the bank as we pulled out at the Eskimo village of Kwethluk, were some friends of ours in much the same fix. The man walked over to me. It was Changsak! I could have almost grabbed him around the neck, so glad was I to see this old rascal with whom we had been through so much. "Changsak, what are you doing here?" I exclaimed, as we tugged on the canoe together. (Bud had gone up to the big house of the teacher.)

"Make converts, maybe. It is freeze-up." He indicated with his inclining head the sliding ice pans which hissed about our feet and even up onto the shore. "You should be in Seward. Winter is no good for white women. What will you do?"

"I guess I'll have to do the same thing you do, Changsak. Ride the grub line."

He smiled broadly, although it is doubtful if he understood. "There is white woman in big house," he suggested. Then, "Native people wait for me. I go now."

"See you later." But I never saw him again, as it happened.

The next morning, we made one more intense effort to get through the still-running ice pack to Bethel, but it was no go. We got into the Kuskokwak to have it pack solid with restless ice stretching out broadly under the white sky for as far as we could see; this, then, was how a river freezes, and it happened before our eyes within a period of fifteen minutes. At first glance it looked clear enough so that we thought we could risk getting through; then just as suddenly it was brought to us forcibly that we were insane even to hope it. For four hours we then broke ice with our paddles and paddled back against the crushing pans, caught in deep water a few yards offshore—just to get back the half mile again to the shelter of Kwethluk. "She sure closes in fast when she once starts to," we agreed, as our benevolent hosts seated us at dinner. And there we were, perhaps for three months, certainly for six weeks.

. The first thing we did, when we became guests of the Indian Service teachers, Betty and Robbin of Kwethluk, was to radiophone in a telegram for an airplane to come from Bethel to pick us up by making a landing on the beach of the Kuskokwak Slough. As it happened, the airplane did not come. I remember Bud was out hunting willow grouse in the woods when a plane flew over and we thought it was for us. Such an event was it to get a plane right away within five days that Betty and Robbin abruptly dismissed both classes of school and had all the Eskimo children out searching the surrounding woods for Bud, while we wildly rang the school bell. Out hunting again—that Bud didn't even hear or know the agonies through which we lived! Once a pilot condescends to make a difficult landing on a mere strip of river beach, you can guarantee he will not try it again. Neither will he wait more than five minutes for the passengers to arrive, if that long, for the crowded airlines are indeed independent in Alaska; everybody is very nice to them. In spite of the fact that Robbin and Bud and I spent a couple of mornings clearing the riverside pasture of willows with scythes, the pilot would not risk a landing.

Betty and Robbin were a wonderful pair to be marooned with, if marooned we had to be. Having been located at this post for eight years, the couple had made of it a real home, with lovely dishes and table service, a real rug, and the most complete and well-selected library of books we had seen on the entire trip.

Betty concocted meals with no seeming effort at all, which is perhaps the proof of the real hostess; she had an Eskimo house girl trained to wash the dishes and tidy up. Robbin was possessed of a couple of university degrees and a remarkably sly sense of humor. Although magnetized mountain ranges blocked radio reception from Fairbanks and Anchorage, as happens so frequently about Alaska, good reception in the Kuskokwim can be attained direct from KGEI at San Francisco, and at this time we first heard the new popular war song, "Praise the Lord and Pass the Ammunition," which immediately set us all to humming, and we knew it was a hit. For a while we had almost forgotten about the war, except to think of it vaguely, but we now had news which set us to thinking of it more concretely again and hastened our anxiety to return to civilization.

As for civilization, we certainly met no more civilized people than Betty and Robbin. They typified exactly the background from which they had sprung—a suburban residential district in Maryland. But like all of us, they were Alaskans now, in concept and attitude. They brought a little bit of Maryland with them, transplanting it, incorporating this into the genuine friendliness of spirit that most people have who move on west.

Every Saturday morning at Kwethluk was wash day for the Eskimo pupils. Water was heated in large drums on the stove. Cold water was supplied from a large barrel which was kept filled with river ice. Betty used her kitchen sink drain, not to run used water into a little closet bucket and have to carry it out again as some people on the Yukon did, but with a real outlet. Drains in the classroom washtubs were also kept open, and soap was there supplied for the Eskimos to use. First Robbin took his boys to wash on Saturday morning, and then Betty took the girls Saturday afternoon.

Keeping clean for Eskimos always has been a different process than that we know. Imagine being an Eskimo and still trying to take baths according to the white man's standards under Eskimo conditions! Ice must be carried into the house and melted. In a land of no trees where seal oil must be used for fuel, no Eskimo can well afford to burn this oil to melt more water than is strictly necessary to drink, for the oil is also food. On adapting to log-cabin life it is certainly inadvisable for the Eskimo to be melting water constantly under these still primitive conditions, for he would live in a constant steam laundry of humidity, which is very conducive to tuberculosis. When primitives start washing too much under primitive conditions they usually become ill. Vilhjalmur Stefansson wrote that early missionaries in the North endeavored to teach cleanliness to the extent that Eskimos should wash their hands several times a day and always before eating and should use towels. The result was that coughing, and colds developed, and the family towel, singular in number, was passed around to all guests months upon end, and spread syphilitic sores (syphilis apparently brought by the whalers) all over the Eskimo population.

In primitive Eskimo society we understand the women never bathe in their lives, but the men have figured out a system for bathing themselves which equals or surpasses any of their other remarkable adaptations to their country: a bath for twenty men takes only a small amount of water. This is the kashima.[1]

Attending the kashima is first of all a social ritual, I should say, and secondarily a bath. It is the community clubhouse for men, and its origins go far back into primitive society. The Eskimo kashima at Kwethluk was about twenty-five feet square and built of timbers. The earth floor was sunken below the level of the ground, and on top of the roof was mounded Kuskokwim earth so that it looked somewhat like a beehive. The entrance was by a long slanting low tunnel, over which hung a bearskin rug to keep in the heat and keep out the cold. Even the white man adopts the tunnel principle to an extent in the North when he adds a storm porch and double doors to his own house, often combined, as with the Yukon cabins, with a roof but seven feet high. Eminent writers and explorers tell us that the Eskimo's original

---

1   There are many variations of this name, from *Kazhim* to *Kozyga* to *Kahreegee* or *Kadrigi*, as one goes north of the dividing line of Unalakleet. Kuskokwim Eskimos, for instance, cannot understand those from the far north.

small compact house built of driftwood or whalebone, over which was stretched skins, and which was banked with earth, was infinitely more windproof and comfortable than today's too large and flimsy log cabin, whose potbellied stove devours cords of wood to the depletion of supply. The kashima at Kwethluk, if an example of these lost arts of native architecture, was indeed well built for its purpose, for it was just as sound as it was over fifty years ago on the day it had been built.

In the middle of the floor of the large single room of the kashima was a pit six feet deep built cone-shape with slanting walls, wide at the top and growing narrower at the bottom. The Eskimos here kept their peculiar shavings or excelsior laid for an instant fire. This fire took but relatively little wood arid gave an immense amount of heat, which was reflected intensely from the low roof. Around the walls next to the pit were the benches on which the men sat, each with his pan of water, with which they wet their naked skins to keep from scorching, and this is how they took their steam baths of the kashima: cleansing was complete, with little water and a large amount of perspiration.

Because the Eskimos had greatly admired and trusted Robbin for many years, Robbin had a standing invitation to attend the kashima at Kwethluk, which is an honor not given to everyone. Aided by Robbin and perhaps by his large stature and red-gold curly beard, Bud made an extremely favorable impression on the village, and within a short time was invited with Robbin to attend the kashima, the sacred clubhouse where no woman may go. When Bud got back from the kashima his skin was flushed and red and he was veiled in what I can only describe as an aura of mystery.

"You act like you'd been initiated into the Masonic Order," I told him. "Well, what did they do?"

"Boy, can those Eskimos take it," was all he would say for some days.

When the hesitating stranger pulls aside the bearskin and enters the kashima for the first time, an especially large fire is built for him. Everyone first undresses and places his clothing in a bundle under the bench, and each person is given a bundle of excelsior to place in his mouth, through which to breathe. As the fire climbs up the pit and is reflected on the walls and roof, the stranger thinks that even his hair is going to catch fire, for it becomes too hot to touch with the hand. One by one the Eskimos crawl under the bench to escape the worst of the heat, and occasionally one runs out the tunnel and plunges headlong into the snow. Incidentally, Bud said that the Eskimo men never tell the young boys of the village that the kashima is not for them; nothing is forbidden. But if an immature boy ventures into this select society, he will usually be sent plunging into the snow, and will not return to the clubhouse again until he is older. It is a select and sacred society, wherein also important tribal events are discussed at times by the elders, or at least much of the gossip and the news of the day. When the fire dies down the sweated and exhausted inmates dress quietly and return to their respective homes in a subdued and amiable frame of mind.

At this kashima the Eskimo girls peeked down the air vent from the roof to see the white man with the red beard and giggled endlessly. But Bud was again invited to attend the kashima for as long as he should remain at Kwethluk. The adolescent girls were shooed away by their elders.

"I think, Bud," said Robbin the next evening at the supper table, "that while you are here we really ought to perform another initiation on you."

"What's that?" asked Bud.

"It's called the Cutting of the Beard. It's done quite frequently in civilized society, you know."

"Yes," added Betty, "we'd like to see, you know, what you really look like behind all that brush. Why don't you cut it now while you're here?"

It was plain that the magnificent beard must go soon. What could be a better time than now? Therefore, we all dragged Bud into the bathroom, and every possible tool in the place was engaged for the operation. Bud looked nervous as the star in such a ceremony, but he was game. When he emerged, the change was unbelievable. Four inches of his long hair and beard had been taken off, and he looked suddenly, instead of a mature man, a naked cherub with protruding ears and a receding chin. The white skin beneath the beard which had escaped being tanned in the weather made his chin recede into his neck, and his nose was now that of a shark. Robbin had humorously left on the long handlebar mustache as a characteristic of his handiwork. "I look like a shark with a mustache," Bud groaned as he looked in the mirror. We noted then that his ordinarily well-filled cheeks had sunken in during the summer beneath the beard and that he was thinner than we had thought he was. After a few days of exposure to the chilling winds, he was his tanned self again, although still slightly infantile and cherubic, I thought, after the beard.

One of the most interesting people we met was "Dummy" of Kwethluk. He was an Eskimo mute who had been driven out of the village by the others and who lived in a cleverly built house down the beach all by himself. Indeed, Dummy was far more clever than many of his companions who could hear and speak. He could carve all kinds of things of wood and he had evolved a sign speech of his own wherein he and Robbin discussed even the more abstract subjects. It was amazing how much Dummy knew, how little escaped his notice.

The first time Dummy came to the house to visit I was almost alarmed by his wild appearance and the animal-like, meaningless sounds which came from his throat when he tried to express himself. "It must be terrible to live in a world of silence and aloneness like that," I mentioned to Robbin.

"No," Robbin contradicted with some impatience. "Dummy's the happiest person you'd want to meet. If you made him feel sorry for himself then you would have something to feel sorry about, but he doesn't know any different. He doesn't know anything else, and he's happy."

Dummy often discussed such things as wartime blackouts, and he understood the need for them at Bethel perfectly, and had his own symbols for airplanes, cannon, and flags. Although he wandered down to Bethel occasionally, it was still beyond us how he could have ever grasped such things as he did, with no one to explain them. His symbol for the Japanese, whom he had never seen, was to hold his fingers slanting over his eyes. He was working on a trail between his house and Bethel to help the Army so that in case it was ever needed the Army could come upriver to Kwethluk quickly in case of retreat. He had a great deal of admiration for the uniforms of the Army and the flag of the United States; no more loyal American ever lived than Dummy, eater of *tipnuk* and raw live blackfish.

As the ice froze solid in the streams and swamps about us, we planned to walk to Bethel of a week end: Robbin would go with us, he said, and help us carry our necessary stuff. It was less than twenty miles by short cuts. The time came after two weeks of waiting when we thought we might attempt it. The day before the attempt was to be made, however, Bud, who had been in the house more or less during this time, was again taken with the urge to go hunting. He wanted to spend this last day running over to the orphanage once again and holding the rabbit and grouse drive which he had once suggested to Jake. I went with Bud on this day, across the frozen lakes and swamps of the intervening tundra. We did not return to Kwethluk. Circumstances beyond our control again intervened and we were caught at the orphanage by a thaw, which now melted the ice so treacherously that it was impossible to walk back.

So, there we were at the orphanage for a while. In addition to the home in which Mr. and Mrs. Schotsnyder, the directors, lived, there were two main large buildings which composed the Moravian orphanage for Eskimo children. In one of these were kitchen, dining room, classrooms, and the girls' dormitory upstairs, with quarters for the teacher and trained nurse who were in constant attendance. In the other, newer building, were laundry, quarters for mission workers, and the boys' dormitory upstairs. It was notable that there was no church. The classroom was the center for church services, biweekly prayer meetings, and the occasional parties which were given the children. Boardwalks three feet above the ground connected all of the beautifully built, hot-air-heated buildings, which rose up like a palatial residence within the scattered spruce trees. About thirty Eskimo juveniles, including one tall girl who looked Japanese, were the orphans.

We stayed with Florence and Jake, who had come from Canada, and who had two little babies, in the building which housed the boys' dormitory. There we plunged with everlasting gratefulness into the first and only bathtub with hot and cold running water which we had seen in four months' traveling in the Interior. Betty and Robbin of Kwethluk had a bathtub, but the water did not run like this. No other person we had met on the Yukon or otherwise had a bathtub.

The lowly paid missionaries and lay missionaries at the Eskimo orphanage worked like ants fourteen to eighteen hours a day to keep the establishment in perfect running order. Everybody worked; there was no room for an idler among them. Everybody seemed to have his whole heart in the task and the mutual cooperation was wonderful to see. If a person has never traveled in the field to see the missionaries at their work, he can have no idea of some people's lives which are lived in humbleness and self- sacrifice as most of us would see it. Everything in this orphanage went to the orphans. Everything was arranged so their welfare * might come first, as the missionaries saw it. Expenses were cut, and personal salaries sometimes dipped into so that the orphans might have clothing; food and clothing were somehow always obtained just in time by prayer and effort.

The superiority of the boarding-school system over the day-school system for quickly Americanizing Eskimos was something which struck us abruptly between the eyes at this really remarkable mission. Used as we were to the stolid, dreary-looking children we had seen all summer, these children were as different as is night from day. You could talk to them in words of more than one syllable; you could expect an intelligent and alert answer. It is no exaggeration to say that the Moravians are doing a wonderful work on the Kuskokwim, a work certainly unexcelled in any place in Alaska from what we know. Nutrition plays probably the largest part in this. The children are fed controlled diets of three square meals a day, including cocoa for breakfast,

milk for lunch (canned, diluted, of course), and tea for supper, and no one who has not seen native childhood conditions in Alaska could possibly realize what this means. All of the children at the orphanage gained pounds of weight after first being taken in, usually in a state of desertion by relatives and in semistarvation; they are weighed regularly and checked by the nurse. Next to nutrition the second big boost to Americanization we believe was the fact that the children were constantly associated with the American patterns of conduct throughout the twenty- four hours of the day, and they spoke English all the time, and with but relatively little accent, too. They not only read about St. Valentine's Day in the standard school reader, but they made valentines and sent them to each other; they celebrated Hallowe'en with an ice-cream party and games and a parade with lanterns in which staff and everybody joined; they celebrated birthdays and Christmas and Santa Claus.

The children developed a keen sense of humor for tricks and escapades of a harmless nature very much like white school children at a private school and thought about much the same things that the white children do. They loved *tipnuk* but were allowed to have it only very occasionally; they got dried fish in between meals sometimes, getting into that which was reserved for feeding the orphanage dog team. Parkas and the reeking mukluks were discarded upon their arrival at the school and were not allowed; they attracted lice and were too smelly and were not comfortable living indoors. Every child was outfitted instead with American-type ski pants and ski jackets of bright colors. And every child had a pair of ice skates!

Ice skating, brought into the country by the whites, has been taken over by the Eskimos, who excel in it. They are so good at it that in villages like Kwethluk the people often contrive to make their own ice skates in the school workshop, and, attaching them to their native mukluks, go skating merrily off along the river with absolutely no arch support except what this moccasin like boot can give—which is exactly none. Mukluks are made of wolf, reindeer, or caribou, often inlaid with fancy pieces of calfskin and bear, and frequently with soles of walrus hide or bearded seal. They usually reach to the knees, where they are tied with bright yarn tassels, although they may reach to the hips. This pretty, lightweight garment, lighter than any leather or rubber boot, is the cold-weather apparel of the North, and is thousands of years old in principle; it has never been improved upon by any other garment by the white man. The natives use insulating insoles of dried grass to absorb the perspiration, but we often use just the felt insole around town because it is handier. Although it is not cold enough on the coasts for mukluks they are worn much of the winter by everybody in a town like Fairbanks, where they have attained great popularity. Muddy or rainy conditions are ruinous to them; they must be worn in a dry climate. Robbin told us he has known Eskimo boys of the village to skate along the river all the way to Bethel and back in a day, simply in mukluks, running on tiptoe over those places where the snow had drifted or rough ice cakes were piled in the way. The loose and sloppy mukluks are the only outdoor boot one sees on anybody all winter at a far western trading post such as Bethel.

Every Sunday afternoon chaperons took all the boys and girls skating together to the lake behind the orphanage, and we went with them one day like this, taking the dog team. I had my first ride in a dog team sled while the whole school, from the smallest one on up, skated beside us across the ice, and Bud at the same time was driving his first dog team on ice skates. Peanuts and candy were thrown to the carefree, rosy-cheeked crowd.

Bud spent the time in taking numerous hunting jaunts for game, with the small boys of the school as his beaters. One evening he played barber and cut half the orphans* hair, and the rest of the time he instructed Jake and Mr. Schotsnyder in making articles in sheet metal, of which the school had a goodly supply but little knowledge in using it. The Eskimo boys with whom he was pals had had a hard time recognizing Bud since the removal of his beard. The day he first appeared at the orphanage one of the little fellows, likening him to the colored pictures which he had seen in Sunday school of people with beards, thought Bud was one of the Disciples of Jesus.

One day I helped the teacher at the orphanage. She was a splendid teacher with a job so big that I wondered how she managed to handle it all by herself. Keeping bright children busy all the time and out of mischief is a task, and these orphans hurried to get every piece of work done as fast as the teacher could assign it. The grades went to the eighth, after which, if the students were good, they would be eligible for the Territorial high school at Eklutna.

Like all orphanage children these youngsters were starved for affection, and they were also starved to know about the outside world, which is unusual in natives. Shy and twittering, as soon as they got me where they wanted me, the older girls pounced upon me, six holding onto either side, and asked questions about the wonderful life in the United States. What kind of clothes did the women wear in the United States? Were all the women as pretty as in the magazines? Had I ever seen a movie actress?

How did these youngsters know so much, is what I wanted to know? Much of this kind of chatter was kept from their ears, and they lived in an extremely isolated place where strangers never stopped. But perhaps that was part of the reason why they were so eager, why they all watched as with one eye the oldest boys who occasionally came by the kitchen window carrying wood. In this convent, guarded largely by unwedded superiors, as is often the case, they lived as cloistered as nuns and, whether their instructors knew it or not, were utterly and wildly man crazy. Their biggest ambition, outside of getting to the United States, was to get to any Alaska town and see the sights, to get to Bethel. I hated to think what their lives might yet be in such a place as Bethel did not the school take the realistic attitude and do important follow-up work in finding some place for them in society after they were let out. An attractive and developing young lady is even more of a problem than a child, as many parents have found.

We had been at the Moravian orphanage for a week when one day Bud came to me quickly. "I believe the ice is going out!" he exclaimed. And that is exactly how it happened. Within an hour Bud and I were released to travel once more, and the friendly mission was relieved of its obligatory guests. The water was running ice again, with plenty of open spots. We caught a ride with a native in his motorboat down to Kwethluk, and losing no time exhumed the old *Queen Beaver* once more from her storage place beneath the Indian Service residence. We could hardly believe that we were still going to be able to paddle our canoe right up to Bethel amid the ice cakes of what was now practically midwinter, but we were going to try it. And something told us that we were going to make it this time; the end of our summer's canoe trip had really arrived at last.

Of the Yukon and the Kuskokwim, we have many memorable pictures. Not the least of these is our race through the drifting ice cakes to Bethel through blue tidewater, with the American goldeneye, the last duck to leave the country in winter, careening overhead. Like the Yukon the Kuskokwim is muddy in summer—so muddy it is small wonder that drowned persons are seldom found because within two hours' time a floating body would become so dragged down and saturated with mud as to be unrecognizable if seen. But at this season the Kuskokwim is truly blue.

We started out about nine-thirty in the morning on this, our last run, taking our old worn places on our canoe seats once again, and wielding paddles which already seemed heavy and unfamiliar from disuse. Robbin went with us, in a one-man kayak in which he skied like a mosquito over the surface, much faster than we could go. The Eskimos in spring and fall water travel often carry a little sled on their kayaks. Then when they come to impassable ice jams they get out and walk, using the little sled to carry the boat. We brought one of these native sleds with us with the same idea in mind. Robbin believed that could we but get beyond the first big ice jam which, according to Dummy, spanned the Kuskokwak at its last bend, we would find ourselves in the clear as far as the Kuskokwim itself, all the way to Bethel.

At first a heavy fog hung over all. Every sound was muffled. The unseen church bell ringing rhythmically for Sunday morning services at Kwethluk receded quickly in the distance as the silent current bore us swiftly away. Robbin, paddling in his kayak alongside through skin ice in the fog which cast no shadow, was a study in black and gray.

The fog strip had lifted and it was bright day when the three of us in our assorted craft reached the ice jam near the mouth of the Kuskokwak, for which we had come prepared.

Leaving the kayak, we loaded the hefty *Queen Beaver* on the little Eskimo sled, and with Bud leading, with the pull rope straining about his chest, we pushed and pulled laboriously along the beach. I was not a great deal of help, but presently, when the going got most tough, an Eskimo friend happened along and lent a hand. We were dragging our load largely across tall grass upon which there was no snow other than a sort of heavy frost, and this was quickly melting and shaking off as we passed, while the sun climbed. Catastrophe called in person when the little sled presently buckled under its load, and both runners went flat. But Bud and Robbin contrived to drive the nails in again, and, holding a match against the still-attached reel of our summer's fishing pole, we melted the line until it could be unwound and used for reinforcement of the sled.

"Look, Robbin, you've been wanting to have a crack at a willow grouse. There's one now." We waited until Robbin had shot, and then Bud walked over to it and with a few deft twists of his wrists plucked the bird of its plumage, dressed it out, and hung it up by the neck in a bush where Robbin could pick it up on his way back. Robbin marveled. Dressing game for many hunters is a messy occupation requiring hours. Not so for Bud; he loved this life and certainly belonged here if ever a human being did. Leaving the wilderness gave us a feeling of loneliness for this pleasant life, as we knew that Bud had here in all probability plucked his last bird for some time to come.

We accomplished the end of the long ice jam and met the Kuskokwim, although there were times when I wondered if we would. Robbin walked out on the last point of land and waved us a laconic and expressive bon voyage, then turned back. He had not accepted any remuneration for our accommodation, although he was going to sell our camping supplies for us through the native co-operative store at Kwethluk which he helped to operate.

It all seemed so final that I could hardly bear it. Why did the summer and the river have to end? Why couldn't they just have gone on forever, as they were?

But we turned our faces downstream now with one thought: to make Bethel today, before night, while the way still held open for our passage. We now had but fourteen miles to go, having come six miles from Kwethluk, and we should easily make it paddling, provided all was well ahead.

Large walls and bergs of ice where the four-inch pans had slid on top of each other to form promontories ten feet high in cases were grounded on the shallow river islands which we passed. Smaller pans of floating ice were all about us, widening and closing alternately, and we made our way cautiously among them in the current, listening to them skid and tinkle musically. This was some place for a canvas canoe! we thought. Already the last rays of the afternoon sun faded as it passed with pale wintry glow to the other side of the world. Abruptly the weather, to those who had lived inside for a month, was indeed cool. It probably would have been cool anyway, even had we continued to practice our theory of immunity to the cold, for this theory will work so far and no farther when one is lightly dressed. If one consistently is underfed and lives continuously outdoors, we found that the body loses heat as each day passes.

Then suddenly the thing which we had been fearing hove into sight—a great ice jam spanning the big bend of the river for as far as we could see.

The pack which had once been soft mush had congealed and solidified in a strange conglomeration several inches thick and under which the cold green water frothed gurglingly. It would be terrible to fall overboard here and be swept under that ice, I thought, as we maneuvered our canoe across the span of the pack, searching every crevice for a hole through. We tried breaking at the ice with our paddles in a small hope of chopping our way right down through the center of the pack, which was still partially mush, but decided against it. Not to mention the fact that it was now freezing since the sun had dropped, such a course would be dangerous and foolish in a canvas canoe and considering the speed of the rushing water. If we got into that pack, we might be like the arctic explorers in their larger boats who never got out.

"I think Bethel's just around the corner. I'm going to see/' said Bud when we had beached the canoe on the shore. He was right. Upon running down the shore myself I could see the early evening lights of the far western trading post, shining from the windows of the houses. The generous town, facing us along the curving bank of the river, looked to me as though it were only two or three miles away, and I was all for attempting immediately to walk there to get some help to carry the canoe out the next day. But Bud studied the situation carefully, observing the long rough and wooded shore line through the glasses. It was every bit of six miles by land yet to Bethel, and it would take a day to walk it.

We had a supper of Russian Mission salmon strips and Kuskokwim water, and went to bed in the canoe, now shorn of its canvas top and all of its equipment other than our sleeping bags and guns. The following morning, we had more fish and water, and presently four soldier boys on special detail came along the beach. They were Southern boys all and were shivering in the cold despite the fact that they were equipped with "siwash" mittens and sheepskin-lined apparel. How often do we remember seeing the new United States soldiers shivering in the cold of Alaska! It is the picture of the day, these boys that one is always so glad to see.

The strong willing backs of those fine boys were the blessing which came along just in time to get us out of our last difficulty. The four of them picked up the canoe on their backs as though it were a feather, walked with it around the ice blockade and deposited it for us by the side of open water, where we thankfully continued traveling in below-zero temperatures. We arrived with the ice cakes successfully at Bethel.

22

Fly Away Home

The Pan-American, seven-passenger Pilgrim taxied down the snow-blown field on wheels, handled by the young pilot who came down to Bethel just once a month and alternatively flew to Nome on what was to be, sometime after the war, Pan-American's future Nome-Asiatic route. These routes were just experimental at this time. A forty-mile wind was sweeping across the tundra as we taxied; I had frosted my nose momentarily on the way to the field. It had taken the pilot, the Eskimo helper, and Bud two hours to warm up the airplane by a plumber's fire pot placed in a fifty-gallon barrel and by keeping the fuselage hooded. The passengers all snapped their safety belts closed and shivered beneath their assorted coats and mukluks in the subzero temperature inside the plane. We hummed down the field quickly and with excited hearts all, and were in the air before we knew it, the hangarless field sailing at angles below us. We ourselves had waited at Bethel seven weeks for this passage, and flying was the only way to get out.

In the winter the wind blows ceaselessly at Bethel. Everyone lives in parkas and mukluks, and some of these garments are beautiful beyond belief to one who has never been acquainted with them before. The white women of the town had many different fur coats and silver, blue, and arctic fox furs to wear around their necks when they took their trips Outside—and many Alaska women are able to take annual trips or a trip every few years at the least. To be willing to live all the time at a place like Bethel they perhaps deserve these things.

Bethel is an unincorporated trading-post town grown to sprawling size and built of boardwalks and shacks above the mud which is being cut into by the turning river: the Army wisely built its quarters on the other side of the river when it came to Bethel. Beluga or small white whales are said to be seen

sporting along the shallow mouth and delta of the Kuskokwim at times. Large seagoing vessels can come within eight miles of Bethel, which lies about one hundred miles up the Kuskokwim. Although on a same latitude with Seward, whose port is open the year round and where never an ice cake is seen, wintertime finds the Kuskokwim Bay and River blocked with ice flows and ice jams, as they are directly exposed to the Bering Sea, which makes the difference. The ground in this area is perpetually frozen and there is no plumbing at Bethel. The same conditions of frozen subsoil are present also in Fairbanks, of course, but Fairbanks keeps the city pipes open by steam, and we must remember that this is a million-dollar proposition. Fairbanks may be the most expensive city of its size to build and maintain in the world, but it maintains itself.

People at Bethel buy their drinking water from a man with a water truck who hauls it from a near-by lake. They get their bathing and kitchen water by catching it from the eaves of their roofs during the rainy summer and bringing it up from the river's edge in the form of chunks of ice by winter. The town health authorities, consisting of the government Indian Hospital with its single physician, have urged the people not to use the river ice for drinking purposes, for at this spot all of the town's sewage is thrown in by summer, not to mention the sewage drifting down with the ice from the villages above, yet many continue to do it.

Eskimos and their dog sleds are to be seen everywhere in and around Bethel; some white people also maintain dog teams. There are twenty thousand reindeer herded in the vicinity for food for the well-fed Eskimos as well as the few whites. It is certainly the real Alaska as Outsiders typically visualize it. It is a center for getting carved ivory from Nunivak and Nelson Islands in the Bering Sea. These islands are nearby air mileage, but otherwise are far. Here reside some of the most primitive Eskimos left in Alaska, and the islands might be described as extremely isolated in that only a few days out of the year do the fog banks and cloud banks lift enough to allow a plane to slip through to them. Almost no planes contacted the islands during the war. The armed forces at the time we were in Bethel had large standing orders for the walrus ivory trinkets, which of course are among the rare treasures of the earth, as the supply is limited and when it is gone there may be no more.

There were perhaps as many as twenty-five white women at Bethel, more than we had seen altogether in five months. Indian Service and reindeer supervision, mission work, and trading are the occupations. The N. C. Company, which took our canoe from us to sell to the soldiers when the next spring should arrive, has built several of the town's houses, as for instance those in which the two rival air lines house their personnel and have offices.

The airlines were at this time up against the problem of transporting out all the miners of the adjacent mining camps, especially Goodnews Bay. Uncle Sam had ordered abruptly that all these mining activities cease, to concentrate on the all-out effort of winning the war. Platinum was still mined at Platinum down the Bay, but Goodnews Bay mines gold, which was considered nonessential in the war effort.

The single clapboard and corrugated-iron-covered roadhouse, six dollars a day room and board or around a hundred dollars for eight days for two people, was crowded with these loafing Good- news miners, awaiting their plane connections to Anchorage and Fairbanks. Since their company had to pay for their accommodations en route and this company at the same time had bought complete ownership of one of the airlines, it was certain that no other passenger could expect accommodations at this time. Flying days only averaged about three days a week; it was estimated that it would take two or three months to get all of the miners out. As for the other private air line, its rival, this had been chartered by the Army bag and baggage to convey officers back and forth for an indefinite period. Civilian travel was at a standstill, it seemed, and we were in a spot.

During the period we were forced to reside at Bethel we came to realize that it was one of those Alaska towns in which it is mighty bad to be "stuck" as a traveler. Indeed, more than one traveler in Alaska, being held up or missing his connections in some way, has gone hundreds and even literally thousands of dollars into debt within a short time in order to live. At one time an airplane passage one way between Nome and Fairbanks, when you could get it, cost eight hundred dollars, open cockpit, and it is not hard to talk with people who remember these days and who still think in terms of thousands and long-range credit. But we ourselves didn't exactly own a gold mine and were as yet too recently from the States to understand this kind of thinking. This was certainly the Alaska over westward that had not changed or caught up with the present times.

Everybody knew as soon as we arrived in town who we were and where we had come from. We were the people who had come down through the ice with a canoe. But if we were prepared to be hailed as conquering heroes arrived at the end of the trail, we were mistaken. It was not that kind of an Alaskan town. It was small enough to be gossipy and clannish and just large enough to be oblivious of the unfortunate. But these were all experiences in meeting the world, we supposed. Not having even enough money for our airplane ride out (for which eventually we made an arrangement with the N. C. Company), we borrowed an ax and made a little lean-to shed where we slept in the snow on the tundra at the edge of town. We lived on ptarmigan Bud shot, and canned ham, cheese, and candy bars (the only thing in Alaska which costs a nickel), which food concentrates upset our systems considerably.

Every day we would go to the air-lines offices, which persuaded us with indefinite promises to come back the next day. Otherwise Bud might have found a job, which he finally did, welding an airplane part, but even at that there were no available houses to rent or buy. As we had already suspected these conditions about Alaska generally, there was naught to do but make the best of it. Presently we were obliged to seek the* shelter of the roadhouse, and there were cast upon the charities of the kind landlady, who allowed us to wash a few dishes, lay linoleums, and "de-soot" the chimney for half our board, which was only an excuse as she already had people hired to perform these tasks.

❧

WE IN THE AIRPLANE WERE bound for Fairbanks. Fairbanks was considerably off our route and the last place Bud and I wanted to go, but it was a way out of Bethel, so we took it, and speeded up to the north again. Under ordinary conditions we should have made connections via Anchorage over Rainy Pass. Going a circular route in order to make connections, we flew far over a thousand miles to get home again, over very wild, rugged and scenic country. The flight from Bethel to Fairbanks was a battle all the way, and we did not make our destination until the close of the second day. We came to realize that even riding in the luxurious Pan-American planes is pioneering in Alaska. For instance, if our pilot had not taken off in a forty-mile wind at Bethel, he probably would not have got off the ground at all for a month.

All of us in the plane were young people, interestingly enough. There was our sheepskin-clad pilot, who was not over twenty- four, his Eskimo helper of the same age, in hooded parka, Bud and I, two part Eskimo boys of seventeen and eighteen, and a young woman probably twenty-six, with a small child in arms and expecting another one. Her husband was sending her to safety Outside for the duration of the war, and her face was red and puffy from tears. She told me the physician at Bethel took no surgical cases, but even sent tonsillectomies over Rainy Pass to Anchorage: cost to the patient to have his tonsils removed, about three hundred dollars for that jaunt.

The boy of seventeen was one-half Eskimo, one-fourth Norwegian, and one-fourth Scotch; the eighteen-year-old was one- half Eskimo, one-fourth Negro, and one-fourth Portuguese. The boy with the negroid features was an especially fine, straight, outstanding type; both were high-school students with college ambitions and had unusually fine and sensitive ideals of what they wanted to accomplish in life. Both had just got out of the Indian Hospital after long convalescences, so that one might say a goodly part of our passengers were in invalided or semi-helpless condition. This was a responsibility that the rest of us felt keenly, in view of the weather and the uninhabited country over which we were ranging for hundreds of miles. It was a dizzy ride and there was much vomiting by the invalids along the way and taking the small child to toilet, which was accomplished by holding paper sacks. Presently almost everybody became upset and was obliged to use the sacks, hiding behind the Eskimo helper and his parka.

The plane became no warmer inside but continued to get colder if anything, the winds tearing through the fabric in spite of heaters.

Radio reports coming in from the trading post of Flat said that there was a seventy-mile ground wind there, so we couldn't land. We battled our way over to McGrath on the upper Kuskokwim and there stayed the night at a construction camp for men who were shortly to be sent from the Aleutians. Sitting around the great roaring drum stove into which whole logs were thrust, we talked with the people on the other plane, the mail plane, who had also left Bethel that morning. The pilots said one of their fellow pilots had checked his signals in at Nulato on the Nome route, and had not been heard of for three days, as he had not reached Nome. We sat helplessly wondering what had become of this flier and one other who had also disappeared in the storm sweeping this area. Both with their parties met their end, as we later ascertained. The pilot on the Nome route and four passengers, including a Civil Aeronautics Inspector who was with him, crashed and were burned to death. Alaska has some of the finest pilots in the world in their brave little ships—ships which are too little sometimes for the tasks that they must undertake. But they must be small in Alaska's present state of development in order to land on small fields and pastures and river ice in servicing all the little "camps" and outposts. All pilots know that if they stay with the game long enough in this country they will eventually spin in. One's luck can't be with him all the time. There are exploits in flying in Alaska that would make all other flying stories any place look dull by comparison.

How we ran short of fuel in the terrific head winds and searched for an hour to find and finally make an emergency landing to refuel at Lake Minchumina; how we flew right over the vicinity of Dick's house by the Tolovana at eight thousand feet and found that remote Dick was only an hour and ten minutes out of Fairbanks; how we saw herds of drifting caribou below at times, and all the mighty frozen rivers looked like ribbons—these things must be abbreviated. When we stepped out of the plane half-frozen at Fairbanks and into the warm Pan-American offices, where all passengers were thawed out by hot coffee, we were suddenly very conscious of our appearance beneath the bright lights and the stares of well-dressed people. Bud and I in our caps of opera cloak and in wolfskin mukluks, genuine urine-tanned by chief Nakotuk's wife (quite different from the commercialized mukluks which civilized people wear), and I with a patch on my pants put on by kind Janet of Tuluksak: we were a sight with our rifles and sleeping

246

bags, and two battered fishing poles in our hands! Even the woman from Bethel who was dressed in a traveling suit looked somewhat out of style here; her suit was two years too long and it didn't hang right. We pioneers had been transported suddenly from the middle of the raging wilderness into the middle of chromium-finished, efficient New York City.

At Fairbanks we learned of the completion of the Alcan Highway to Edmonton and New York, and the completion of a new highway called the Glenn Highway which now linked Anchorage to the Richardson Highway, and hence to Valdez and Fairbanks and Edmonton and New York. Fairbanks was jammed with Army and civilians. Russian aviators at Fairbanks were ferrying planes back and forth to Russia. No hotel rooms were available, and true to historic Fairbanks hospitality, the housewives opened their homes to travelers wherever a room or a part of a room or a basement was available.

After a delay of five days at Fairbanks we got on another plane bound for Anchorage, a plane filled with entirely different passengers from our original pioneer friends. These people were well-dressed, confident Alaska businessmen who expected no accident to befall them any more than one would expect a similar accident in taking elevated and bus all the way across New York City in an afternoon. Presently, 20,300-foot Mt. McKinley, highest mountain in North America, reared up beside us—that is, the peak itself was seventy-five miles away as we cut along Broad Pass in the Alaska Range. Mt. McKinley's glacier tongues wound like broad highways from his valleys, which in the rays of the setting sun were gold and silver and purple. It all looked like a miniature model, but since we were flying at a hundred miles an hour it took the great peak an hour and a half to slide by us; it seemed to stay in one place. Finally, the clouds of night swallowed it up, and suddenly the wheels hit the runway and we were at Anchorage, where the streets were bustling with cars and all the shop lights were twinkling.

At Anchorage we saw the first loan and hock shop, which had come into Alaska in our absence, although there may have been one at some other town at some other time in the past. It seemed that civilization was on the march. Army nurses, who some people thought were the WAC's, were to be seen in uniform on the streets. Christmas toys were beginning to show in the windows. The Pay'N Takit concern had set up a branch store in Anchorage, and in a land where everything is habitually done by credit in large orders, and where the customer scarcely ever bothers to add up his account, gained little popularity except with the newcomers for whom it had been erected. A Pay'N Takit clerk said that the store had to pay shipment on all the pennies which it was using on "bargains" after the policy practiced in the States, but it was a losing proposition, because the store kept importing and importing pennies and never got its pennies back. "They give them to their children to play with," the clerk told me. We had to smile at how Pay'N Takit had brought the penny into Alaska on its one-way trip. However, some of the drugstores were beginning to use pennies now, too, in Anchorage, and a new clerk started to charge a customer for an extra short piece of wrapping twine until she was told not to.

Ammunition, about which we had worried for the sake of the natives, had been specially ordered for Alaska by the War Production Board in our absence. Ammunition was still considered vital for civilians in Alaska, as were walking shoes and almost all food commodities which were now to be rationed, as we had more or less expected, in the States.

After a wait of three days in Anchorage, we again boarded a plane with a third group of passengers, and presently our wheels came down upon the rough familiar field at Seward, from whence we had started this trip.

Seward, like Anchorage and Fairbanks, swarmed with pretty new young working girls who had recently come into Alaska in view of the war effort. One could see them soon on a sunny day of summer bicycling along the dusty roads in gay costume and enjoying nature despite the whistles of the soldiers. We who had been in Alaska really only a short time were now pioneers in comparison to this new horde of people. Alaska had certainly changed during our absence from town; in fact, the changes were unbelievable. We were not sorry—especially to see the young people come. The soldier boys and their girls who met at the Service Club were the same boys and girls meeting at similar Service Clubs practically everywhere all over the world now; they ate the same kind of hamburgers—thousands of them, and how good they tasted!—and they discussed the same topics. Being in Alaska now was like belonging to a great fraternity which linked all lands. It was the spot of the day. These kids wouldn't be able to walk down a street in Seattle after the war without hailing and being hailed by friends from

Alaska who covered the globe, like a meeting of the Alaska fraternity. Youth was on the march again, and we hoped that we ourselves in our own small explorations had been with the forerunner of that march. The magnitude of these changes which were occurring in the world was something to think about!

An old Navy man had got Bud interested in the Navy more than the Army while we were at Bethel. At one-time Bud had been talking all Army, but now it was Navy for him. He wrote immediately volunteering for training in naval flying, for which he believed he was eligible, but we were surprised to learn that the Navy was not yet accepting married men into that division; shortly thereafter came the President's order that there could be no more volunteering at all.

"Well," said Mr. Cox at Fort Raymond, after we had been home a month, "you can come back to work here. We've got some new material." And so, we went back, working very hard to win this war which was to be won by Alaskan civilians with lunch buckets as well as by the soldiers who came to engage in combat. Uncle Fred was very glad to have us home, where we spent the first three days doing almost nothing but reading our mail from Outside, which had accumulated for five months. We were still going to continue to be Alaskans for a while.

Of course, we had many memories of the trip: how we got so we could live on fish all the time, just like Japanese; the time the Indians reported to the white people ahead that we had been drowned; the "walking" whirlpools of the Tanana with their long sweepers, and the portage, and all the many fish camps. Sailing right up to the Army reservation at Bethel in a mistaken impression that we should report to the Major himself; that pilot we met in Bethel who said he saw us on the Yukon one day from his airplane and so practically knew us; Dick and Mary and Tommy on the Tolovana; fifty-seven below zero at Fairbanks and the air being kind of smoky to the taste and heavy to breathe, but otherwise not particularly cold at all in the stillness; such a delightful climate at Fairbanks, and how of course the people like the winter season most of all, and how they pass you from one friend to another in getting acquainted fast; and lightly dressed students on the campus popping in one door and out the other between classes, but, well, hardly lingering in their • walks as people of other climes do. "And do you remember that perfectly awful jam we got into down by the Bering Sea once?" we'll be able to say to each other casually someday. And we met a wonderful girl who was half Eskimo but she didn't know it, so she acted just like a white person.

One of the points about the Alaska natives we want to make, aside from our active interest in their education and progress in the modern world, is the hope that the adoption of orphaned children will become popular in the United States. With the great war, many children will, we hope, be adopted by parents in America. Not the least of these we hope will be our own Alaska children, whose parents have not been killed in the war perhaps, but whose situation has just recently been brought before the public as Alaska is observed by that public as a whole for the first time. It is with regret that we have heard that the Bureau of Indian Affairs has fought these adoptions and has tried in every way up till now to keep the Alaska natives in Alaska. It is our humble opinion that now is the time for the turning of the tides. Legislation and publicity should encourage adoptions to give these children a chance. Many states have in the past prevented or discouraged out-of-state adoptions of children by simply requiring the prospective parents to put up a bond of $5000 or more on each child. This is unfortunate if much adopting of war orphans is to be done, and it is also unfortunate from the standpoint of Alaska, where there are not enough resident white families who have facilities to engage in these enterprises. We have mentioned before that Alaska has a very transient population, mostly male. Furthermore, it is people closest to the scene who are oftentimes most ignorant of what they should know, and it sometimes takes those far away to have the right kind of detached, unprejudiced viewpoint. Native children in Alaska's cities who are going on to higher education have a hard time because of local prejudices with which they are constantly confronted.

The way to get around the prohibitive state bonds is for people who wish to "take" Alaska Eskimo or Indian children in the United State to get these children through the Department of Public Welfare, having a relative or close friend in Alaska hold the legal adoption papers. These papers may eventually be transferred to the true adoptive parents after some time has elapsed.

Another project which Alaska citizens could take directly upon themselves most readily is each year to finance a certain number of exceptional students in college, that Eskimos and Alaska Indians may be represented with equal chances of opportunity in our democracy.

There are many cases who are definitely college material if given the proper guidance; a limited few have already made some fame and fortune of their own, but certainly more must inevitably in the enlightened future. The colleges of the United States should at this time make a special effort to open their doors to these newcomers from Alaska who, cast into a strange alien world, have talent but do not know how to go about getting higher education without advice and encouragement.

There have been a few Army marriages to Indians and Eskimos, as might be expected, but unfortunately these will not always be found to be of the higher type; gradually the good qualities of native culture will be incorporated into the white life, however. Some native traditions are popular now in Alaska, and will reach out to other places,'adding a flavor distinctly their own. The officers' club at Anchorage has been dubbed the Kashim, which there could be no better or more appropriate name.

Up till this time the Eskimos and Indians have been displayed in pictorial views of basket-weaving and at their hunting and fishing, which are all true and interesting, but in this observation we have tried to show them in terms of their social quotient: what their health is, their economic status, how they are adapting as Americans in America, what they are accomplishing at present and what they may be expected to accomplish in the future, looked at not only with individual sympathy but from the standpoint of population health as a whole according to the standards by which we look at the world today.

We do not pretend to have seen all of Alaska—few indeed have—and of course conditions differ widely in different localities, for Alaska is above all a land of contrasts, where one meets the unexpected at every turn. Our attitudes have been determined in considerable part by our reflections while canoeing on the Yukon.

Alaska is a big place which will not be changed overnight. We were glad to be there and live there—the newest pioneers in the newest land.

About the Author

Constance Helmericks paddled into the Alaskan wilds in 1942, and spent twelve years exploring the Arctic with her husband. She wrote a series of bestselling books about their adventures, and co-filmed and produced three documentaries that were shown on national lecture tours and early television. Their story and photographs were twice featured in *LIFE* Magazine, including the cover. Later wilderness travels with her young daughters in Canada and Australia were subjects of her seventh and eight books. She was a thoughtful early environmental activist. She died in 1987.

CPSIA information can be obtained
at www.ICGtesting.com
Printed in the USA
FSHW020007030519
57799FS